PSYCHOLOGY OF DECISION MAKING IN RISK TAKING AND LEGAL CONTEXTS

PSYCHOLOGY OF DECISION MAKING IN RISK TAKING AND LEGAL CONTEXTS

RACHEL N. KELIAN
EDITOR

Nova Science Publishers, Inc.
New York

For permission to use material from this book please contact us:
Telephone 631-231-7269; Fax 631-231-8175
Web Site: http://www.novapublishers.com

NOTICE TO THE READER

The Publisher has taken reasonable care in the preparation of this book, but makes no expressed or implied warranty of any kind and assumes no responsibility for any errors or omissions. No liability is assumed for incidental or consequential damages in connection with or arising out of information contained in this book. The Publisher shall not be liable for any special, consequential, or exemplary damages resulting, in whole or in part, from the readers' use of, or reliance upon, this material. Any parts of this book based on government reports are so indicated and copyright is claimed for those parts to the extent applicable to compilations of such works.

Independent verification should be sought for any data, advice or recommendations contained in this book. In addition, no responsibility is assumed by the publisher for any injury and/or damage to persons or property arising from any methods, products, instructions, ideas or otherwise contained in this publication.

This publication is designed to provide accurate and authoritative information with regard to the subject matter covered herein. It is sold with the clear understanding that the Publisher is not engaged in rendering legal or any other professional services. If legal or any other expert assistance is required, the services of a competent person should be sought. FROM A DECLARATION OF PARTICIPANTS JOINTLY ADOPTED BY A COMMITTEE OF THE AMERICAN BAR ASSOCIATION AND A COMMITTEE OF PUBLISHERS.

LIBRARY OF CONGRESS CATALOGING-IN-PUBLICATION DATA
Available upon request

ISBN 978-1-60021-854-5

Published by Nova Science Publishers, Inc. ✦ New York

CONTENTS

Preface   **vii**

Chapter 1   Causes, Impact, Prevention and Medicolegal
                 Aspects of Child Abuse and Neglect   **1**
                 B. R. Sharma

Chapter 2   From Abstinence to Safer Sex: Ambiguities and Dialectics   **29**
                 Donna E. Howard, Robin Sawyer and Jessica Brewster-Jordan

Chapter 3   Adolescent Sexual Risk Behavior: Associations with
                 Family, Peers and School Environment   **47**
                 Aleksandra Jovic-Vranes and Boris Vranes

Chapter 4   Sexual Aggressions amongst Underaged:
                 Vulnerabilities, Risk Factors, Signs of Calling for Help   **61**
                 Philippe Bessoles in collaboration with Myriam Linnell-Boutaud

Chapter 5   Predictors of Middle School Youth Educational
                 Aspirations: Health Risk Attitudes, Parental
                 Interactions, and Parental Disapproval of Risk   **75**
                 Regina P Lederman, Wenyaw Chan and Cynthia Roberts-Gray

Chapter 6   Risk Mitigation: Individual and Market Behavior   **85**
                 Jamie Brown Kruse and Kevin M. Simmons

Chapter 7   Frequency-domain versus Time-domain
                 Estimates of Risk Aversion from the C-CAPM:
                 The Case of Latin American Emerging Markets   **101**
                 Ekaterini Panopoulou

Chapter 8   Hurricane Risk: Perceptions and Preparedness   **117**
                 John C. Whitehead

Chapter 9   Risk Avoidance and Risk Taking
                 in Mental Health Social Work   **131**
                 Shulamit Ramon

Chapter 10   Do Outsider-Dominated Boards and
                     Large Board Size Curtail Firm Risk Taking?   **149**
                     Michael Graham and Alfred Yawson

Chapter 11   Risk Perception and the Value of Safe Rooms as a
                     Protective Measure from Tornadoes: A Survey Method   **165**
                     Ozlem Ozdemir

Index   **181**

PREFACE

In a fast-moving world, the necessity of making decisions, and preferably good ones, has become even more difficult. One reason is the variety and number of choices perhaps available which often arenot presented or understood. Alternatives are often unclear and complex paths to them confusing and misleading. Thus the process of decision making itself requires analysis on an ongoing basis. Decision making is often made based on cultural factors whereas the best alternative might be quite different. The subject touches ethics aspects as well as psychological considerations. This new book presents important research on the psychology of decision making and risk taking.

Chapter 1 - Abuse and neglect of children and adolescents continue to be major public health problems all over the world. It has been found to be correlated with emotional and behavioral problems, suicidal behavior, substance abuse, and many psychiatric disorders including post-traumatic stress disorder. However, despite the high prevalence and the mental health consequences of childhood abuse for the victims, insufficient efforts are being made to recognize these consequences and there are too few resources available to provide the needed mental health services to these victims and their families. On the other hand, exciting advances have taken place regarding care of sexual abuse victims. Clinical research has demonstrated the effectiveness of psychotherapies and suggested the efficacy of medications in ameliorating the behavioral and emotional consequences of childhood abuse. Specific clinician interviewing strategies have been developed to avoid suggestion and interference with sexual abuse-associated litigation. However, psychiatry and allied mental health professionals have much to contribute in terms of advocacy for abuse victims and an increased understanding of the need for provision of rehabilitation opportunities to these children. Medical professionals can also contribute to lower the high acquittal rate in cases of child sexual abuse by proper documentation of the history and examination findings.

Chapter 2 - Despite a steady decrease in teen pregnancy, birth rates and abortion since 1991, adolescents in the United States continue to experience unintended pregnancy at higher rates than their peers in nearly all other industrialized nations and are at high risk for Sexually Transmitted Infections (STIs). At the same time, debate rages over whether comprehensive sexuality education or abstinence-only curricula should be taught in schools. Additionally, there is growing concern, among adolescent sexual behavior researchers, that our limited ability to affect changes in sexually risky behavior may be related to discordance between the survey questions pertaining to adolescent sexual behavior and actual youth practices. That is, research suggests that a significant proportion of data purporting to accurately gauge adolescent participation in specific acts of sexual behavior may be not only incomplete but flawed. This chapter will review the debate over sexuality education, examine the language used on current national health surveys that assess the sexual behavior of adolescents and young adults and provide recent findings from an exploratory study which examined the denotative meaning of sexual terms among a convenience sample of late adolescent university students. In this study, it was found that there still exists little consensus among adolescents about the behavioral referents for the terms *safe* and *safer* sex. Information in this chapter will help inform the development of rigorous investigations to further examine ambiguities surrounding the language and practice of sexual behavior among adolescents and consider how this imprecision affects policy and programmatic decision making.

Chapter 3 - During the dynamic period of adolescence when the passage from childhood to maturity takes place, sexuality takes on new dimensions; feelings become more intense, relationships become more complex, and the consequences of sexual behavior are radically altered. In general, earlier puberty, later marriage, a decline in the family leading to less control and more autonomy, and intense exposure to sexual stimuli via the mass media and travel across cultural boundaries have made pre-marital adolescent sexual activity more common. Adolescent sexual risk behavior places them at risk of unwanted pregnancy and childbirth, induced abortion in hazardous circumstances, HIV infection, and other sexual transmitted diseases. Objective of the study was to achieve a picture of adolescent sexual risk behavior. It also provides better material for the planning of specific preventive activities.

Random cluster sample consisted of 1540 15-year old adolescents, 822 female and 718 male. The multiple choice questionnaire included 119 items, covering topics such as: demographic characteristics, psychosocial determinants of health, leisure time behavior, family and peer context, risk behavior (tobacco use, alcohol and drugs consumption, sexual activity), and perceptions of school and the school's influence. Descriptive statistics, Chi-square test and logistic regression were applied for statistical analyzes.

Thirteen percent of adolescent reported that they had sexual intercourse before age 15 years. Average age of first sexual intercourse was 13.88. Average number of sexual partners they had was 3.10. One out of three never used condom. Eight percent reported multiple sex partners, and fourteen percent alcohol use before intercourse. Factors associated with adolescent sexual risk behavior include other form of risk behaviors, family and peer context, and school environment.

Adolescent relationships are complex and future research should consider not only causality of adolescent sexual risk behavior, but also the etiology of the satellite behaviors.

Chapter 4 - Post-trauma notion of vulnerability, following a sexual aggression, appears too general in infantile clinical psychopathology to be sufficiently operating. Differences regarding criteria for symptomatological assessments, differential diagnosis with post-trauma disorders, personality changes inherent to child development, specificity (or not) of a post-traumatic semiology inherent to under fifteen, etc. add to the complexity of the question. According to research, vulnerability can be, at once, synonym of psycho-social factors of risk, signs of victimarius call for help or badly circumscribed psychological vulnerabilities. International studies often diverge as investigation methodologies are so contradictory and epidemiological data not consensual enough... Notions of abuse, touching, incest, remain blur and badly defined despite a number of publications in which categorizations are suggested by searchers like M. Montés de Oca, C. Yohant and A. Markowitz (1990), who differentiate:

- *Sexual abuse without body contact*: public or private exhibitionism, pornographic pictures, verbal incitation towards sexual activity, and erotic talk on sex in front of children.
- *Sexual abuse with body contact*: erotic caresses or kisses, touching, calls for masturbation.
- *Sexual abuse with penetration*: rape attempt or rape with anal, vaginal or oral penetration (the French penal code completes this definition of rape "*with the use of any object*".

Legal, clinical or medical definitions overlap or oppose themselves. Inside a research field, contradictions add to the complexity of psychopathological and therapeutic aims such as "*compliant hymen*" regarding medico-legal expertise or the statute of limitation after 10 years in the case of rape. Legal expertise is paradigmatic of these difficulties.

In this relatively complex context and based on the authors' clinical victimology consultations in the ward of clinical forensic (CHU Montpellier, France – University Hospital Center), the authors have taken an interest (over a period of three years; 1998-2000) in two major questions on ill-treatments inflicted to underage:

1st question: *by differentiating sexual and non-sexual ill-treatments, what is the proportion of girls or boys who are affected?*

2nd question: *amongst observed disorders, do vulnerabilities, specific to under 15, exist that could lead to the hypothesis of a post-sexual-abuse syndrome?*

Chapter 5 - School-wide surveys in five middle schools were used to measure educational aspirations, attitudes toward sexual health risk behaviors and drug use, and perceptions of parental interactions and disapproval of risk behavior at baseline and one year later. Participants were male and female students of Black ($n = 222$), Hispanic ($n = 317$), White ($n = 216$), and Asian or other heritage ($n = 85$), ages 11 to 14. Analyses were performed for three factors with Cronbach's alpha coefficients ≥ 0.65 (youth's attitudes, discourse with parents, and parents' disapproval of risk behavior), and three single items inquiring about use of alcohol, use of marijuana, and sexual behavior. Generalized Linear Model (GLM) with logit link was used to evaluate the contribution of these measures at baseline as predictors of educational aspirations at the one-year follow-up. Results showed race/heritage ($p < .001$), attitudes toward health risk behaviors ($p < .01$), extent to which youth talked with parents about use of drugs and other health risk behaviors ($p < .05$), and perceptions of their parents' disapproval of risk behavior ($p < .05$) each made significant contributions in predicting educational aspirations. Gender did not contribute to the prediction of educational aspiration nor did self-report of actual risk behavior. These results indicate that youth interactions with parents regarding health risk behaviors is worthy of further exploration to develop interventions to reduce adolescent health risks and increase educational aspirations.

Chapter 6 – The authors will examine the relationship between individual bidding behavior and the aggregative properties of a market for full insurance. They utilize a Vickrey auction to sell from one to six policies. A Vickrey auction is a sealed-bid auction in which participants each simultaneously submit bids. The auctioneer discloses the identity of the highest bidder(s) who is declared the winner. The price paid by the winning bidders is equal to the highest bid that does not win the object(s). This format is named after William Vickrey who first described it and pointed out that bidders have a dominant strategy to bid their true values. Participants in the laboratory experiment reported here either acquire one of the available insurance policies in the auction or face exposure to the risk of a two-dollar loss. There is a rich literature in Psychology and Economics that has contributed to our current understanding about decision under risk. The authors describe a few of the important papers in the next section. This is followed by their experimental design, results and conclusions.

Chapter 7 - Campbell confirms the equity premium puzzle in an international context based on the Consumption-CAPM and cross-country evidence on implausibly large coefficients of relative risk aversion. In this paper the authors adopt a spectral approach to re-estimate the values of risk aversion over the frequency domain for six Latin American emerging markets. They complement the authors' analysis with the traditional time series approach and confirm the results of existing literature of large coefficients of relative risk aversion. Their frequency domain findings, however, indicate that at lower frequencies risk aversion falls substantially across countries, thus yielding in many cases reasonable values of the implied coefficient of risk aversion.

Chapter 8 - In this paper the authors measure wind and flood risk perceptions and five determinants of hurricane preparedness in surveys of North Carolina coastal residents conducted after hurricane Bonnie (1998) and hurricanes Dennis and Floyd (1999). These data allow an analysis of changes in risk perceptions and preparedness and their interrelationship. They explore a two-stage model. In the first stage, objective risk factors, hurricane experience, and demographics are determinants of risk perceptions. In the second stage, risk perceptions, hurricane experience, and demographics are the determinants of hurricane preparedness.

In the rest of the paper the authors describe the surveys and data. Then they use multivariate regression models to analyze the determinants of risk perception and preparedness. Finally they discuss their results and offer some conclusions.

Chapter 9 - This chapter will look at issues related to risk in mental health social work, especially the over-focus on risk avoidance and the need to create space for calculated risk taking. Examples from Britain and continental Europe will be utilised.

Chapter 10 - This chapter examines the impact of board composition and board size on three firm risk taking variables; strategy risk, stock returns risk, and income instability risk. There is recognition in the literature that corporate governance processes need to encompass mechanisms for motivating board and managerial behavior towards enhancing firm risk taking. Agency theory and regulatory recommendations advocate for an increasingly greater roles for outsiders on the board of directors. The evidence documented here indicates a positive relationship between majority independent board composition and firm risk taking. The literature also suggests board size affects firm activities independent of other board attributes and that there are biases against risk taking as board size grows. The authors do not, however, find any evidence to support the proposition that large board size influences firm risk taking. Thus, whereas the recommendation of increasing independent members on board of directors by regulatory bodies as well as the Cadbury and Hampel facilitate wealth creation by firms, the total representation on the board of directors does not exert any measurable influence on firms' wealth creation.

Chapter 11 - The purpose of the current study is to investigate the relationship between risk perception and willingness-to-pay for increased safety in LPHC risk situations. A tornado is chosen as the LPHC risk and willingness-to-pay for an in-residence storm shelter (safe room) is specified as the mitigation measure. The probability that a damaging tornado will strike a given location is miniscule, even in "high" tornado risk areas. However, the prospect of injury or loss of life due to a tornado is frightening. Brown, Kruger and Bos place tornadoes "among the most violent and lethal of all natural disasters."

In: Psychology of Decision Making in Risk Taking ...
Editor: Rachel N. Kelian
ISBN 978-1-60021-854-5
© 2008 Nova Science Publishers, Inc.

Chapter 1

CAUSES, IMPACT, PREVENTION AND MEDICOLEGAL ASPECTS OF CHILD ABUSE AND NEGLECT

B. R. Sharma[*]

Department of Forensic Medicine and Toxicology,
Govt. Medical College and Hospital, Chandigarh, India

ABSTRACT

Abuse and neglect of children and adolescents continue to be major public health problems all over the world. It has been found to be correlated with emotional and behavioral problems, suicidal behavior, substance abuse, and many psychiatric disorders including post-traumatic stress disorder. However, despite the high prevalence and the mental health consequences of childhood abuse for the victims, insufficient efforts are being made to recognize these consequences and there are too few resources available to provide the needed mental health services to these victims and their families. On the other hand, exciting advances have taken place regarding care of sexual abuse victims. Clinical research has demonstrated the effectiveness of psychotherapies and suggested the efficacy of medications in ameliorating the behavioral and emotional consequences of childhood abuse. Specific clinician interviewing strategies have been developed to avoid suggestion and interference with sexual abuse-associated litigation. However, psychiatry and allied mental health professionals have much to contribute in terms of advocacy for abuse victims and an increased understanding of the need for provision of rehabilitation opportunities to these children. Medical professionals can also contribute to lower the high acquittal rate in cases of child sexual abuse by proper documentation of the history and examination findings.

---

[*] Correspondence: Dr. B. R. Sharma, #1156 – B, Sector – 32 B, Chandigarh – 160030. India. E-mail: drbrsharma@yahoo.com and drbrsharma@gmail.com

INTRODUCTION

Child abuse and neglect is a terrible misfortune for millions of children and families, for communities, and for society. It affects children of all colors, social classes, ethnic groups, and religions. It damages young people in infancy, childhood and adolescence. The term child abuse refers to any act or failure to act that violates the rights of the child that endangers his or her optimum health, survival or development. Definitions of child abuse inevitably vary according to the uses for which they have been devised. There ought to be differences of emphasis between definitions that are intended for legal purposes, clinical diagnostic purposes or to suit the needs of a research study. Cultural relativity may be a significant issue, for certain behaviors that are construed as abusive by some cultures or subcultures may not be regarded in the same light by others. Definitions of abusive behaviors that are essentially the acts of commission may need to be distinguished from neglectful care taking, which is characterized by the acts of omission. Neglect may refer to deprivation or non-provision of necessary and societally available resources due to proximate and proscribed human actions that create the risk of permanent impairment to development or functioning. Child abuse or maltreatment is commonly divided into five categories; physical abuse, emotional abuse, sexual abuse, neglect and exploitation. Although any of these forms may be found separately, but more often they occur together.

According to a World Health Organization estimate about 40 million children aged 0 - 14 around the world suffer form abuse and neglect and require health and social care [1]. In 2000, nearly 2 million reports of alleged child abuse or neglect were investigated by child protective services agencies, representing more than 2.7 million children who were alleged victims of maltreatment and who were referred for investigation [2]. Of these children, approximately 879,000 were found to be victims of maltreatment, meaning that sufficient evidence was found to substantiate or indicate the report of child maltreatment. This reflects a national rate of approximately 12.2 children per 1,000 children younger than 18 years of age in the general population who were found to be substantiated or indicated victims of maltreatment. Nearly two-thirds of child victims (62.8%) suffered neglect, including medical neglect, while nearly one-fifth (19.3%) suffered physical abuse and approximately 10 percent suffered sexual abuse.

The 2000 Annual Report from the National Child Abuse and Neglect Data System (NCANDS) indicates that national child abuse incidence rates increased in each year from 1990-1993, and decreased in each year through 1999. The rate of victimization was 13.4 per 1,000 children in 1990. The rate peaked at 15.3 children per 1,000 in 1993, then decreased to 11.8 per 1,000 in 1999, while increasing slightly to 12.2 children per 1,000 in 2000 [3]. Meanwhile, the Third National Incidence Studies (NIS-3) found that rates of child maltreatment under the *Harm* Standard increased 149 percent from the time the first NIS study (NIS-1) was conducted [4]. In the 2003-2004 financial year, Kids Help Line counselors responded to 452 contacts from children and young people in Western Australia with concerns about child abuse. Among those seeking help, 50% cases were that of physical abuse, 38% of sexual abuse, 6% emotional abuse, and 5% of neglect [5].

However, available figures on the incidence of child abuse are undoubtedly underestimates for three main reasons. Firstly, there is often failure to detect the signs and symptoms that are indicative of abuse, especially if these are psychological rather than physical in nature. Secondly, even if the signs and symptoms are recognized it may not be realized that they result from abuse. Thirdly, even if the true etiology is suspected, the case may not be reported and so cannot enter into any official statistics. Furthermore, recognition and diagnosis of child abuse are compromised by denial that pervades all aspects of the phenomenon: perpetrators routinely deny that they did it; abused children sometimes deny that any thing had happened to them; otherwise concerned adults, such as neighbors, teachers, and emergency department physicians, may overlook and underreport abuse for any number of personal reasons; complex legal requirements may make it hard to convict the abusers; and generalized societal denial protects people from awareness of an unpleasant side of life.

Child abuse and neglect affects the healthy and normal course of development. It causes deviation from an expected trajectory, preventing the developing child's negotiation of sequential tasks and disrupting the normal transaction between different facets of development. The evaluation and management of child abuse require cooperation of diverse professional groups, including pediatricians and other primary care physicians, emergency department staff, radiologists, pathologists, law enforcement agencies, social service personnel, mental health professional, and forensic experts. Therefore child abuse and neglect is the very antithesis of adequate childcare and rearing posing a major threat to human development.

NEGLECT

Child neglect has been difficult to define [6]. Definitions have varied across disciplines agencies and states, in accordance with differing goals and thresholds [7]. Some authors have proposed broad definitions that incorporate not only caregiver acts and omissions, but also societal and institutional conditions (for example, hunger, lack of health insurance) that affect children [8]. More commonly, child neglect has been narrowly defined as parental or caregiver acts of omission or failure to provide for a child's basic needs. However, this perspective is limited and may not afford adequate protection to children since societal factors (e.g., poverty) that compromise the abilities of parents to care for their children also impair children's health and development and as such 'neglect' must be evaluated within a societal context. Any definition of child neglect must take into account the heterogeneity within the phenomenon. Different forms of neglect, of varying severity and chronicity, and within differing contexts, require a range of responses tailored to the individual situation. For example, a parent's ignorance of a child's nutritional needs requires a very different response from protecting children from lead or any other poisonous substance in the environment. On the other hand, it is also important to recognize the variability among children and their response to specific situations. Being a latchkey child might be appropriate for a mature child with adequate neighborhood supports, but endangering for another [9].

Child neglect, thought to be the most common of the five categories of maltreatment and probably the most life threatening may be further classified as: 1) Physical as for example, lack of appropriate supervision or failure to provide necessary food, shelter, or medical care. 2) Educational as for example, failure to educate a child or attend to special education needs. 3) Emotional as for example, inattention to a child's emotional needs or exposure to domestic violence, however, these situations do not always mean that a child is neglected. Sometimes cultural values, the standards of care in the community, and poverty may be contributing factors, indicating that the family is in need of information or assistance. When a family fails to use information and resources, and the child's needs continue to be unmet, then further child welfare professional intervention may be required.

In considering the impact of a situation on a child and the possibility of neglect, several factors need to be evaluated: whether actual or potential harm occurred, the severity of harm involved, and the frequency / chronicity of the behavior / event(s). In current practice, neglect is often considered only when actual harm has occurred, however, in some situations, the potential for moderate to serious harm needs to be an important consideration, as many forms of neglect have no immediate physical consequences, although there may be substantial and long-term psychological harm [10]. Severity of neglect is typically based on the degree of harm involved. A serious injury is apt to be seen as more severe neglect than a minor injury and any injury is likely to be seen as more severe than a potential injury. Pattern of omissions in care has been an important criterion of neglect, although single or occasional lapses in care are often considered 'only human' and are not regarded as neglect. But, even a single omission in care can have devastating results, such as an unattended toddler drowning in a swimming pool. In contrast, some omissions in care are unlikely to be harmful unless they are recurrent. For example, for a child to miss asthma medications occasionally may involve little risk, but that risk is far greater if medications are missed repeatedly.

PHYSICAL ABUSE

Physical abuse is the physical assault of a child by any person having custody, care, or charge of that child. It includes physical injury (ranging from minor bruises to severe fractures or death) as a result of punching, beating, kicking, biting, shaking, throwing, stabbing, choking, hitting (with hand, stick, strap, or other object), burning, or otherwise harming a child. Such injury is considered abuse regardless of whether the caretaker intended to hurt the child or not. Cruelty towards children has been described throughout history, with children viewed as parental property, however, the problem, was unveiled by Silverman (1953) and Wooley and Evans (1955) in its exact shape, magnitude and significance, who established the deliberate trauma character of certain specific types of pathological lesions [11], earlier detected by J. Caffey, a pediatric radiologist (Caffey's Syndrome) [12].

Physical abuse occurs at all ages, although biological sequelae are more severe in infancy. There is no association with ethnic groups, but a strong one with low socioeconomic status among the under fives, becoming weaker throughout the childhood and disappearing by adolescence [13]. Children with developmental disabilities have a raised risk [14]. Families in which physical abuse occurs are more likely to support mutually abusive coercive communications and interactions than controls. Partner abuse and domestic violence is relatively more common, combined with evasive hostility and decreased cohesion. Discussion, positive display of affection, and encouragement of prosocial behaviors are less common than in non-maltreating families [15].

The Third National Incidence Study which sampled child protective services, law enforcement, juvenile probation, public health, hospital, school, day care, and mental health and social services agencies for the child maltreatment prevalence data, reported that physical abuse had increased to 5.7 per 1000 children as compared to 4.3 per 1000 and 3.1 per 1000 reported by Second and the First National Incidence Study respectively [4]. According to a U.S. Department of Health and human Services report, there were 903,000 victims of child maltreatment nationwide, of which, neglect involved 53.5%, and physical abuse involved 22.7% of cases [3].

Physical abuse is detected through the observation of physical injuries without an alternative non-abusive explanation [16]. Usually, the diagnosis is based upon a discrepancy between the physical findings and the history provided. When an explanation is forthcoming, trigger events or developmental challenges are common – for example, persistent crying in infancy, problem of toileting or feeding among toddlers, or issues of discipline in later childhood. There may have been previous episodes of similar or lesser concern.

In the usual course of prognosis, some physically abused children may have neurological and other physical sequalae as a result of their injuries [17]. Educational difficulties are consistently found on follow-up. These children are less sensitive to social cues and less skilful at managing personal problems. Their capacity for emphatic concern with the everyday problems of their peers becomes blunted. Not surprisingly therefore, chronic oppositional and aggressive behavior is the most consistently documented outcome. These children may range from the socially withdrawn and avoidant to those who demonstrate fear, anger, and aggression [13]. Approximately 20 to 30% of physically abused children become delinquent in their teenage years. They are at increased risk of running away from home, alcohol and illicit drug use, self-destructive behavior, suicide, teenage pregnancy, etc [15].

SEXUAL ABUSE

Child sexual abuse was once regarded as the 'hidden pediatric problem' that Kempe referred to in 1977. By the latter half of nineteenth century, three French physicians, Tardeu, Bernard, and Brouardel, had each tried to expose the problem. Near the turn of the twentieth century, Sigmund Freud initially tried to uncover it, but like children who attempt to disclose, he recanted and created a myth that children's accounts of sexual abuse were the result of childhood desires and fantasy. This myth was accepted more readily than was the truth. In the course of last three decades, we have witnessed awakening concern, increasing public awareness, and organized backlash about child sexual abuse. Statements like "children never lie" and "children always lie" have been shown to be myths. Management of sexual abuse began as an art, and the scientific basis for the art continues to be laid down.

There is no universal definition of child sexual abuse. Most definitions cover a wide range of sexual activities, including situations with no physical contact. Kemp [18] defined child sexual abuse as the involvement of children and adolescents in sexual activities they do not understand, to which they cannot give informed consent, or that violate social taboos. Some definitions emphasize the unwanted, manipulative and exploitative factors while recognizing the importance of age and developmental level differences between participants [19, 20]. A simple definition of child sexual abuse, however, should include activities by a parent or caretaker such as fondling a child's genitals, penetration, incest, rape, sodomy, indecent exposure, and commercial exploitation through prostitution or the production of pornographic materials [21]. The definition of child and adolescent sexual abuse used in the

Third National Incidence study [4] involves a child younger than 18 years of age having experienced one of the following types of sexual acts: intrusion, defined as evidence of oral, anal, or genital penile penetration or anal or genital digital or other penetration; molestation with genital contact, but without evidence of intrusion; or other acts that involved contact with non-genital areas of a child's body (e.g., fondling of breasts or buttocks, exposure) or inadequate or inappropriate supervision of sexual activities when the perpetrator was a parent, parent substitute, or other.

Child sexual abuse is the product of complex factors involving the victims, the perpetrator, and the environment. Intrafamilial sexual abuse or incest is fostered by an environment that allows poor supervision or poor choice of surrogate caretakers, or fails to set appropriate sleeping and role boundaries [22]. Likewise, extra-familial sexual abuse is fostered by factors that increase the child's vulnerability. Children with unmet emotional needs are easier to victimize. Adolescence defiance and peer pressure place some children at increased risk of sexual abuse. The risk-taking child is even less likely to disclose the abuse out of the fear of blame or punishment, or concern about angering or upsetting the peer group [23]. Finkelhor [24] described four preconditions for sexual abuse. The first precondition is an abuser whose motivation to abuse children comes from 'emotional congruence', often secondary to abuse a child, sexual arousal by children, and the inability to have appropriate sexual relationships with peers. The second precondition is the ability of the abusers to overcome their own internal inhibitions or moral standards to abusing children. The third precondition requires overcoming external inhibitors to abuse, such as the protective parent or normal boundaries between family members or between children and adult in general. The fourth precondition is overcoming the resistance of the child through use of pressure, seduction, or coercion.

The process of sexual victimization usually occurs in the context of relationship and is accompanied by behaviors designed to engage the child in the sexual activity and permit the abuse to go on over time. Initially, the child is targeted for victimization, and a non-sexual relationship is established. Typically, the sexualization of the relationship appears to take place gradually. The child's cooperation and silence are maintained through a variety of forms of coercion, often by exploiting a child's normal need to feel valued [22]. Summit [25] used the term 'child sexual abuse accommodation syndrome' to describe the process by which the perpetrator gains access to the child, initiates the abuse, and assures cooperation and secrecy using threats or rewards. The child accommodates to the increased sexual demands with an increasing sense of betrayal and feelings of guilt, and may develop behavioral symptoms. The children who disclose often find an unsupportive response, which may lead to repeated attempts at partial disclosure. If the unsupportive reactions continue, the child retracts the complaint of abuse. The child's false retraction is quickly accepted, leaving the child vulnerable to continued abuse.

Victims of child sexual abuse may present in many ways. Some children are brought for medical evaluation after the disclosure of abuse. Masked presentations, however, are more common. Some children present initially with physical or behavioral complaints and, on further investigation, the history of sexual abuse is obtained. Common masked complaints include genital symptoms, abdominal pain, constipation or rectal bleeding, straddle injury, and various other somatic and behavioral problems [26, 27]. Chronic or recurrent urinary tract infections may be another masked presentation [28], however, symptoms mimicking a urinary tract infection are more common than actual urinary tract infection in sexually abused children [29].

A child's direct statement describing sexual abuse is the most definitive historical indicator of abuse. The child may also provide a history of abuse during evaluation of a particular physical problem or behavioral problem. Both types of disclosures should be taken seriously and should be investigated. Physical indicators of abuse may be used to corroborate the history of abuse. Common behaviors, often categorized as behavioral indicators of child sexual abuse, although may reflect the child's response to any emotional conflict, but should not be considered diagnostic of sexual abuse. However, they may be considered supportive evidence of sexual abuse [30, 31].

In the course of prognosis, a wide range of psychological sequlae in childhood and adult life are associated with prior childhood sexual abuse [32]. However, these are linked with the effects of both the quality of the family environment at the time of abuse, and the nature of the subsequent life events [33]. In particular, factors such as family disharmony and violence, existence of other forms of abuse and neglect, and parental mental health difficulties in addition to subsequent events, such as losses through death or separation, combined with the child's own method of coping with the abuse and ameliorative effects of positive school or social relationships all contribute to the outcome. According to reports, about one-third of children are symptom free. Approximately 10% of children show worsening symptoms over time, including depression and post-traumatic symptoms. While in some cases, the effects on personality and social relationships can be disabling during development, other children are unaffected [34].

EMOTIONAL ABUSE

Preferably referred to, as 'psychological maltreatment' is any pattern of behavior that impairs a child's emotional development or sense of self-worth. It encompasses the acts of omission and commission, which are considered potentially psychologically damaging, by conveying to children that they are worthless, flawed, unloved, unwanted, endangered, etc [35]. It may occur in institutional settings as well as in families. Psychological maltreatment can be direct or indirect, for example, being terrorized by witnessing domestic violence directed towards a loved parent, or observing parental involvement in anti-social activities such as drug abuse.

In all six forms of psychological maltreatment have been described, though most cases involve mixture of the following: spurning (hostile rejection or degradation) terrorizing, isolating, exploiting or corrupting, denying emotional responsiveness (ignoring) and mental health, medical and educational neglect [13]. 'Spurning' includes both verbal and non-verbal acts that reject and degrade the child through demeaning, belittling, degrading, ridiculing, shaming or consistently singling out for criticism or humiliation. 'Terrorizing' involves behavior that threatens the child directly or indirectly through threatening the child's attachment figures. 'Isolating' means the consistent denial of the child's opportunities to meet and interact, for example through confining or unreasonably limiting the child's freedoms. 'Exploiting and corrupting' incorporates those acts, which encourage the child to develop inappropriate or antisocial behaviors, for example criminal activities, or sexually illegal activities such as involvement in pornographic productions or prostitution. 'Denying emotional responsiveness' includes inattention to the child's emotional needs, requirements for nurturing, or emotional well-being. It represents failure to give both love and affection, as well as attentiveness to the child's emotional cues. 'Medical care neglect' refers to the failure or denial to provide the necessary medical treatment (including immunizations, prescribed medications, surgery and other interventions) for serious diseases or injuries. 'Mental health neglect' refers to parent's refusal to comply with the recommended therapeutic procedures in situations where children have serious, treatable psychiatric disorders. Although less well recognized, it can be an issue in anorexia nervosa, pervasive refusal syndrome, or chronic fatigue syndrome. 'Educational neglect' is normally linked with regulations and laws concerning the responsibility of parents to ensure that their children attend school. It is not uncommon, however, for cases involving physical and psychological neglect to also include educational neglect.

Reports of emotional abuse in children become more frequent throughout childhood into adolescence. According to a report, psychological maltreatment constituted 0.5 per 1000 in the United Kingdom, accounting for 17% of the caseload of child protection agencies in 1999 [36]. Reported cases are more likely to be linked with lower socioeconomic status. There is no particular link with racial or ethnic groups. Psychological maltreatment is frequently integral to other forms of maltreatment and so distinguishing different etiological factors and consequences is difficult.

Recognition of emotional abuse usually follows detection of other kinds of child abuse, or when domestic violence or parental substance abuse is uncovered. It also occurs when children are referred to child developmental or mental health clinics, or through reported observations of neighbors or professionals (e.g., teachers). Diagnosis requires detailed history, direct observations of parent-child interactions, and interviews with older child.

CAUSES OF CHILD-ABUSE AND NEGLECT

Abuse and neglect of children occurs in families from all walks of life, and across all socioeconomic, religious, and ethnic groups. There is no single, identifiable cause of child maltreatment; rather, it occurs as a result of an interaction of multiple forces impacting the family. For example, lack of preparation or knowledge of critical issues surrounding parenting, financial or other environmental stressors, difficulty in relationships, stress of single parenting, and depression or other mental health problems can all lead to abusive or neglectful behavior. Parents may lack an understanding of their children's developmental stages and hold unreasonable expectations for their abilities. They also may be unaware of alternatives to corporal punishment or how to discipline their children most effectively at each age. Parents also may lack knowledge of the health, hygiene, and nutritional needs of their children. These circumstances, combined with the inherent challenges of raising children, can result in otherwise well-intentioned parents causing their children harm or neglecting their needs. However, while certain factors related to parents, children, families, and the environment are commonly associated with a greater incidence of child maltreatment, the presence of these factors alone is not sufficient for abusive situations to develop. Stated differently, the presence of known risk factors does not always lead to family violence, and factors that may cause violence in one family may not result in violence in another family [37].

There is no single cause of child abuse and neglect, rather multiple and interacting factors at the individual (parent and child), familial, community and social levels contribute to child maltreatment. Maternal problems in emotional health, intellectual abilities and substance abuse have been reported to be associated with child neglect. Emotional disturbances, including depression, have been a major finding among mothers of neglected children [38]. Polansky [39] described the apathy-futility syndrome in mothers of neglected children, characterized by an emotional numbness, loneliness, interpersonal relationships that involve desperate clinging, a lack of competence in many areas of living, a reluctance to talk about feelings, the expression of anger through passive aggression and hostile compliance, poor problem-solving skills, a pervasive conviction that nothing is worth doing, and an ability to evoke a sense of futility in others. Mothers of neglected children have been described as more bored, depressed, restless, lonely, and less satisfied with life than the mothers of non-neglected children [40] and more hostile, impulsive, stressed and less socialized than either abusive or non-maltreating mothers [41]. Intellectual impairment, including severe mental retardation and a lack of education, also have been associated with child neglect [42, 43].

Theories of child development and child maltreatment emphasize the importance of considering children's characteristics because caregivers respond differently to these characteristics. For example, parents of children who are temperamentally difficult report more stress in providing care and the situations that lead to parental stress may contribute to child maltreatment. This association is supported by research that has, for example, found increased depression and stress in parents of chronically disabled children [44]. Several studies have found low birth weight or prematurity to be significant risk factors for abuse and neglect [45, 46], because these babies usually receive close pediatric follow-up as well as other interventions. In addition, medical neglect might be expected to occur more often among children who require frequent health care because their increased needs place them at risk for these needs not being met [10]. Some studies have reported increased neglect, but not abuse, among disabled children who had been hospitalized [47].

Problems in parent-child relationships have been found among families of neglected children. Research on dyadic interactions indicated less mutual engagement by both mother and child [48] and frequent disturbances in attachment between mother and infant [49, 50]. Several studies reveal that the mothers of neglected children may have unrealistic expectations of their young children with a lack of knowledge concerning child developmental milestones [51 - 52]. Kadushin [54] described chaotic families with impulsive mothers, who repeatedly demonstrated poor planning and judgment. He further described the negative relationships that many mothers of neglected children have with the fathers of their children, particularly because the fathers had often deserted the family or were incarcerated. Most of the studies on child neglect and high-risk families focuses on mothers and ignores fathers. This bias probably reflects the greater accessibility of mothers, and suggests that the frequently modest involvement of fathers in these families might be an additional contributor to child neglect, and a type of neglect in and of itself. An investigation of families with 5-year old children found that father involvement protected children against neglect [55]. Neglect has been associated with substantial social isolation [56]. Single parenthood without support from a spouse, family members, or friends poses a risk for neglect. In one large controlled study, mothers of neglected children perceived themselves as isolated and as living in unfriendly neighborhood [57]. Crittenden [58] described three types of neglect associated with deficits in cognitive processing, affective processing or both: a) disorganized, b) emotionally neglecting and c) depressed. Families, who respond to the immediate affective demands of situations, with little regard for the cognitive demands, characterize the first type – 'disorganized'. These families operate in crisis mode and appear chaotic and disorganized. Children may be caught in the midst of this crisis, and consequently, their needs are not met. The second type, 'emotionally neglecting', includes families in which there is minimal attention to affect or to the emotional needs of the child. Parents may handle the demands of daily living, but pay little or no attention to how the child feels. The third type, 'depressed', represents the classic image of neglect. Parents are depressed and therefore unable to process either cognitive or affective information. Children may be left to fend for themselves emotionally and physically. Although the intervention for these three different family patterns differs, they all rely on a family system approach in which parent and child behavior are considered in context.

The community context and its support systems and resources influence parent-child relationships and are strongly associated with child maltreatment [59]. A community with a rich array of services, such as parenting groups, high quality and affordable child care, and a good transportation system, enhances the ability of families to nurture and protect their children Informal support networks, safety, and recreational facilities also are important in supporting healthy family functioning. Garbarino and Crouter [59] described the feedback process whereby neighbors may monitor each other's behavior, recognize difficulties, and intervene. This feedback can be supportive and diminish social isolation, and may help families obtain necessary services. Studies have reported that the families in a high-risk environment are less able to give and share and might be mistrustful of neighborly exchange. In this way, a family's problems seem to be compounded rather than ameliorated by the neighborhood context [60]. Socioeconomic factors (poverty) and parent's negative perceptions of the quality of life in the neighborhood have been reported to be strongly associated with increased child maltreatment [59]. In summary, communities can serve as a valuable source of support to families or they may add to the stresses that families are experiencing.

IMPACT OF CHILD ABUSE AND NEGLECT

It has been reported that the impact of child maltreatment is far greater than its immediate, visible effects. Abuse and neglect are associated with short- and long-term consequences that may include brain damage, developmental delays, learning disorders, problems forming relationships, aggressive behavior, and depression [61 – 72]. Survivors of child abuse and neglect may be at greater risk for problems later in life—such as low academic achievement, drug use, teen pregnancy, and criminal behavior—that affect not just the child and family, but society as a whole. Social and emotional handicaps are perhaps the most serious long-term consequences of maltreatment. Physically abused children are generally more aggressive with their peers than children who have not been abused, have more troubled interpersonal relationships and have more depressive symptoms and affective disorders. Sexually abused children, in addition to their depressive and aggressive symptoms have an increased frequency of anxiety disorders and problems with sex roles and sexual functioning [73]. Furthermore, abused children when they become adults have 2 or 3 times as many problems with substance abuse and depression. Still further, abused children, when they become parents have a tendency to abuse their own children. However, the physical, behavioral and emotional manifestations will vary between children, depending on the developmental stage at which the abuse occurs and its severity.

Walker et al. [74], reported a broad array of adverse adult health outcomes with which child sexual and physical abuse are associated, including disturbances in emotional, social, and role functioning; mental health problems; risky health practices including substance abuse; a broad array of physical symptoms and health disorders reaching clinical threshold. Felitti et al. [75], found a strong graded relationship between exposure to abusive or neglectful conditions in childhood and risk of certain adult disorders, including ischemic heart disease, cancer, chronic lung disease, skeletal fractures, and liver disease.

Findings of these studies call for an explanation as to how do abusive and neglectful family environments in childhood affect mental and physical health decades later? An important route involves alterations in autonomic and endocrine responses. The consequences of early exposure to abuse or neglect appear to be potentially irreversible disruptions in biological systems that may, perhaps also in conjunction with genetic predisposition, produce significant differences in susceptibility to stress, to biological markers of the cumulative effects of stress, and to stress related physical and mental health disorders [76]. For example, alterations in sympathetic nervous system reactivity in response to stress appear to begin in childhood, in part as a result of exposure to abusive or neglectful circumstances. These include elevated blood pressure and heart rate responses, as well as prolonged sympathetic response to stress. Alterations in hypothalamic-pituitary-adrenocortical reactivity in response to stress also appear to be related to adverse family history. In families characterized by conflict, anger, and aggression, for example, there may be disruptions of the normal rise and fall of serum cortisol levels in response to acutely stressful circumstances, such that a protracted cortisol response, or in extreme cases a flattened cortisol response, may develop. In contrast, a warm and supportive family environment may actually foster a less elevated cortisol response to potentially stressful circumstances or one that rapidly habituates to stress [77]. There is evidence too, for serotonergic dysregulation in offspring of abusive and neglectful families. Difficulty in moderating aggressive impulses, problems in developing and maintaining social relationships, and risky health-related behaviors, especially substance abuse, are among the outcomes consistently seen in response to the abusive or neglectful childhood family environment, and serotonergic dysfunction may be implicated in these patterns.

The adverse long-term health effects of childhood abuse cannot be understood solely in terms of biological dysregulations and behavioral pathways that follow from, exacerbate, and interact with biological dysregulations are at least as important. Two important psychosocial mechanisms whereby the long-term adverse effects of abuse may be maintained into adult hood include: deficits in emotion regulation skills and low social competence. In the warm and supportive household, children learn emotion regulation strategies, including how to recognize their emotions when they occur, and how to control those emotions when interacting with others. Children from families in which there has been abuse or neglect have difficulty monitoring, identifying, reacting to, and regulating their emotions, including emotional intensity, range, and duration. Among the consequences of poor emotional regulation are social rejection and isolation. Children who are unable to express or control their emotions or respond appropriately to the emotions of others are more likely to be bullied by others, act as bullies themselves, or be socially ignored or isolated – problems that lay the groundwork for difficulties in adulthood [78].

Deficits in appropriate emotion regulation and social regulation skills take their toll on adult health in many ways. People who lack these vital skills interact poorly in the social environment. As adults, they may have difficulty forming long-term social relationships, such as romantic relationships and friendships, and compromise their work-related relationships as well. Social isolation and lack of social support have been related to a greater risk of mortality from all causes, as well as more protracted courses of illness and recovery from several acute and chronic disorders. Emotion dysregulation and low social competence, in turn, increase the likelihood of substance abuse, aggression, risky behavior, and other poor health habits. Poor control over emotions and the social fallout that results may thus be essential components of the sustaining pathways that explain the long-term effects of childhood abuse on social, mental and physical health. Emotional dysregulation as a risk factor for mental illness is implicated in almost half of the DSM-IV axis I psychiatric disorders and in almost all of the axis II disorders. Emotion regulation is implicated in physical health, in that people who are emotionally reactive are also likely to be physiologically reactive. For example, emotions such as anger and hostility have been related to the development and exacerbation of hypertension and coronary heart disease. In summary, child neglect and abuse can justifiably be viewed as a public health problem with immediate and long-term social, mental and physical health consequences.

An association between abuse and suicide has been found in studies of abused children and adolescents, of adolescent suicide attempters, and of mothers who attempt suicide. Self-mutilation has been reported in abused and neglected children [79]. Adolescents who attempt suicide have more often been reported as abuse victims [80]. High rates of suicide attempts have been reported in adolescent runaways [81]. Kaplan et al., [82] reported that conduct disorders, substance abuse, depression, family discord, and family histories of suicide, and other exposure to suicide appear to be risk factors for adolescent suicide. Child-abusive behaviors were also found more often in mothers who attempted suicide than in a comparison group of non-suicidal mothers [83]. Studies have reported that physically abused adolescents have significantly more risk factors for suicide than do non-abused adolescents [84]. Though the origin of the association between suicidal behavior and physical abuse remains to be studied, it may be secondary to modeling of aggressive behavior within the family or to exposure to the suicidal behavior of family members. [85, 86]

PREVENTION

Prevention of child abuse and neglect has taken on many forms since the 1960s when the Battered Child Syndrome was identified. Policy makers, legislators, professionals, and concerned citizens have struggled to find effective ways to prevent violence against children. The goal of child abuse prevention is simple—to stop child abuse and neglect from happening in the first place, sparing children and family's emotional and physical trauma and decreasing the need for costly intervention and treatment services. Many principles of prevention have been suggested from time to time.

Mrazek et al., [87] have categorized prevention programs along three dimensions: universal, selected and indicated. 'Universal' or population-based interventions are designed to prevent child maltreatment for the entire population of children and are mass distributed. Examples include child protection policies, mass media campaigns, and public service announcements to draw public attention to the importance of protecting children and promoting their optimal development. 'Selected' interventions are directed towards families who are at high risk for child neglect and abuse. Their goal is to reduce the incidence of child maltreatment, often by reducing the risk factors that are associated with child neglect and abuse. Thus selected interventions are often targeted to families experiencing social isolation, high stress, few resources, poverty and substance abuse. 'Indicated' interventions are directed towards families in which child neglect / abuse has already occurred and aim at minimizing the negative effects of neglect or abuse on the child and breaking the cycle by preventing further occurrence. In a review of prevention strategies for neglect, Holden et al., [88] recommended the need for theory-driven, longitudinal programs that extend beyond the prevention of neglect to the promotion of healthy care-giving practices.

The best way to prevent child abuse and neglect is to support families and provide parents with the skills and resources they need. It has been established that those in closest proximity to the child perpetrate a considerable amount of child maltreatment. While it is accepted that maltreatment can occur because of wider societal system, organizations and processes, it's also agreed that a major step in developing preventive strategies is to recognize those dangers, which are in the control of individuals closest to the child. These individuals are most frequently family and community members and in some cases strangers whom the child encounters within his / her day-to-day environment. Interventions can be at the primary, secondary or tertiary level. Primary prevention aims at proving education to the parents to be, about good parenting. At the secondary level those parents who were abused, as children should be given education regarding child rearing. Once the abuse has occurred tertiary prevention helps to avoid recurrence of the same.

MULTIDISCIPLINARY TEAM APPROACH

Effective assessment of the alleged child victim and intervention in the field of child maltreatment is the result of collective insights of many professionals. The mechanism for achieving consensus and thus shared responsibility is the multidisciplinary team. Each discipline holds one piece of the puzzle, and until all of the interlocking pieces are joined, a full understanding of the child's experience and the needs of the victim and family will not be appreciated. The multidisciplinary team is the mechanism to ensure improved coordination, better information gathering, and thus a more comprehensive assessment of an allegation. A comprehensive assessment assists in providing direction for the law enforcement, mental health, and the child-protection system to respond, when coordinated intervention occurs in a coordinated manner, appropriate service needs can be identified early in delivered timely.

The legal system can respond without compromising its focus and taking into account the needs of the victims and their families. Although valid statistics are lacking, the multidisciplinary team is likely to lead to more successful prosecution when appropriate. The artificial turf issues in each discipline and the boundaries that exist to form the turf diminish with time, and all disciplines begin to interact to reflect a more global understanding of the system and the victim's needs. The issue of confidentiality of the communication as well as discovery rules may vary from state to state and must be addressed, with particular attention to how the team's discussions and recommendations are recorded.

A multi-disciplinary protection team should include representation from the medical, mental health, education, social service and legal professions working with government agencies. Non Governmental Organizations can also play a lead role. An emotionally secure infancy is a fundamental requirement for a stable adulthood. Hence treatment services must focus on the child as well as the parent. They must help children develop feelings of self worth and learn interpersonal skills and coping mechanism. For this to happen the basic needs of the family and the community should be met. World Health Organization is active in the areas of improving mother and child interaction, in promoting life skills education for children and adolescents and in promoting child-friendly schools. Parents need to rediscover the art and skill of our yester year grandmothers, in preventing child sexual abuse in the families, in a subtle way by anticipating situations and acting appropriately in time. As professionals, the health care workers need to be committed to protect the rights of the children by motivating the parents to be more proactive and systematically sensitizing the other agencies like the police and judiciary about the various aspects of the problem.

Providing ongoing support to the victims of childhood abuse may include assisting young people to:

- Regain trust and establish supportive relationships;
- Understand the effects on their current thoughts and feelings;
- Validate the normality of their thoughts and feelings;
- Manage impacts on other relationships;
- Rediscover their strengths and value what is special about them;
- Help them to make meaning from their experiences; and
- Help them to make the changes they want to make, at their pace.

WHY DOES PREVENTION MATTER?

Through prevention activities such as parent education, home visitation, and parent support groups, many families can find the support they need to stay together and care for their children in their homes and communities. Prevention efforts help parents develop their parenting skills, understand the benefits of nonviolent discipline techniques, and understand and meet their child's emotional, physical, and developmental needs. Prevention programs also can help parents identify other needs they may have and offer assistance in getting that additional support.

Prevention of socially undesirable and hazardous behaviors may not only save lives, but also resources. While it is impossible to entirely eradicate certain kinds of behavior that can have tragic human consequences, including the maltreatment of children, human service professionals have been buoyed by improvements over time across numerous major indices that measure the health and well-being of individuals and families.

INTERVENTION AND TREATMENT

The primary concern of child welfare agencies has been child protection and safety. Increasingly, in Australia, the United States and the United Kingdom there have been movements to redress the imbalance, so that child- and family-support services achieve much greater importance. This may be welcomed, because maltreated children and their families are typically embedded within a range of family difficulties and social stresses, which need to be tackled to obtain positive outcomes for children. Intervention therefore is multifaceted and may involve several professionals working together [89]. The overall objectives of management are to help the child and his or her family by:

- Stopping abuse or reversing neglect and ensuring adequate care-taking;
- Improving the capacity for positive interpersonal relationships between family members;
- Treating symptoms of psychological disorders;
- Stopping sexually aggressive, violent, or exploitative behavior that is either directed towards child or which is likely to have an impact on him or her;
- Facilitating understanding by the child and his or her parents of the nature and dynamics of maltreatment.

The process of treatment may be conceptualized in three phases: first, an initial acknowledgement of the problem; second, improving parental competence and sensitivity to their child's needs and third, a resolution phase, either in the direction of alternative care or, if possible within the family [89].

Treatment of child sexual abuse requires a psycho-educational component, so that the nature of sexual exploitation and the way in which children become coerced into sexual activity can be understood by the child without a sense of personal blame. Cognitive-behavioral treatments have been particularly helpful especially when combined with a program of intervention for the non-abusive caretaker [33]. Abusers should be assessed for their potential to respond to psychological treatment [90]. In the field of physical abuse, cognitive-behavioral treatment and family therapy have been shown to be more effective than routine community services at reducing the levels of violence and parental distress, as well as family conflict [13]. Psychological treatments in the field of neglect have concentrated on improving parenting skills and sensitivity through direct encouragement of positive interactions in feeding, play and general care, combined with individual therapy for parents themselves, who have frequently experienced multiple deprived childhoods. Psychiatric treatment of parental mental health problems, such as depression or substance abuse, is critical. Mobilizing community-based supports and networks to overcome social isolation, and linking neglectful mothers with other parents who can provide role modeling and support, appears to be promising approach.

FORENSIC ASPECTS OF INTERVIEWING
ALLEGEDLY ABUSED CHILDREN

Since there is currently no valid syndrome for child sexual abuse and there is a strong likelihood of child sexual abuse symptoms having multiple explanations, short of a valid offender confession [91] and incontrovertible medical evidence, the crucial aspect of a proper forensic evaluation of suspected sexual abuse in children is usually the interview itself, which must be done in an 'ethically permissible manner' [92]. Mandatory state and provincial reporting laws require the health care professionals as well as others in positions of trust to report the suspected child sexual abuse to child protection services or the police. However, since the initial disclosure interview with the child is usually the most valid one, the clinical practitioner should be prepared to provide minimally optimum standards of forensic interviewing at this crucial juncture. Furthermore, there has been increasing recognition that, under certain circumstances, false memories of abuse may develop in children [93]. Pre-schoolers, in particular, have been found vulnerable to confusion and false memories because of faulty interview techniques. Recent studies inform clinical practice by suggesting that children are most likely to be misled during interviews if (a) they feel it is preferable to 'guess' or 'pretend' during interviews rather than to acknowledge 'not knowing' [94]; (b) their memories are 'weak' [95]; (c) they are confused about 'adult' language that does not take the child's development level into account; (d) the interviewer is seen as unfriendly, intimidating, or authoritarian [96]; or (e) the interviewer has a preconceived bias about the event.

Statement validity analysis is a serious attempt to construct a valid and systematic forensic interview schedule for children that emphasizes free recall as its key component. There also is a general consensus that the use of open-ended questions when interviewing children suspected to have been sexually abused, although associated with lowest risk of confusion, also is associated with the generation of least information. In contrast, leading questions, which pressure a child to agree with the interviewer, can lead to a permanent distortion of memory for what happened. Focused questions, which fall between free recall and leading questions, have been found to be necessary by many clinicians when faced with a child reluctant to discuss abuse [97]. To minimize suggestibility in forensic interviews of allegedly abused children, Reed [98] has recommended that interviewers systematically clarify to children what is expected of them by specifically teaching children to state when they are 'confused' or 'do not know' answers to the questions.

Several structured and semi-structured interview protocols have been introduced that were designed to maximize the amount of accurate information and to minimize mistaken or false information provided by children. These approaches include the 'cognitive interview', which encourages witnesses to search their memories in various ways, such as recalling events forward and then backward. The step-wise interview is a funnel approach that starts with open-ended questions and, if necessary, moves to more specific questions. The interview protocol developed at the National Institute of Child Health and Human Development includes a series of phases and makes use of detailed interview scripts [99].

Although these protocols may be particularly important in a forensic context, experienced clinicians endorse flexibility to size up the situation and use techniques that are likely to help the youngster become comfortable and communicative. One victim might need a favorite object (e.g., a teddy bear or a toy truck); another might need to have a particular person included in the interview. Some children are comfortable talking; others prefer to draw pictures. An unrelated joke, a shared cookie, or a picture on the evaluator's wall may lead to a disclosure of abuse. Important comments may be made while chatting during the break time, instead of during the structured interviews. The interviewer should remember the following principles:

- Audiotape or videotape the interview, if possible;
- Use a minimum number of interviews, as multiple interviews may encourage confabulation;
- Avoid repetitive questions, either-or questions, leading and suggestive questions;
- Use restatement, that is, repeat the child's account back to the child (This allows the interviewer to see if the child is consistent and ensures that the interviewer understands the child's report);
- Conduct the interview without the parent being present, however, if the child is young, consider having a family member in the room;
- Use an examination technique that is appropriate to the child's age and developmental level;
- Determine the child's terms for body parts and sexual acts; do not educate or provide new terms.

However, the interview should not take the form an interrogation. The interviewer should note the child's affects while discussing the topic and be tactful in helping the child manage anxiety. The 'step-wise interview, which is primarily intended for forensic evaluation, consists of the following components: building rapport, asking the child to describe two specific past events to assess the child's memory, establishing the need to tell the truth, introducing the topic of concern, eliciting a free narrative, posing general questions, posing specific questions, using interview aids etc., while trying to explore:

- Whether the child was told to report or not to report anything;
- Who the alleged perpetrator was;
- What the alleged perpetrator did;
- Where did it happen;
- When it started and when it ended;
- Number of times the abuse occurred;
- How the child was initially engaged and how the abuse progressed over time;
- How the alleged perpetrator induced the child to maintain secrecy;
- Whether the child is aware of specific injuries or physical symptoms associated with the abuse;
- Whether any photography or videotaping took place.

FORENSIC EVIDENCE COLLECTION IN CHILD SEXUAL ABUSE

It is first necessary to consider what the legal system views as scientifically useful evidence and how this applies to behavioral testimony, whether given by psychologists, psychiatrists, or social workers. Such psychological considerations are quite different from clinical ones in a variety of ways, which turn on the rigor of findings (i.e., probability), their admissibility in court (i.e., relevancy) and our avoidance of biasing the jury. Although there is a good deal of variation in how these 'rules of evidence' are interpreted and administered in courts at various states and provincial levels, these legal tools are nevertheless broad guidelines to good forensic practice in general. When science and the law work well together, there is a relatively smooth transition between the two as to the validity of data. Thus, if one's assessment is knowingly to be used in court, then it should be prepared as a scientific exhibit rendered interpretable according to common law rules of evidence. This need not be an obscure task as data that are reliable and valid are often consistent with the spirit of good evidence.

Several general guidelines about evidence should be addressed before outlining a more specific approach to specimen collection. First, specific details of collection, labeling and packaging of specimens should be worked out with the laboratory processing the specimens. Second, a specimen collection protocol should be used to ensure that all appropriate specimens are collected for both routine and non-routine circumstances. Third, collection kits should be standardized, providing containers, collection devices, and checklists to assure proper collection of specimens. Fourth, the procedures for collecting specimen are best explained in advance to the child and the caretakers, because cooperation is the key to the collection of proper specimens. Fifth, proper consent must be obtained from the parent and child before performing the examination and collecting evidence. Finally, the handling of collected specimens should be documented to maintain the 'chain of evidence'.

Forensic evidence collection, usually done at the same time as the physical examination, has been recommended when the examination occurs within 72 hours of acute sexual abuse [100]. This recommendation is based at least in part on the fact that seminal fluid and other foreign substances are rarely recoverable after 72 hours of the sexual contact. The types of evidence sought include sperm, seminal fluid, and foreign materials on the victim's body surface or clothing. Semen, blood, saliva, body hair, bite marks, and other materials occasionally found on the body of the victim can also be used to identify the perpetrator with the help of genetic markers. DNA typing or profiling is the most specific development in the identification of the perpetrator of sexual abuse [101]. Christian et al., [102] recommended that guidelines for evidence collection for adult sexual assault victims may not be appropriate for pre-pubertal victims and the clothing and linens that yield the majority of evidence should be vigorously pursued for analysis.

MEDICOLEGAL ASPECTS OF CHILD ABUSE AND NEGLECT

All states have reporting laws mandating that professionals in the areas of health care, social service, law enforcement, and education report suspected cases of child abuse or neglect. Conversely, the ethical principles of medicine, nursing and other professions require professionals to safeguard confidential information. But in legal proceedings, the presence or absence of a privilege is important. In court, a professional may have to answer questions that require disclosure of information the professional is ethically bound to protect.

Confidentiality arises from three sources: (a) the broad ethical duty to protect confidential information, (b) laws that make certain records confidential, and (c) privileges that apply in legal proceedings. Communication between a patient and a professional is privileged when three requirements are fulfilled. First, the communication must be between a patient and a professional with whom privileged communication is possible. The fact that a third person is present when a patient discloses information may or may not eliminate the confidentiality required for a privilege. Second, the patient must consult the professional to obtain advice or therapy. Despite the fact that a patient may consult a physician who refers the patient to a second professional, communication between the patient and the referring physician is privileged even though the patient does not receive treatment from the referring physician. Third, only communications that the patient intends to be confidential are privileged. Furthermore, privileged communications remain privileged when the relationship with the patient ends as in case of death of the patient. It must be stressed that the privilege belongs to the patient, not the professional. In legal parlance, the patient is the 'holder' of privilege and as a privilege holder; he can prevent the professional from disclosing privileged information in legal proceedings. When the patient is a child, parents normally have authority to make decisions about confidential and privileged information. However, when a parent is accused of abusing or neglecting a child, it may be inappropriate for the parent to make decisions regarding the child's confidential information. In the event of a conflict between the interests of the child and the parents, the court may appoint someone else, such as a 'guardian ad litem', to make decisions about confidential and privileged information.

Child abuse reporting laws require professionals to report suspected child abuse and neglect to designate authorities [103]. The reporting laws override the ethical duty to protect confidential client information. Moreover, the reporting requirement overrides privileges for confidential communications between professionals and their patients. However, although reporting laws abrogate privileges, abrogation usually is not complete. In many states, professionals may limit the information by reporting the specific information required by law. Information that is not required to be reported remains privileged.

Statement of the abused child recorded during examination and interview has medical as well as legal significance [1]. If children's statements are properly documented they may be admissible in subsequent legal proceedings. In some cases, the child's statements to the professionals are the most compelling evidence of maltreatment. However, the rule in all states is that 'hearsay' is inadmissible in criminal and civil litigation unless the particular hearsay statement meets the requirements of an exception to the rule against hearsay. In these cases, a child's words are hearsay if three requirements are fulfilled: (a) the child's words were intended by the child to describe something that happened; (b) the child's words were spoken before the court proceedings at which the words are repeated by someone who heard the child speak and (c) the child's words are offered in court to prove that what the child said actually happened [104 – 106].

An 'excited utterance' is a hearsay statement that relates to a startling event. The statement must be made while the child is under the acute emotional stress caused by the startling event. Excited utterances can be used in court even though they are hearsay. Accordingly a professional can document the following important factors:

- Nature of the event;
- Amount of time elapsed between the startling event and the child's statement relating to the event (the more time that passes between a startling event and a child's statement describing it, the less likely a court is to conclude that the statement is an excited utterance, however, exceptions are there);
- Indications that the child was emotionally upset when the child spoke (whether crying, frightened or otherwise upset);
- Extent to which the child's statement was spontaneous (the more spontaneous the statement the more likely it meets the requirements of this exception);
- Number and type of questions used to elicit the child's statement (asking questions does not necessarily destroy the spontaneity required for the excited utterance exception, however, as the questions become leading, spontaneity may dissipate, undermining the applicability of this exception);

First safe opportunity to disclose what happened (in many cases, abused child remains under the control of the abuser for hours after the abusive incident and has the first safe opportunity to disclose when released. A child's statement at the first safe opportunity may qualify as an excited utterance even though considerable time has elapsed since the abuse occurred)

A child's initial disclosure of sexual abuse may be admissible in court under an ancient legal doctrine called 'fresh complaint of rape or sexual assault'. In most states, a child's fresh complaint is not, technically speaking, hearsay.

Most states have an exception to the hearsay rule for certain statements to professionals providing diagnostic or treatment services, commonly called the 'diagnostic or treatment exception'. The primary rationale for this exception is that hearsay statements to these professionals are reliable. Reliability exists because the patient has a strong incentive to be truthful with the professional. To increase the probability that a child's statements satisfy the diagnosis or treatment exception to the rule against hearsay, the professional can take the following steps:

- Discuss with the child the clinical importance of providing accurate information and of being completely forthcoming.
- The diagnosis or treatment exception requires that information supplied to the professional be pertinent to diagnosis or treatment. Thus it is important to document how information disclosed by the child is pertinent to diagnosis or treatment.
- If the child identifies the perpetrator, the professional should document why knowing the identity of the perpetrator is pertinent to diagnosis or treatment. For example, knowing the identity of the perpetrator may be important to determine whether it is safe to send the child home or the physician needs the perpetrator's identity if sexually transmitted disease is a possibility.
- Document the foregoing factors in the child's chart.

Many states have a hearsay exception known as 'residual or catch all exception', which allows use in court of a reliable hearsay statement that does not meet the requirements of one of the traditional exceptions. Some states also have a special hearsay exception for statements by children in child abuse cases. These 'child hearsay exceptions, and residual exceptions allow use in court of children's reliable hearsay statements that do not fit into another exception.

Proper documentation by the medical professionals is needed not only to preserve the child's words, but also to preserve a record of the factors indicating that the child's hearsay statements meet the requirements of an exception to the hearsay rule. Without careful documentation of exactly what questions are asked and exactly what the child says, the professional will not likely remember months or years later, when called as a witness and asked to repeat what the child said. Furthermore, uncorroborated clinical inference and contaminated interviewing have no place in preparing scientifically informed child abuse evidentiary material. When clinical descriptions of children are improperly elevated to the status of empirically contentious syndromes, disorders or even simple profiles, numerous psycho-legal errors and miscarriages of justice can result because they do not sufficiently reduce uncertainty below reasonable doubt and can then bias the trier of fact and invade the province of jury. It is also essential to know the scientific limitations of one's discipline to provide a balanced and useful forensic evaluation.

CONCLUSION

Many efforts are directed towards identification of victims, and yet prevention is the ultimate goal in the management of child abuse and neglect. Multidisciplinary teams provide an excellent opportunity for clinicians to become involved in the child protection system and to take leadership role in their community. Medical professionals functioning as a part of team can educate team members concerning the scope of medicines' contribution in the field. At the same time, they can learn to appreciate the complexity of the system and then advocate for necessary changes that will positively affect children and their families. However, different professionals, particularly those of medicine and law sometimes seem like ships passing in the night, yet if children are to be protected, all must work together. Only genuine interdisciplinary cooperation holds realistic hope of reducing the tragic number of abused and neglected children. Furthermore, given the presumption of innocence in common law and the need to protect the rights of both the accused and the victims, it is especially incumbent upon health professionals and allied service providers to adhere to very high scientific standards when assessing child sexual abuse. Regrettably, however, most health-care professionals and lawyers are not specifically versed in terms of valid child sexual abuse interviewing. Presumably then, their knowledge of valid behavioral manifestations of child sexual abuse is also likely to be deficient. Accordingly, there is a pressing need for more user-friendly literature that integrates behavioral and legal issues.

REFERENCES

[1]   Sharma BR. Medicolegal aspects of child abuse. *Physician's Digest 2005;* 14 (1): 41 – 48

[2]   U.S. Department of Health and Human Services, Administration on Children, Youth and Families: Child Maltreatment 1998: reports from the States to the National Child Abuse and Neglect Data System. Washington, DC, US Government Printing Office, 2002

[3]   U.S. Department of Health and Human Services, Administration on Children, Youth and Families: *Child Maltreatment 1998*: *reports from the States to the National Child Abuse and Neglect Data System.* Washington, DC, US Government Printing Office, 2000

[4]   Sedlak A, Broadhurst MLA. *Third National Incidence Study of Child Abuse and Neglect Washington DC,* U.S. Department of Health and Human Services, 1996

[5]   *Kids Help Line report 2003 – 2004*, available at *www.kidshelp.com.au*

[6]   Black MM. The roots of child neglect. In Rees RM. Ed. *The treatment of child abuse.* Baltimore; Johns Hopkins University Press; 2000

[7]   Zuravin SJ. Child neglect: a review of definitions and measurement research. In Dubowitz H. ed. Neglected children; Thousand Oaks CA: *Sage Publication 1999*; 24 – 46.

[8]   Helfer RE. The neglect of our children. *Pediartic Clin North Am. 1990*; 37: 923.

[9]   Berman BD, Winkleby M, Chesterman E. et al. After-school child care and self-esteem in school-age children. *Pediatrics 1992*; 89: 654

[10]   Jaudes PK, Diamond LJ. Neglect of chronically ill children. *Am J Dis Child 1986*; 140: 655

[11]   Nandy A. *Principles of Forensic Medicine, 1st Ed. 1995;* New Central Book Agency (P) Ltd.: 352 - 357

[12]   Caffey J. Multiple fractures in the long bones of infants suffering from chronic subdural hematoma. *Am J Rontgenol 1946*; 56: 163 – 173.

[13]   Skuse D, Bentovim A. Physical and emotional maltreatment. In M Rutter, E Taylor, L Hearsov eds. Child and Adolescent Psychiatry, *Blackwell Science, Oxford, 1994,* 209 – 229.

[14]   Westcott HL, Jones DPH. Annotation: the abuse of disabled children. *J Child Psychology and Psychiatry 1999;* 40: 497 - 506

[15]   Kolko D. Child physical abuse. In J Briere, L Berliner J Bulkley et al., eds. The APSAC hand book on child maltreatment , *Sage , London, 1996,* 21 - 50

[16]   Feldman K. Evaluation of physical abuse. In R. Helfer, R Kempe and R Krugman eds. The Battered Child, *University of Chicago Press, (5th edn) 1997,* 175 - 220

[17]   Cicchetti D, Toth S. A developmental psychopathology perspective on child abuse and neglect. *J Am Acad Child and Adolescent Psychiatry 1995*; 34: 541 – 565

[18]   Kempe CH. Sexual abuse, another hidden pediatric problem. *Pediatrics 1978*; 62: 382 – 389

[19]   Finkelhor DH, Hotaling GT. Sexual abuse in the National Incidence Study of Child Abuse and Neglect: an appraisal. *Child Abuse Negl 1984*; 8: 23 – 32

[20]   Wyatt GE, Peters SD. Methodological consideration in research on the prevalence of child sexual abuse. *Child Abuse Negl 1986*; 10: 241 – 251

[21]   Sharma BR, Gupta M. Child abuse and its implications. *J Clinical Forensic Medicine 2004; 11 (5)*: 258 – 266

[22]   Beriner L, Conte JR. The process of victimization: the victim's perspective. *Child Abuse Negl 1990*; 14: 29 – 40

[23] American Prosecutors Research Institute National Center for Prosecution of Child Abuse. *Investigation and prosecution of child abuse, Alexandria, VA*: American Prosecutor's Institute, 1987

[24] Finkelhor D. The victimization of children: a developmental perspective. *Am J Orthopsychiatry 1995*; 65: 177 – 193

[25] Summit RC. The child sexual abuse accommodation syndrome. *Child Abuse Negl 1983*; 7: 177 - 193

[26] Hunter RS, kilstrom N, Loda F. Sexually abused children: identifying masked presentations in a medical setting. *Child Abuse Negl 1985*; 9: 17 – 25

[27] Seidel JS, Elvik SL Berkowitz CD, et al. Presentation and evaluation of sexual misuse in the emergency department. *Pediatr Emerg Care 1986*; 2: 157

[28] DeJong AR, Emans SJ, Goldfarb A. Sexual abuse: what you must know? *Patient Care 1989*; 23: 145

[29] Klevan JL, deJong AR. Urinary tract symptoms and urinary tract infection following sexual abuse. *Am J Dis Child 1990*; 144: 242 – 244

[30] Meadow R. *ABC of child abuse*, BMJ Publishing London, 3rd Ed. 1997

[31] Jones DPH, Lynch MA. Diagnosing and responding to serious child abuse. *BMJ 1998*; 317: 484 - 485

[32] Jones DPH. Management of the sexually abused child. *Advances in Psychiatric Treatment 1996*; 2: 39 – 45

[33] Jones DPH, Ramchandani P. *Child sexual abuse – informing practice from research*, Radcliffe Medical Press, Oxford, 1998.

[34] Rind B, Tromovitch P, Bauserman R. A meta-analytic examination of assumed properties of child sexual abuse using college samples. *Psychological Bulletin 1998*; 124: 22 – 53

[35] Brassard M, Hardy D. Psychological maltreatment. In R. Helfer, R Kempe and R Krugman eds. *The Battered Child*, University of Chicago Press, (5th edn) 1997, 392 – 412

[36] Department of Health, Health and personal social services statistics for England, HMSO London, 2000. Website *http://www.Doh.gov.uk/HPSSS/INDEX.HTM*

[37] Sharma BR, Harish D, Gupta M. Innocence abused: an overview of the nature, causes and prevention of child abuse. *J Indian Academy of Forensic Medicine 2003*; 25 (3): 87 - 92

[38] Zuravin S. *Child abuse, child neglect and maternal depression: is there a connection?* National Center on Child Abuse and Neglect: child neglect monograph: proceedings from a symposium. Washington DC: Clearinghouse on child abuse and neglect information, 1988.

[39] Polansky N. *Damaged parents: an anatomy of child neglect.* Chicago: University of Chicago. 1981

[40] Wolock I, Horowitz H. Child maltreatment and maternal deprivation among AFDC recipient families. *Soc Serv Res 1979*; 53: 175.

[41] Friedrich WN, Tyler JA, Clark JA. Personality and psycho-physiological variables: its abusive, neglectful and low- income control mothers. *J Nerv Ment Disord 1985*; 173: 449

[42] Martin M, Walters S. Familial correlates of selected types of child abuse and neglect. J *Marriage Family 1982*; 44: 267.

[43] Ory N, Earp J. Child maltreatment and the use of social services. *Public Health Rep 1981*; 96: 238.

[44] Shapiro J. Family reactions and coping strategies in response to the physically ill or handicapped child. *Soc Sci Med 1983*; 17: 913

[45] Benedict M, White K. Selected perinatal factors and child abuse. *Am J Public Health 1985;* 75: 780.

[46] Herrenkohl EC, Herrenkohl RC. *Some antecedents and developmental consequences of child maltreatment.* In Rizley R, Cicchetti D, eds Developmental perspectives on child maltreatment. San Francisco: Jossey-Bass, 1981.

[47] Glaser D, Bentovim A. Abuse and risk to handicapped and chronically ill children. *Child Abuse negl 1979;* 3: 565

[48] Dietrich KN, Starr RH, Weisfeld OE. Infant maltreatment: caretaker-infant interaction and developmental consequences at different levels of parenting failure. *Pediatrics 1983;* 72: 332.

[49] Crittenden PM. Maltreated infants: vulnerability and resilience *J Child Psychol Psychiatry 1985*; 26: 85.

[50] Egeland B, Brunquell D. An at-risk approach to the studies of child abuse and neglect. *J Am Acad Child Adolesc Psychiatry 1979*; 18: 219.

[51] Azar S, Robinson DR, Hekimien E. Unrealistic expectations and problem solving ability in maltreating and comparison mothers. *J Consult Clin Psychol 1984*; 52: 687

[52] Twentyman C, Plotkin R. Unrealistic expectations of parents who maltreat their children: an educational deficit that pertains to child development. *J Clin Psychol 1982*; 38: 497.

[53] Herrenkohl RC, Herrenkohl EC, Egolf BP. Circumstances surrounding the occurrence of child maltreatment. *J Consult Clin Psychol 1983*; 51: 424.

[54] Kadushin A. Neglect in families. In Nunnally EW, Chilman CS, Cox FM. Eds Mental illness, delinquency: addictions and neglect. Newbury Park: sage, 1988.

[55] Dubowitz H, Black MM, Kerr M, et al. Fathers and child neglect. *Arch Pediatr Adolesc Med 2000*; 154: 135

[56] Polansky NA, Ammons PW, Gaudin JM. Loneliness and isolation in child neglect. *Social Casework 1985*; 66: 38

[57] Polansky NA, Gaudin JM, Ammons PW, et al. The psychological ecology of the neglectful mother. *Child Abuse Neglect 1985*; 9: 265

[58] Crittenden PM. Child neglect: causes and contributors. In Dubowitz H eds Neglected Children. Thousand Oaks, CA: *Sage publications 199*9; 47 – 68.

[59] Garbarino J, Crouter A. Defining the community context of parent-child relations. *Child Dev 1978*; 49: 604

[60] Garbarino J, Sherman D. High-risk neighborhoods and high-risk families: the human ecology of child maltreatment. *Child Dev 1980*; 51: 188

[61] Rimsza ME, Berg RA. Sexual abuse: somatic and emotional reactions. *Child Abuse Negl. 1988*; 12: 201 - 208.

[62] Walker E, Katon W, Harrop J, et al. Relationship of chronic pelvic pain to psychiatric diagnosis and childhood sexual abuse. *Am J Psychiatry 1988*; 145: 75 - 80.

[63] Arnold RP, Rogers D, Cook DA. Medical problems of adults who were sexually abused in childhood. *BMJ 1990*; 300: 705 - 708.

[64] Koss MP, Koss PG, Woodruf WJ. Deleterious effects of criminal victimization on women's health. *Arch Intern Med. 1991*; 151: 342 - 347.

[65] Walker EA, Katon WJ, Roy-Byrne PP. Histories of sexual victimization in patients with irritable bowel syndrome or inflammatory bowel disease. *Am J Psychiatry 1993*; 150: 1502 - 1506.

[66] Moeller TP, Bachmann GA, Moeller JR. The combined effects of physical, sexual and emotional abuse during childhood: long term health consequences for women. Child *Abuse Negl. 1993*; 17: 623 - 640.

[67] Lodico MA, DiClemente RJ. The association between child hood sexual abuse and prevalence of HIV related risk behaviors. *Clin. Pediatr. 1994*; 498 - 502.

[68] Golding JM. Sexual assault history and physical health in randomly selected Los Angeles women. *Health Psychol. 1994*; 13: 130 - 138.

[69] Taylor ML, Trotter DR, Csuka ME. The prevalence of sexual abuse in women with fibromyalgia. *Arthritis Rheum. 1995*; 38: 229 - 234.

[70] Golding JM. Sexual assault history and women's reproductive and sexual health. Psychol. *Women Quart. 1996;* 20: 101 - 121.

[71] Golding JM. Sexual assault history and limitations in physical functioning in two general population samples. *Res. Nurs. Health 1996;* 19: 33 - 44.

[72] McCauley J, Kern DE, Kolodner K, et al. Clinical charasteristics of women with a history of childhood abuse: unhealed wounds. *JAMA 1997;* 277: 1362 - 1368.

[73] Sharma BR, Gupta M. Child rape – save the innocents. *Social Welfare 2004*; 51 (9): 3 – 8

[74] Walker EA, Gelfand A, Katon WI, et al.. Adult health status of women with histories of childhood abuse and neglect. *Am J Med 1999*; 107: 332 – 339

[75] Felitti VJ, Anda RF, Nordenberg D, et al. Relationship of childhood abuse and household dysfunction to many of the leading causes of death in adults. *Am J Prevent Med 1998*; 14: 245 – 258

[76] McEwen BS. Protective and damaging effects of stress mediators. *NEJM 1998*; 338: 171 - 179

[77] Gunnar MR. Quality of early care and buffering of neuroendocrine stress reactions: potential effects on the developing human brain. *Prevent Med 1998*; 27: 208 – 211

[78] Taylor SE. The lifelong legacy of childhood abuse. *Am J Med 1999*; 107: 399 – 400

[79] Green A. self-destructive behavior in battered children. *Am J Psychiatry 1978*; 135: 579 – 582.

[80] Deykin E, Alpert J, McNamarra J. A pilot study of the effect of exposure to child abuse or neglect on suicidal behavior. *Am J Psychiatry 1985*; 142: 1299 – 1309

[81] Farber E, Kinast C, McCord W, et al. Violence in families of adolescent runaways. *Child Abuse Negl 1984*; 8: 295 – 299

[82] Kaplan S, Pelcovitz D, Salzinger S et al. Adolescent physical abuse: risk for adolescent psychiatric disorders. *Am J Psychiatry 1998*; 155: 954 – 959

[83] Hawton K, Roberts J, Goodwin G. The risk of child abuse among mothers who attempt suicide. *Br. J Psychiatry 1985*; 146: 486 – 489.

[84] Kaplan S, Pelcovitz D, Salzinger S et al. Adolescent physical abuse and suicide attempts. *J Am Acad of Child Psychiatry 1997*; 36: 799 – 807.

[85] Sharma BR, Sharma V, Harish D. Suicides in Northern India – causes, Methods used and Prevention thereof. *J Med. Sci. Law 2003;* 43 (3): 221 - 229.

[86] Schmidt P, Muller R, Dettmeyer R, Madea B. Suicide inchildren, adolescents and young adults. *Forensic Science International 2002*; 127: 161 - 167

[87] Mrazek PJ, Haggerty RJ. Reducing risks for mental disorders: frontiers for preventive intervention research. Washington DC: *National Academy Press, 1994*

[88] Holden EW, Nabors L. the prevention of child neglect. In Dubowitz H. ed Neglected children. Thousand Oaks CA: *sage Publications, 1999*; 174 – 190

[89] Jones DPH. Treatment of the child and the family where child abuse or neglect has occurred. In R. Helfer, R Kempe and R Krugman eds. *The Battered Child*, University of Chicago Press, (5th edn) 1997, 521 – 542

[90] Becker J. Offenders: characteristics and treatment. Future of Children 1994; 4: 176 – 197

[91] Kassin SM. The psychology of confession evidence. *Am Psychol 1997*; 52: 221 – 233

[92] Bruck M, Ceci SJ, Hembrook H. Reliability and credibility of young children's report: from research to policy and practice. *Am Psychol 1998*; 53: 136 – 151

[93] Ceci S, Bruck M. Suggestibility of the child witness; a historical review and synthesis. *Psychol Bull 1993*; 113: 403 – 439

[94] Saywitz KJ, Moan-Hardie S. Reducing the potential for distortion of childhood memories. *Conscious Cogn 1994*; 3: 408 – 425

[95] Saywitz KJ, Goodman GS, Nicholas E, et al. Children's memories of physical examinations involving genital touch: implications for reports of child sexual abuse. *J Consult Clin Psychol 1991*; 59: 682 – 691

[96] Goodman GS, Batterman-Faunce JM, Kenney R. *Optimizing children's testimony: research and social policy issues concerning allegations of child sexual abuse.* In Cicchetti D, Toth S eds Child Abuse, Child Development and Social Policy. Norwood, NJ, Ablex, 1992

[97] Saywitz KJ, Goodman GS. Interviewing children in and out of court: current research and practical implications. In Briere J, Berliner L, Bulkley J. et al., eds The APSAC hand Book on Child maltreatment. Thousand Oaks, CA, *Sage, 1996,* 297 – 318

[98] Reed LD. Findings from research on children's suggestibility and implications for conducting child interviews. *Child Maltreatment 1996*; 1: 105 – 120

[99] *American Professional Society on the Abuse of Children, Guidelines for psychosocial evaluation of suspected sexual abuse in young children,* Chicago, American Professional Society on the Abuse of Children, 1997

[100] American Academy of Pediatrics Committee on Child Abuse and Neglect, Guidelines for the evaluation of sexual abuse of children: subject review. *Pediatrics 1999*; 103: 186 – 191.

[101] Gill P, Jeffreys AJ, Werrette DJ. Forensic application of DNA fingerprints. *Nature 1985*; 318: 577 - 579

[102] Christian CW, Lavelle JM, DeJong AR, et al. Forensic evidence collection in prepubertal victims of sexual assault. *Pediatrics 2000*; 106: 100 - 104

[103] Kalichman SC. *Mandated reporting of suspected child abuse: ethics, law and policy.* Washington, DC: American Psychological Association, 1993

[104] Mueller CB, Kirkpatrick LC. Federal evidence, 2nd ed. Rochester, NY: Lawyers Cooperative Publishing, 1994

[105] Myers JEB. *Evidence in child abuse and neglect cases, 2nd ed.* New York: Aspen Law and Business, 1997

[106] Myers JEB. Legal issues in child abuse and neglect practice, 2nd ed. Thousand Oaks, CA: Sage, 1998

In: Psychology of Decision Making in Risk Taking ...   ISBN 978-1-60021-854-5
Editor: Rachel N. Kelian   © 2008 Nova Science Publishers, Inc.

Chapter 2

FROM ABSTINENCE TO SAFER SEX: AMBIGUITIES AND DIALECTICS

Donna E. Howard, Robin Sawyer and Jessica Brewster-Jordan
Department of Public and Community Health
University of Maryland, College Park, MD USA

ABSTRACT

Despite a steady decrease in teen pregnancy, birth rates and abortion since 1991, adolescents in the United States continue to experience unintended pregnancy at higher rates than their peers in nearly all other industrialized nations and are at high risk for Sexually Transmitted Infections (STIs). At the same time, debate rages over whether comprehensive sexuality education or abstinence-only curricula should be taught in schools. Additionally, there is growing concern, among adolescent sexual behavior researchers, that our limited ability to affect changes in sexually risky behavior may be related to discordance between the survey questions pertaining to adolescent sexual behavior and actual youth practices. That is, research suggests that a significant proportion of data purporting to accurately gauge adolescent participation in specific acts of sexual behavior may be not only incomplete but flawed. This chapter will review the debate over sexuality education, examine the language used on current national health surveys that assess the sexual behavior of adolescents and young adults and provide recent findings from an exploratory study which examined the denotative meaning of sexual terms among a convenience sample of late adolescent university students. In this study, it was found that there still exists little consensus among adolescents about the behavioral referents for the terms *safe* and *safer* sex. Information in this chapter will help inform the development of rigorous investigations to further examine ambiguities surrounding the language and practice of sexual behavior among adolescents and consider how this imprecision affects policy and programmatic decision making.

INTRODUCTION

The Debate over Sexuality Education

Although birth rates and abortion have decreased in the United States since 1991, American adolescents continue to experience unintended pregnancy at higher rates than their peers in nearly all other industrialized nations (Guttmacher Institute, 2004). Although such reductions are obviously a positive development, recent data from the national Youth Risk Behavior Survey (YRBS, 2005) suggest that adolescents continue to be sexually active and engage in unprotected sexual behavior. According to a 2003 study of adolescent risk behavior, 33% of ninth graders reported that they had experienced sexual intercourse; the proportion of sexually active adolescents in the older grades were as follows: 44% of tenth graders, 53% of eleventh graders and 62% of twelfth graders (CDC, 2003). In addition to unplanned pregnancy, adolescent sexual behavior can lead to the acquisition and communicability of sexually transmitted infections (STIs). The Centers for Disease Control and Prevention (CDC) estimates the transmission of over 19 million STIs annually, with almost half occurring among young people, ages 15-24 (CDC, 2004). Recent estimates suggest the direct medical costs to diagnose and treat STIs in the United States is approaching 13 billion dollars annually (Chesson, Blandford, Gift, Tao, and Irwin, 2004). The consequences of early sexual activity are all too apparent with implications for both adolescents and the larger society. Outcomes associated with teen childbearing include lower educational achievement, higher rates of poverty, greater welfare use, lower rates of school completion, less stable employment, lower rates of marital stability and additional non-marital births (Chase-Lansdale, 1995; Chesson, Blandford, Gift, Tao, and Irwin, 2004).

Despite the widespread recognition of serious health, psychosocial and economic consequences of adolescent sexual behavior there exists little consensus in the United States regarding the appropriate approach to this issue. The current battle being waged between proponents of abstinence-only-until-marriage education and advocates of a more comprehensive approach to sex education is indicative of other political schisms apparent in the United States today. Issues related to human sexuality, i.e., school-based sex education, gay marriage, mandatory HPV (Human Papilloma Virus) vaccination, stem cell research, and emergency contraception (the "morning after pill") have become highly politicized and polarized. Furthermore, they have become lightning rods for political wrangling over issues of religion, morality, and ethics.

Attempting to restrict comprehensive sexuality education is not new, and in fact, began in 1981. In that year the Office of Population Affairs began administering the Adolescent Family Life Act (AFLA) that was designed to prevent teen pregnancy by advocating chastity and self-discipline (Saul, 1998). In 1993, as a result of a suit by the American Civil Liberties Union, AFLA programs were forced to adjust their curricula to: not include religious references, be medically accurate, and to respect the principle of self-determination regarding contraceptive referral for teenagers (Saul, 1998). The AFLA continues to fund abstinence-only programs today, despite two decades of programming without rigorous evidence to suggest that the programs are effective at changing adolescent sexual behavior (Bartels et al., 1996; Kirby, 2002). The abstinence-until-marriage only movement began to flourish in 1996, when the federal government attached a provision to a welfare reform law establishing a federal entitlement program for abstinence-only-until-marriage education. This program, Section 510(b) of Title V of the Social Security Act appropriated 250 million dollars over five years for state initiatives promoting abstinence-only sex education (Social Security Act, 1996). To ensure that the abstinence-only message was not diluted, the law (PL 104-193, Section 510 of the Social Security Act) stipulated that the term "abstinence education" refers to an educational or motivational program that includes the following eight elements:

(1) has as its exclusive purpose, teaching the social, psychological, and health gains of abstaining from sexual activity;

(2) teaches abstinence from sexual activity outside of marriage as the expected standard for all school-age children;

(3) teaches that abstinence is the only certain way to avoid out-of-wedlock pregnancy, STDs, and associated health problems;

(4) teaches that a mutually faithful monogamous relationship within marriage is the expected standard of human sexual activity;

(5) teaches that sexual activity outside of marriage is likely to have harmful psychological and physical effects;

(6) teaches that bearing children out-of-wedlock is likely to have harmful consequences for the child, the child's parents, and society;

(7) teaches young people how to reject sexual advances and how alcohol and drug use increases vulnerability to sexual advances;

(8) teaches the importance of attaining self-sufficiency before engaging in sex. (Section 510, p. 1).

Regardless of the requirement's lengthy and overtly moralistic undertone, the wording fails to accurately define the term *abstinence*. This obvious flaw creates methodologic and pragmatic issues when attempting to evaluate the efficacy of abstinence-only programming. How can researchers truly evaluate what has not been defined? Indeed, there is a paucity of existing research examining the effects of the abstinence-only approach to sexuality education. In 2002, Advocates for Youth performed an evaluation of findings from ten states that were implementing abstinence-only sex education. In addition to definitional problems, the evaluation was complicated by poor research design and inconsistent statistical analysis. Their review was unable to establish any positive outcomes for the abstinence-only programs (Kirby, 2002). In 2005, the Department of Health and Human Services published a report on the first year impact of abstinence education programs and although the findings indicated greater support for abstinence among students participating in the program, there was no available evidence of a change in intention to abstain from sexual activity (Mathematica Policy Research, 2005).

The Department of Health and Human Services attempted to refine its definition of abstinence, when in June of 2006, a notice of federal grant availability saw the abstinence education themes expand from eight to thirteen and, for the first time, the terms abstinence and sexual activity were defined: "Abstinence means voluntarily choosing not to engage in sexual activity until marriage. Sexual activity refers to any type of genital contact or sexual stimulation between two persons including, but not limited to, sexual intercourse" (Administration for Children and Families, 2006). This more specific definition of abstinence may have been intended as a response to data suggesting that adolescents were turning to "alternate" sexual activity such as oral or anal sex to maintain their abstinent status (Lewin, 1997; Stepp, 1999). In 2006, 46 states applied for the abstinence education funds, with only California, Maine, New Jersey and Pennsylvania rejecting the opportunity (Kaiser, 2007).

Newly revised federal guidelines for the 2007 abstinence education program included the expansion of the program's scope to include unmarried adults up to age 29 (Health and Human Services, 2007). The logic for this quite dramatic increase in target audience seems to rest on the fact that the age group most likely to bear children out of wedlock is 19-29 year olds; thus, the Department of Health and Human Services considers this group a prime target for abstinence education. Once again, alarm has been raised that common sense is being trumped by extra-scientific, political motives rooted in religious doctrinaire. Attempting to proselytize abstinence to an age group in which 90% of individuals in their late twenties are already sexually active may appear not only impractical but paternalistic. That is, this approach ignores the committed, monogamous couple who choose not to wed, it narrowly defines healthy sexuality and could be construed as a negation of sexual behavior that is not linked to procreation. Recently, the Society for Adolescent Medicine (SAM) published a position paper regarding their stance on abstinence-only education(Santelli, Ott, Lyon, Rogers, and Summers, 2006a). The SAM statement supported abstinence education, but not as the sole option; indeed they argued that "abstinence only" education lacked both ethical and scientific integrity. A comprehensive health education program, however, which includes, among other things, information on abstinence, contraceptives and protection from STIs, is endorsed by the SAM (Santelli, Ott, Lyon, Rogers, and Summers, 2006a; Santelli, Ott, Lyon, Rogers, Summers, and Schleifer, 2006b).

Disagreement exists not only among policy makers and scientists but between legislators and the constituencies that are affected by abstinence-only educational policy. For example, several nationwide polls provide evidence that a significant percentage of Americans support comprehensive sexuality education, rather than abstinence-only curriculum (Kaiser Family Foundation, 2004; Hickman-Brown Research, Inc., 1999). In fact, in a 2000 national poll conducted by Kaiser Family Foundation, the majority of parents, teachers, principals, and students were in favor of offering sexuality classes to high school students covering a variety of sexual behavior related topics (Kaiser Family Foundation, 2000). In a recent study in which parents of North Carolina youth were asked for feedback on the health education provided in their public schools (Ito, Gizlice, Owen-Dowd, Foust, Leone, and Miller, 2006), the viewpoints of the parents regarding comprehensive sexuality education did not correspond with the legislated abstinence curriculum for the state of North Carolina. That is, most parents were against legislators setting the sexuality education curriculum and thought parents and health professionals should determine the content of such courses. In addition, parents identified the following sexuality education topics as being important: transmission and prevention of STIs, HIV, and AIDS; how to handle the pressure to have sex; what to do if someone is sexual assaulted; and how to talk with partner about not having sex (Ito, Gizlice, Owen-Dowd, Foust, Leone, and Miller, 2006).

An Examination of Sexual Health Behavior Terminology

As noted above, a core ambiguity surrounding abstinence education is the lack of an accepted definition for terms like abstinence and sex, and perhaps, more importantly, a total lack of consensus among adolescents as to their interpretation of these terms. In 1998, the American public received an unexpected presidential primer on the definition of sex as President Clinton adamantly defended his "non-sexual" relationship with Monica Lewinsky. In the wake of this highly publicized event, a magazine survey of 15-19 year olds reported that 40% of respondents felt that oral sex was not "sex" (Seventeen, 2000), while a 2000 Internet survey indicated that 18% of 13-19 year-old girls believed that oral sex was something you did with your boyfriend before you were ready to have sex (Birnbaum, 2000).

Elsewhere, a group of Midwestern adolescents, who were receiving abstinence education, were asked how they interpreted the term abstinence. The students had great difficulty arriving at a definition and responses ranged from "kissing is OK" to "anything but intercourse" (Bell, 2000). Another study conducted with Midwestern adolescents, concluded that these individuals conceptualized abstinence as a "waiting period" and part of a continuum of natural development (Ott, Pfeiffer, and Fortenberry, 2006). In a 1998 study of over 1,000 college freshmen and sophomores, 61% of respondents considered mutual masturbation to be abstinence, 37% thought oral sex was also abstinence and 24% believed that anal intercourse was not sex (Horan, Phillips and Hagan, 1998). Even health professionals have shown little evidence of consensus with 30% of a sample of health educators responding that oral sex was abstinent behavior while 30% believed that mutual masturbation was not abstinence (Mercer, 1999). In a recent study where a four-item measure to assess sexual abstinence behavior was being developed, the researchers grappled with the definitional meaning of the term abstinence in the context of a person's virginity status (Norris, Clark and Magnus, 2003). These authors argued that those committed to sexual abstinence are more often virgins, yet virginity is not a prerequisite for sexual abstinence.

As the federal government came to understand, the promotion of abstinent behavior necessitates definition of the terms abstinence and sexual activity. A number of studies have been conducted to clarify the meaning of these terms among adolescents and young adults. A 1999 study of college students (Sanders and Reinisch,1999) demonstrated that penile-vaginal intercourse was the only sexual activity that respondents could agree constituted "sex" ; 60% reported that oral-genital contact was not considered as having "sex." To add further complexity to this definitional quandary, research suggests that adolescents' perceptions of what is considered "sex" often differs by contextual factors (Bogart, Cecil, Wagstaff, Pinkerton, and Abramson, 2000; Cecil, Bogart, Wagstaff, Pinkerton, and Abramson, 2002). Bogart et al. (2000) provided undergraduate students with a series of scenarios involving sexual behavior in an effort to glean their interpretation of the sexual acts performed between two hypothetical male and female actors. Over 90% of the sample felt both actors would perceive vaginal and anal intercourse as sex and the female actor was projected to identify a broader range of sexual behaviors to constitute sex. Cecil et al. (2002) also distributed sexual behavior items to college students to illicit feedback on what actions between the male and female actors signify their status as sexual partners. Couples who had engaged in vaginal or anal intercourse rather than oral sex were more often labeled as sexual partners. In addition, findings suggested that the frequency of the sex behavior and the dating status of the couple also played a in role in judgments regarding their status as sexual partners.

One of the most common items used on sexuality surveys is the term "sexual intercourse." Although most researchers may *infer* penis-vagina intercourse when they use this term, (Bell, 2000; National College Health Risk Behavior Survey, 1995; NBC/People, 2005) survey respondents may *perceive* the meaning in a different way. For example, among a sample of undergraduate students asked to define the term, "sexual intercourse," 36% defined it as vaginal intercourse, 36% characterized it as including vaginal and anal intercourse, while 20% of the sample explicitly excluded oral intercourse from their definition (Sawyer, Howard, Brewster-Jordan, Gavin, and Sherman, 2007). Although the term, "vaginal intercourse" is slightly more specific than "sexual intercourse" possible ambiguity still exists. National behavioral risk surveillance systems routinely survey adolescents and young adults about a host of risk behaviors, including sexual risk (Youth Risk Behavior Survey, 2005). A common survey item reads, "Have you had sexual intercourse in the past three months?" (NBC/People, 2005). Without any clarifying definition, the difficulty with accurately interpreting responses to this question is all too obvious: does a "yes" response indicate penis-vagina intercourse, oral intercourse, and/or anal intercourse? The ability to make meaningful inferences, let alone programmatic decisions based on responses to an ambiguous item simply asking about "sexual intercourse" appear to be highly compromised.

The concept of virginity has also been found to be highly ambiguous. There is a high degree of subjectivity among individuals in terms of what embodies the transition from virgin to non-virgin status. Carpenter (2001) explored virginity loss through in-depth interviews with 61 men and women ages 18 to 35. She found consensus among participants that first time vaginal-penile intercourse constituted a loss of virginity; however, discrepancies between other sexual acts that individuals could engage in and still be considered a virgin were apparent (i.e., oral sex, same-sex intercourse, anal sex). She concluded that virginity can be viewed alternatively as a gift, stigma, or part of an inevitable or advantageous rite of passage in life depending on other contextual factors discussed in the interviews. Elsewhere (Stevens-Simon, 2001), virginity and abstinence have each been described as possibly a "state of mind" rather than of body, in that many young people who report being abstinent or a virgin may in fact be sexually active. Clearly, further exploration into the denotative and connotative meaning of the term virginity is warranted in order to better understand its relationship to adolescent sexual beliefs, intentions and behaviors.

Another important area of research surrounds the study of oral sex or oral intercourse. During the past decade, sexuality researchers seem to have been so preoccupied with studies related to unintended pregnancy prevention and its concomitant focus on penis-vagina intercourse that research on other important sexual behaviors, including oral sex, has largely been ignored. Despite much anecdotal information in the popular press suggesting an increase in oral sex among adolescents (Stepp, 1999), there exists very little empirical data in peer-reviewed research journals. This is despite the clinical findings linking oral sex to the transmission of STIs like Gonorrhea, Herpes, and Chlamydia (Hook, and Handsfield, 1999; Lafferty, Downey, Celum, and Wald, 2000; Kashima, Shah and Lyles, 1992). In a study of ninth-grade adolescents, more respondents reported having experienced oral sex (19.6%) than penis-vagina intercourse (13.5%), viewing oral sex as less risky (Schuster, Bell and Kanouse, 1996). A 2002 study reported that 55% of males and 54% of females aged 15-19 in the U.S. had engaged in oral sex, (Mosher, Chandra, Jones, 2005) while a United Kingdom study reported an almost identical rate of experience with oral sex in a population of students aged 16-18 years (Stone, Hatherall, Ingham, and McEachran, 2006). Notwithstanding the high prevalence of oral sex among adolescents, major surveys purported to monitor adolescent engagement in health-risk behaviors, such as the national Youth Risk Behavior Survey, fail to include a single item on this behavior. Developing a complete and useful picture of adolescent sexual behavior would seem difficult without the inclusion of items that examine one of the most common adolescent sexual activities. However, recent research would seem to suggest that simply including an item that reads, "Have you had oral sex?" would be insufficient. A recent study found almost 25% of the sample disagreed as to the meaning of the term oral sex, leading the authors to conclude that more often the person performing oral sex was viewed as *not* having oral sex in comparison to the person on the receiving end (Sawyer, Howard, Brewster-Jordan, Gavin, and Sherman, 2007).

Recently Sawyer et. al., (2007) conducted an exploratory study to examine the denotative meaning of sexual terms in a convenience sample of late adolescent university students. Three anonymous surveys were developed to capture students' interpretations of the terms sexual intercourse, virgin, abstinence, and oral sex. Upon receiving Institutional Review Board approval from the university, questionnaires were distributed to students enrolled in three large survey courses offered by a department of public and community health.

Sexual Intercourse

Slightly over one-third of the sample (36%, n=117) defined sexual intercourse as meaning vaginal sex. A similar proportion of the sample interpreted sexual intercourse to include vaginal and/or anal and oral sex (35%, n=112). Just under 20% (n=63) of the sample did not include oral sex as part of the definition of sexual intercourse, but did include vaginal and/or anal sex. Only a small proportion of the sample specifically used the term penetration (6%, n=18) in their definition. A smaller percent perceived oral sex alone as synonymous with sexual intercourse (2%, n=5). There were gender differences regarding the designation of oral sex in that males were more likely than females to list oral sex as a sexual activity included in the term sexual intercourse; these differences, however, were non-significant.

Virgin

Vaginal intercourse was the singular behavior that was most likely to negate a person's virginity status by both females and males. Five percent (n=16) of the sample included penetration as a behavior associated with loss of virginity. About 19% (n=62) also considered a virgin to be a person who has never participated in vaginal or anal sex. Another 14% (n=46) included oral sex, in addition to vaginal and/or anal sex, as an action that would terminate one's status as a virgin. There were no significant gender differences in the behaviors that would constitute a non-virgin identity.

Abstinence

A large proportion of students indicated that if anal or vaginal *penetration* occurred, they did not consider themselves abstinent (anal 157, 86%, vaginal 174, 95%,); however, over a third of the sample recorded that anal or vaginal *touching* by a penis still signified abstinent behavior. The sample was nearly split as to whether performing or receiving oral sex, defined either as a tongue penetrating or touching another's vagina or penis penetrating or touching another's mouth, could be practiced while still considering oneself abstinent. Sexual behaviors that could be practiced while still considering oneself abstinent displayed minimal gender variability with one exception. More males (14%) believed that if their penis penetrated a female's anus they could remain abstinent while only about 6% of females believed they could be abstinent if they were on the receiving end of penis-anal penetration.

Oral Sex

In this survey, university students were presented with the statement, "Jamie performs oral sex on Chris." The students were then asked to respond to the following questions: "In your opinion, has Jamie had oral sex? In your opinion has Chris had oral sex?" Although 76% of the sample felt that both individuals had experienced oral sex, fully 20% of respondents believed that Jamie (the person performing oral sex) had *not* experienced oral sex. In addition, 5% of respondents believed that the person receiving oral stimulation had not experienced oral sex (Sawyer, Howard, Brewster-Jordan, Gavin, and Sherman, 2007). That is, almost 25% (n=38) of the sample differentiated between "giving" and "receiving" when defining oral sex. In summary, the person on the receiving end was more often seen as having oral sex than was the person performing the oral sex.

These findings have implications for research, clearly bringing into question the accuracy and reliability of data gathered from questionnaires. When as many as one-fifth of a survey population responds "no" to an item regarding oral sex because they had performed and not received oral sex, then the interpretability of survey results are obviously questionable. The findings from this study suggest little consensus among adolescents about the behavioral referents of the term abstinence and related terms such as virginity, sexual intercourse, and oral sex. Regardless of whether elicitation of definitions occurred via open-ended or closed-ended probes, these terms appear to have highly personalized and often contradictory interpretations among college students, with one important exception. Findings from this study support previous research that has determined penis-vagina intercourse as the one sexual behavior that an individual cannot perform and still consider him or herself to be abstinent (Sanders and Reinisch, 1999; Bogart, Cecil, Wagstaff, Pinkerton, and Abramson, 2000; Pitts and Rahman, 2001). Penis-anus penetration was the only other sexual behavior that a large majority of the sample in this study believed could not be practiced for one to still be abstinent. Adding to the uncertainty surrounding the definition of terms such as abstinence, sex and virginity are issues related to the actual practice of oral sex, which was evident in the results reported by Sawyer et al., (2007). Many of the nationally representative adolescent surveys do not include items on oral sex, and those that do, only ask "Have you had oral sex?" without providing a definition for the term; indeed, the ambiguities surrounding its meaning may call into serious question the results obtained from such surveys (Youth Risk Behavior Survey, 2005; National College Risk Behavior Survey, 1995; American College Health Association College Health Assessment, 2003; Halpern-Fesher, Cornell, Kropp, and Tschann, 2005).

In summary, the need to accurately define what is meant by abstinence, and other related terms such as sexual intercourse and virginity is critically important on many levels. If adolescents are encouraged to be abstinent, then they need a precise definition of what that really means. Furthermore, if program planners and researchers are to implement and evaluate abstinence-only interventions, operational definitions must be developed that are robust.

Unless survey items are constructed with precise definitions of the referenced sexual behavior terms, interpretation of data may be difficult and prevalence estimates of abstinence may be inflated. Inevitably, related terms like sexual intercourse and virginity will also need precise definitions as they are relevant to our understanding of abstinence. Furthermore, without such specificity, adolescents will continue to be confused about the nomenclature surrounding their sexual behavior and health professionals will have great difficulty evaluating sexuality data, in general, and the success of abstinence-only education, in particular.

The lack of consensus surrounding definitions of sexual behavior may well have a considerable impact on the ability of researchers to collect meaningful data. Although surveillance reports measuring the prevalence of unintended pregnancy and rates of STI are considered to be accurate, due in large measure to the clinical nature of the data and the generation of accurate medical records, adolescent sexuality data collected through large surveys with a self-report format may well be flawed or incomplete. Accuracy of data can only be achieved if the researcher and respondent have a common understanding of the definitional meaning of individual terms in survey questions.

An Examination of Sexual Language Used on National Surveys

The ambiguities discussed in the prior sections raise a host of concerns regarding the sexual terminology incorporated into national surveys which aim to monitor adolescent health-related risk behaviors, particularly sexual behaviors. As a result, Howard, Sawyer and Brewster-Jordan conducted a comprehensive literature review to examine the specific language used on current national health surveys that assess the sexual behavior of adolescents and young adults. The aim was to evaluate the extent to which that language is vague or limited in scope. The decision to examine national surveys was based on the fact that they are representative in nature, rigorously designed, and often guide policy and funding decisions at various levels within the public health infrastructure.

The literature review was conducted using multiple large research databases containing published journal articles and abstracts. A total of eight national surveys meet eligibility criteria and underwent thorough review. These eight surveys included: American College Health Association - National College Health Assessment (ACHA-NCHA); Kaiser Family Foundation and Seventeen Magazine National Survey of Teens: Safer Sex, Condoms and the Pill; Middle School Youth Risk Behavior Survey (MSYRBS); 1995 National College Health Risk Behavior Survey (NCHRBS); National Longitudinal Study of Adolescent Health (Add Health); National Survey of Family Growth (NSFG); NBC News/People Magazine: National Survey of Young Teens Sexual Attitudes and Behaviors; and Youth Risk Behavior Surveillance Survey (YRBSS).

A review of the surveys found inconsistent sexual health behavior terminology being used with most lacking descriptions of the behaviors being queried. All the surveys asked about intercourse, either using the specific phrase "vaginal intercourse" or the more general phrase "sexual intercourse". Very few surveys asked about "anal sex" and/or "oral sex", however, one of the surveys asked about both sexual behaviors and included explanations of these acts. Surveys administered through an interview methodology, as opposed to a self-administered questionnaire, were more apt to delve into detailed sexual behavior questions. The findings from this study further exhibit the need for researchers to provide specific descriptions of adolescent sexual health terms in order to enhance the validity and reliability of measures designed to investigate and understand an adolescent sexual behavior.

Exploratory Study of the Connotative Meaning of Safer Sex

As previously mentioned, nearly half of all HIV infections and two thirds of all sexually transmitted STIs occur among youth and young adults under the age of 25, yet there is currently no federal mandate to teach sex education in public school (Starkman, and Rajani, 2002). Indeed, federal funding for programs that focus on abstinence-only, which exclude information on sexuality and contraception, has increased. Teachers appear stymied in their ability to adequately educate youth about human sexuality; they report being more and more handicapped in their ability to provide answers to sexuality questions that are not included in the more restrictive abstinence-only educational curricula (Darroch, Lanfdry, and Singh, 2000). This shift comes at a time where a majority of Americans say they favor courses that teach contraception and condom use, in addition to abstinence (Wilson, 2000). Findings from the Annenberg National Health Communication Survey, conducted in 2006 to gauge U.S. adults preference for the teaching of sex education in public schools, found that a plurality of adults (82% of respondents) favor abstinence-plus programs which emphasize not only abstinence but other methods of preventing pregnancy and STIs (Bleakley, Hennessy, and Fishbein, 2006). One of the potential downsides from the aforementioned substantive changes in sexuality education is growing confusion, among young adults, as to whether one can practice safe sex and what constitutes safe sex.

The term, *safe sex*, whose coinage was associated with the emergence of a global AIDS crisis in the 1980's (Hillier, Harrison, and Warr,1998), has evolved into the language of *safer* sex; perhaps in acknowledgement of an ongoing dialectic between risk *elimination*, a seemingly unattainable goal, and risk *reduction*, a more modest approach but pragmatically more achievable (Moore, 1997). There is an implication that the term safe sex is an oxymoron; in essence, the only way to avoid risks associated with sexual contact is to abstain completely from sexual activity (Wikipedia, 2006). The intent of developing the terms safe and safer sex has been largely an attempt to reduce potentially risky sexual behavior and its negative consequences; practical recommendations for safe(r), versus risky activities have become commonplace in sexuality communications and interventions during the past two decades. Unfortunately, despite the development of various definitions for this term (Medline Plus, 2006), the nomenclature of safe(r) sex appears susceptible to the same ambiguities as other terms that reference sexual behavior. Indeed, as noted by Moore (1997), "within the categories of "possible safe" practices, ideas about what constitutes safer sex are constantly being reformulated" and exist on a continuum rather than seen as a polarity. This confusion clearly impedes the development of interventions that seek to address effective measures to limit sexual risk-taking.

In some contexts, safe sex is seen as synonymous with both safer sex and protected sex and refers to a set of practices that are intended to reduce the risk of acquiring a STI. Yet, at times, the term is associated with a series of seemingly divergent messages that aim to transform sexual practices (Moore, 1997). Hillier et. al., (1998) contend that usage of the term safe sex has been overly simplified and sanitized and has been reduced to a simple equation: safe sex equals condom use. By contrast, unsafe sex refers to unprotected sexual behavior, i.e., sexual intercourse without use of any barrier contraception or prevention against STIs (Wikipedia, 2006). Yet, it also has been argued that sexual behavior must not be placed in the same context as other risk behavior, since human sexuality is both normative and healthy- it is only certain sexual practices that constitute risk (Dailard, 2001). In fact, there is some concern that endorsement and promotion of abstinence only practices such as virginity-until-marriage pledges may have the unintended consequence of leaving youth vulnerable to unplanned pregnancy and STI if and when they do break these pledges, because evidence suggests they are less likely to engage in protected sex (Bearman and Bruckner, 2000). The significance of this finding may lie in the fact that by 1995 more than 2 million adolescents, or 12% of all adolescents, had taken such pledges (Bruckner and Bearman, 2005). Based on data drawn from the National Longitudinal Study of Adolescent Health (Add Health), Bruckner and Bearman (2005) examined the effectiveness of virginity pledges in decreasing STD infection among youth aged 8-24. They found that while those who pledge may initiate sexual intercourse later than youth who do not make such pledges most will eventually engage in premarital sex; more importantly, when they do they are less likely to use a condom at first intercourse. For those youth who do not have premarital sex, they are likely to substitute oral and/or anal sex for vaginal sex.

It has been argued that there is a direct relationship between the high rate of negative sexual health outcomes among youth in the U.S. and negative attitudes toward sexuality, an "erotophobia" of sorts, as promulgated by ideologically conservative and religious fundamentalists (Dodge, Sandford, Yarber, and de Wit, 2005; Weeks, 2002; Weeks, 1989). Furthermore, evidence is accumulating that the message of safe sex is equally as potent as an abstinence message in reducing the amount of unprotected sex, yet the political climate may dictate that abstinence-only programs remain a cornerstone to educational efforts for youth (AIDS Alert,1998). Finally, the best evidence available, i.e., based on rigorously designed and evaluated trials, suggests that abstinence-only curricula have failed to demonstrate efficacy in delaying initiation of sexual intercourse (Santelli, Ott, Lyon, Rogers, and Summers, 2006a; Santelli, Ott, Lyon, Rogers, Summers, and Schleifer, 2006b). In fact, Santelli et al. (2006b), maintain that the problem with abstinence- only programs is not abstinence but *only* abstinence and raise important scientific, human rights and ethical concerns with the federal funding requirements surrounding sexuality education.

Research conducted over the past 30 years suggests that the meaning of sexual terms changes over time, there are often gender differences in the how sexual terms are used and interpreted and what may constitute sexual behavior may also differ by demographics (Bogart, Cecil, Wagstaff, Pinkerton, and Abramson, 2000). Bogart et al., (2000) found that broad cultural definitions influenced subjective judgments regarding sexual activity and virginity status along with contextual considerations such as the nature of the behavior, whether and who experienced orgasm. This has been echoed by Dodge et al., (2005) who argue that human sexual behavior involves a complex socio-cultural set of dynamics. Indeed, when applying terms such as safer sex and risk in the context of sexual health messages and prevention efforts, it is appropriate to consider personal and situational factors if the goal is to facilitate decision-making to reduce risk (Moore, 1997). Perhaps because the concept of safe sex derived from a model designed for gay men, it neglects certain psychosocial implications of sexual activity that specifically apply to women, including a sullied reputation and the concomitant social sanctions that are associated with such behavior, particularly when the relationship is not sustained (Hillier, Harrison, and Warr, 1998).

In light of these ambiguities and contradictions, the following exploratory study aimed to examine the denotative meaning of the term *"safer sex"*.

METHODS

Data used for this study were gathered from administration of an opened-ended survey on safer sex to students enrolled in two undergraduate courses at a large mid-Atlantic university. The two courses where participants were recruitment from were a 100 level Personal and Community Health course and a 300 level Psychology of Women course. Students were provided with a brief explanation of the purpose of the study followed by instructions for survey completion. Study team members emphasized the anonymity of the collected responses and that participation was completely voluntary.

Survey Administration

A 1-item survey was designed to capture open-ended feedback from students about their interpretation of the concept *safer sex.* The item asked students, *"When someone says he or she is practicing "safer sex", what do YOU think he or she means?* The open-ended responses for this item were systematically coded by the research team using a master coding dictionary developed specifically for that purpose. Responses were reviewed and coded twice by different study team members to establish inter-rater reliability.

The development of the master coding dictionary began with the identification of six coding categories. These categories reflected an initial review of written responses collected from the Personal and Community Health course. The six coding categories were: (1) general description (not specifying a particular form of contraception or behavioral protection), (2) behavioral act of protection, (3) contraception, (4) protection, (5) abstinence, and (6) other. Each coding category was labeled and included examples taken directly from student surveys; collectively they constituted the coding dictionary. Using these six categories, surveys from the Psychology of Women course were reviewed to determine whether additions and/or changes to the coding dictionary were required. While no additional categories were needed, additional examples were included into the master coding dictionary to further illustrate differences across the six categories. Surveys from both courses were independently reviewed twice to confirm the final coding. Collected data from this survey was entered into SPSS 13.0 for analysis (Shad, 1997). Overall frequency distributions were computed along with sub-analyses by gender.

RESULTS

An overwhelming majority of students listed either contraception or protection as the behavioral referent for the term "practicing safer sex" (see Table 1). Males were more likely to use the more narrow term contraception, while females were more apt to define the practice of safer sex in a broader sense, i.e., protection. Only 1 student defined safer sex as abstinence.

Table 1. Denotative meaning of the term "practicing safer sex"[1]
(N= 123; 91 females, 28 males) [2,3]

Sexual Behaviors	% (N)	Females	Males
General description, no behavioral referents[4]	6.5 (8)	0.07 (6)	0.07 (2)
Activation of behavioral protection[5]	1.6 (2)	0.02 (2)	0 (0)
Contraception[6]	39.0 (48)	0.34 (31)	0.50 (14)
Protection[7]	48.8 (60)	0.55 (50)	0.36 (10)
Abstinence[8]	0.8 (1)	0	0
Other	3.3 (4)	0.02 (2)	0.07 (2)

[1] Actual question asked: "When someone says he or she is practicing "safer sex", what do *YOU* think he or she means?"

[2] Data were gathered from an introductory health class, HLTH 140- Personal and Community Health (n = 53) and a midlevel psychology class, PSYCH 336- Psychology of Women (n = 70)

[3] 4 participants did not indicate gender

[4] Examples included: "Being more moderate and less dangerous", "Means doing something you weren't doing before, but doesn't mean practicing safe sex", "Taking more precautions"

[5] Examples included: "Getting checked out", "Limiting sexual activities to just one person, not engaging in casual sex"

[6] Examples included: "Condoms", "Birth Control", "Spermicides", "More than one form of protection", "Birth Control", "Using condoms more often", "One or more forms of contraception"

[7] Definitions incorporated the term protection; category further divided into 9 sub-domains

[8] Definitions incorporated the term abstinence.

Table 2. Meaning of "Protection" as regards the practice of safer sex[1]
(N= 60; 50 females, 10 males)

Sexual Behaviors	% (N)	Females	Males
Using precautionary measurements/using > 1 method	30 (18)	0.30 (15)	0.30 (3)
Having control over actions + contraceptives	8.3 (5)	0.10 (5)	0
Contraceptives + other means of having "safe sex"	3.3 (2)	0.02 (1)	0.10(1)
Using protection + getting tested	5.0 (3)	0.06 (3)	0
Improving own personal methods of protection	20.0 (12)	0.18 (9)	0.30 (3)
Birth control + condoms + pulling out	1.7 (1)	0.02 (1)	0
Working towards being less sexually active + contraception	23.3 (14)	0.24 (12)	0.20 (2)
Checking up on sexual health of partners + contraceptive	5.0 (3)	0.04 (2)	0.10 (1)
Taking precautions (i.e., using condoms) some of the time	3.3 (2)	0.04 (2)	0

[1] Pertains to the subset of students who answered question in Table 1 and provided specification on the meaning of protection as a strategy for practicing "safer sex

[2] Table 1 data were gathered from an introductory health class, HLTH 140- Personal and Community Health (n = 53) and a midlevel psychology class, PSYCH 336- Psychology of Women (n = 70).

For those students who used the term protection to describe the practice of safer sex (50.4%) many provided additional detail as to the meaning of this term (see Table 2). The most common definition of protection included using precautionary measures, that is, more than 1 method of protection. Next frequent were statements indicating the use of contraception, but also sentiments related to "working towards being less sexually active". Frequent reference was also made to improving one's personal methods of protection. Some interesting gender differences emerged. Only females mentioned "having control over one's actions" or "getting tested" as a measure of safer sex. Additionally, females were much more likely to indicate that "working toward being less sexually active" was a means of being protected.

DISCUSSION

The findings from this exploratory study suggest that being protected and/or using contraception is seen as synonymous with the practice of safer sex. Only 1 student equated safer sex with abstinence. Examples of contraception provided by students included using condoms, spermicides or birth control. Clearly, these methods are not equivalent in terms of preventing both pregnancy and STIs. Furthermore, in elaborating on the use of contraception, some participants interpreted the practice of safer sex to mean more frequent use of contraception or use of more than one form of contraception. This raises questions regarding the regularity of contraception use and contextual factors that might determine whether and which additional forms of contraception are used. Clearly, more needs to be learned about the decision-making process and factors that influence the nature, extent and choice of contraception use among college students.

The meaning of protection, in the context of practicing safer sex, was wide ranging. Some students discussed protection in terms of behavioral referents, i.e., "using more than one method" and "getting tested". Some females referred to cognitive factors such as "having more control over one's actions". For some males and females, being protected included "working toward being less sexually active", conceivably endorsing implicitly the notion that safe sex equates to abstinence.

CONCLUSION

As noted by Abraham and Sheeran more than a decade ago (1993), perhaps the thrust, so to speak, of future adolescent sexuality research should be away from biology to social psychology and a search for a psychology of safer sex promotion. While emphasizing the complex social skills that are embodied in the practice of safe sex attention must also be placed on how environmental and cultural forces shape and reinforce sexual attitudes and behavior. As part of an advocacy agenda for 2010, Wilson (2000) argues that proponents of responsible sex education must continue to remind the public that an overwhelming majority support the teaching of contraception and disease prevention in addition to abstinence and point out to politicians that there does not exist scientifically credible evidence that abstinence-only education has delayed the onset of sexual intercourse or reduced sexual activity. Researchers, as well, must be pressed to be more explicit and exacting when using sexual terminology, assessing sexual behavior and interpreting sexuality-related survey data.

Surely, we have our work cut out for ourselves.

REFERENCES

Abraham, C., Sheeran, P. (1993). In search of a psychology of safer-sex promotion; beyond beliefs and texts. (1993). *Health Education Quarterly*, 8, 245-254.

Administration for Children and Families. (2006). Request for proposals for community-based abstinence education programs, Family and Youth Services Bureau. Accessed from: http://www.acf.hhs.gov/grants/open/HHS-2006-ACF-ACYF-AE-0099.html

American College Health Association. (2003). National College Health Assessment. Accessed from: http://www.acha.org/projects_programs/sample_ncha.pdf.

Bartels C, Wilcox B, Limber S, O'Bierne H. (1996). Adolescent Abstinence Promotion Programs: An Evaluation of Evaluations. Paper presented at the Annual Meeting of the American Public Health Association, No. 18, New York, NY.

Bell, H.A. (2000). Just because you see their privates doesn't mean you're not a virgin: adolescents' understanding of sexual terminology. Unpublished thesis, Iowa State University, Ames, IA.

Bearman, P.S., and Bruckner, H. (2000). Promising the future: Virginity pledges as they affect transition to first intercourse. *Institute for Social and Economic Theory and Research*, 1-63.

Birnbaum, C. (2000). The love and sex survey, *Twist*, Oct/Nov. 2000, 54-56.

Bleakley, A., Hennessy, M., and Fishbein, M. (2006). Public Opinion on Sex Education in US Schools. *Archives of Pediatric and Adolescent Medicine*, 160, 1151-1156.

Bogart, L.M., Cecil, H., Wagstaff, D.A., Pinkerton, S.D., and Abramson, P.R.. (2000). Is it sex? College students' interpretations of sexual behavior terminology. *Journal of Sex Research*, 37, 108-116.

Bruckner, H., and Bearman, P. (2005). After the promise: the STD consequences of adolescent virginity pledges. *Journal of Adolescent Health*, 36, 271-8.

Carpenter, L. (2001). The ambiguity of "having sex": The subjective experience of virginity loss in the United States. *The Journal of Sex Research*, 38, 127-139.

Cecil, H., Bogart, L.M., Wagstaff, D.A., Pinkerton, S.D., and Abramson, P.R. (2002). Classifying a person as a sex partner: The impact of contextual factors. *Psychology and Health: An International Journal*, 17, 221-234.

Centers for Disease Control and Prevention. (2003). Youth Risk Behavior Surveillance MMWR, (53) SS-2,: United States, 2003, May 21, 2004. Accessed from: http://www.cdc.gov/mmwr/PDF/SS/ SS5302.pdf.

Centers for Disease Control and Prevention. (2004). STD Surveillance. Trends in Reportable Sexually Transmitted Diseases in the United States. Accessed from: http://www.cdc.gov/std/stats/trends 2004.htm.

Chase-Lansdale, P.L. (1995) Who's Responsible? An historical analysis of the changing roles of mothers, fathers, and society. In: PL Chase-Lansdale and J Brooks-Gunn (Eds.), *Escape from Poverty: What makes a difference for children?* (pp11-37) New York: Cambridge University Press.

Chesson, H.W., Blandford, J.M., Gift, T.L., Tao, G., and Irwin, K.L. (2004). The estimated cost of STD in American youth,. Abstract P075. 2004 National STD Prevention Conference, Philadelphia, PA.

Dailard, C. (2001). Recent Findings from The 'Add Health' Survey: Teens and Sexual Activity. *The Guttmacher Report on Public Policy,* 4, 1-3.

Darroch, J.E., Singh, L., and Singh, S. (2000). Changing emphases in sexuality education in U.S. public schools, 1988-1999. *Family Planning Perspectives*, 32, 204-211 and 265.

Dodge, B., Sandfort, T.G.M., Yarber, W.L., and de Wit, J. (2005). Sexual health among male college students in the United States and the Netherlands. *American Journal of Health Behavior*, 29, 172-182.

Editorial staff. (1998). Safe sex vs abstinence: which is more effective. *AIDS Alert*, 78-79.

Guttmacher Institute. (2004) *U.S. Teenage Pregnancy Statistics: Overall trends, trends by race and ethnicity and state-by-state information*, updated February 19, 2004. Accessed from: http://www.guttmacher.org/pubs/state_pregnancy_trends.pdf

Halpern-Felsher, B.L., Cornell, J.L., Kropp, R.Y., and Tschann, J. (2005). Oral versus vaginal sex among adolescents: perceptions, attitudes and behavior. *Pediatrics*, 115, 845-851.

Health and Human Services. (2007). FY 2007 Program announcement, section 510, Abstinence Education Program. Accessed from: www.acf.hhs.gov/grants/open/HHS-2007-ACF-ACYF-AEGP-0143.html., November 3, 2006.

Hickman-Brown Research Inc. (1999). Public Support for Sexuality Education Reaches Highest Level. SIECUS and Advocates for Youth. Accessed from: http://www.siecus.org/parent/pare 0003.html

Hillier, L., Harrison, L., and Warr, D. (1998). "When you carry condoms all the boys think you want it": negotiating competing discourses about safe sex". *Journal of Adolescence*, 21, 15-29.

Hook, E.W. and Handsfield, H.H. (1999). Gonococcal infections in the adult. In: Holmes K.K., Mardh, P.A., Sparling, P.F., et al., eds: *Sexually Transmitted Diseases*. 3rd ed., New York,NY:McGraw-Hill:p.456.

Horan, P.F., Phillips, J., and Hagan, N.E. (1998). The meaning of abstinence for college students. *Journal of HIV/AIDS Prevention and Education for Adolescents and Children*, 2, 51-66.

Ito, K.E., Gizlice. Z., Owen-O'Dowd, J., Foust, E., Leone, P.A., and Miller, W.C. (2006). Parent opinion of sexuality education in a state with mandated abstinence education: does policy match parental preference? *Journal of Adolescent Health,* 39, 634-641.

Kaiser. (2007). Daily women's health policy: Federal guidelines expand the scope of abstinence education funds to include people up to age 29. Accessed from: http://www.Kaisernetwork.org. October 31, 2006.

Kaiser Family Foundation. (2000). Sex Education in America: A View from Inside the Nation's Classrooms. Accessed from: http://www.kff.org/youthhivstds/3048-index.cfm

Kaiser Family Foundation. (2004). Sex Education in America: General Public/Parents Survey. Accessed from, http://www.kff.org/newsmedia/7017.cfm

Kaiser Family Foundation and Seventeen Magazine National Survey of Teens: Safer Sex, Condoms and the Pill (2000). Accessed from: http://www.kff.org/entpartnerships/upload/SexSmarts-Survey-Safer-Sex-Condoms-and-the-Pill-Toplines.pdf

Kashima, H.K., Shah, F., and Lyles, A.A. (1992). A comparison of risk factors in juvenile-onset and adult-onset recurrent respiratory papillomatosis. *Laryngoscope*, 102, 9-13.

Kirby, D. (2002). Do Abstinence-Only Programs Delay the Initiation of Sex Among Young People and Reduce Teen Pregnancy? Washington DC: Campaign to Prevent Teen Pregnancy, October 2002.

Lafferty, W.E., Downey, L., Celum, C., and Wald, A. (2000). Herpes simplex virus type 1 as a cause of genital herpes: impact on surveillance and prevention. *Journal of Infectious Disease*, 81, 1454-1457.

Lewin, T. (1997). Teenagers alter sexual practices, thinking risks will be avoided, *New York Times*, April 5, 1997, A1.

Mathematica Policy Research, Inc. (2005, June). *First Year Impacts of Four Title V, Section 510 Abstinence Education Programs*. Princeton, NJ.

Medline Plus. "Safe" sex. updated June 6, 2006. Accessed from: http://www.nlm.nih.gov/medlineplus/ ency/article/001949.htm.

Mercer, J.G. (1999). Defining and teaching abstinence: an e-mail survey of health educators. Unpublished thesis, North Carolina State University, Raleigh, NC.

Middle School Youth Risk Behavior Survey. (2005). Accessed from: http://www.cdc.gov/ HealthyYouth/yrbs/pdf/questionnaire/2005middleschoolquestionnaire.pdf

Moore, L. (1997). "It's like you use pots and pans to cook. It's the tool": The technologies of safer sex. *Science, Technology, and Human Values*, 22, 434-471.

Mosher, W., Chandra, A., Jones, J. (2005). Sexual behavior and selected health measures: men and women 15-44 years of age, United States, 2002. *Advance Data from Vital and Health Statistics* September 15, 2005; No. 362:21-26.

Nanchahal, K., Wellings, K., Barrett, G. Copas, A., Mercer, C., Macmanus, S., Macdowall, W., Fenton, K., Erens, B., and Johnson, A. (2005). Changes in the circumstances of young mothers in Britain: 1990 to 2000. *Journal of Epidemiology Community Health*, 59, 828-833.

National College Health Risk Behavior Survey (1995) Updated November 14, 1997. Accessed from: http://www.cdc.gov/mmwr/preview/mmwrhtml/00049859.htm.

The National Longitudinal Study of Adolescent Health (Add Health). Accessed from: http://www.cpc.unc.edu/addhealth

National Survey of Family Growth (NSFG). (2002). Accessed from: http://www.cdc .gov/nchs/nsfg.htm

NBC/People (2005) National survey of young teens' sexual attitudes and behaviors, 2005, updated January 31, 2005. http://www.msnbc.msn.com/id/6839072.

NBC /People: National Survey of Young Teens Sexual Attitudes and Behaviors. (2004). Accessed from: http://msnbcmedia.msn.com/i/msnbc/Sections/TVNews/Dateline %20NBC/ NBCTeenTop line.pdf

Norris, A. E., Clark, L. F., and Magnus, S. (2003). Sexual abstinence and the Sexual Abstinence Behavior Scale. *Journal of Pediatric Health Care,* 17, 140-144.

Ott, M.A., Pfeiffer, E. J., and Fortenberry, J.D. (2006). Perceptions of sexual abstinence among high- risk early and middle adolescents. *Journal of Adolescent Health*, 39, 192-198.

Pitts, M., and Rahman, Q. (2001). Which behaviors constitute "having sex" among university students in the UK? *Archives of Sexual Behavior*, 30, 169-176.

Sanders, S.A. and Reinisch, J.M. (1999). Would you say you "had sex" if ...? *Journal of the American Medical Association*, 281, 275-277.

Santelli J., Ott, M.A., Lyon, M., Rogers, J., Summers D.. (2006a). Abstinence-only education policies and programs: a position paper of the Society for Adolescent Medicine, *Journal of Adolescent Health*, 38, 83-87.

Santelli J., Ott, M.A., Lyon, M., Rogers, J., Summers D., and Schleifer, R. (2006b). Letters to the editor: Abstinence and Abstinence-Only Education, *Journal of Adolescent Health*, 39, 152-154.

Saul, R. (1998). "Whatever Happened to the Adolescent Family Life Act?" *Guttmacher Report on Public Policy*, 1, 5-11.

Sawyer, R.G., Howard, D.E., Brewster-Jordan, J., Gavin, M., and Sherman, M. (In press, 2007). "We didn't have sex … did we?" College students' perceptions of abstinence. *Journal of Health Studies.*

Schuster M.A., Bell R.M., and Kanouse D.E. (1996). The sexual practices of adolescent virgins: genital sexual activities of high school students who have never had vaginal intercourse. *American Journal of Public Health*, 86, 1570-1576.

Seventeen. (2000, February 28). News Release: National survey conducted by *Seventeen* finds that more than half of teens ages 15-19 have engaged in oral sex.

Shad, B.W., Barnwell P.S., and Bieler G.S. (1997). Software for the statistical analysis of correlated data: User's manual. Research Triangle Park, NC: Research Triangle Institute.

Social Security Act, P.L. (1996), 104-193, Section 510(b) of Title V.

Starkman, N. and Rajani, N. (2002). The case for comprehensive sex education. *AIDS Patient Care STDS*, 16, 313-318.

Stepp, L.S. (1999). Parents are alarmed by an unsettling new fad in middle schools: oral sex. Washington Post, July 8, 1999, p.A1; and Stepp, LS, Talking to kids about sexual limits, Washington Post, July 8, 1999, p. C4.

Stevens-Simon, C. (2001). Virginity: a state of mind…but not necessarily of body. *Journal of School Health*, 71, 87-88.

Stone, N., Hatherall, B., Ingham, R., McEachran, J. (2006). Oral sex and condom use among young people in the United Kingdom. *Perspectives on Sexual and Reproductive Health*, 38, 6-12.

Weeks, J. (2002). The social construction of sexuality. In Peiss K, (ED). Major Problems in the History of American Sexuality. Boston: Houghton Mifflin Company, 2-9.

Weeks, J. (1989). Sex, politics and society: the regulation of sexuality since 1800 (2nd edition). London: Longman, 1-326.

Wikipedia. (2006). Safe sex. Accessed from: http://en.wikipedia.org/wiki/Safe_sex

Wilson, S. (2000). Sexuality education: Our current status, and an agenda for 2010. Family Planning Perspectives, 32:252-254.

Wilson, S.N. (2000). Sexuality education: Our current status, and an agenda for 2010. *Family Planning Perspectives*, 32, 252-254.

Youth Risk Behavior Surveillance – United States, 2005. Morbidity and Mortality Weekly Report 2006; 55(SS-5):1-108.

Youth Risk Behavior Surveillance Survey. (2005). Accessed from: http://www.cdc.gov/HealthyYouth/yrbs/pdf/questionnaire/2005/

ISBN 978-1-60021-854-5
© 2008 Nova Science Publishers, Inc.

Chapter 3

ADOLESCENT SEXUAL RISK BEHAVIOR: ASSOCIATIONS WITH FAMILY, PEERS AND SCHOOL ENVIRONMENT

Aleksandra Jovic-Vranes[1,] and Boris Vranes[2]*

[1] Institute of Social Medicine, Medical School University of Belgrade, Dr Subotica 15, 11000 Belgrade Serbia

[2] Institute of Gynecology and Obstetrics, Clinical Center of Serbia

ABSTRACT

Objectives

During the dynamic period of adolescence when the passage from childhood to maturity takes place, sexuality takes on new dimensions; feelings become more intense, relationships become more complex, and the consequences of sexual behavior are radically altered. In general, earlier puberty, later marriage, a decline in the family leading to less control and more autonomy, and intense exposure to sexual stimuli via the mass media and travel across cultural boundaries have made pre-marital adolescent sexual activity more common. Adolescent sexual risk behavior places them at risk of unwanted pregnancy and childbirth, induced abortion in hazardous circumstances, HIV infection, and other sexual transmitted diseases. Objective of the study was to achieve a picture of adolescent sexual risk behavior. It also provides better material for the planning of specific preventive activities.

Methods

Random cluster sample consisted of 1540 15-year old adolescents, 822 female and 718 male. The multiple choice questionnaire included 119 items, covering topics such as:

* e mail: aljvranes@yahoo.co.uk

demographic characteristics, psychosocial determinants of health, leisure time behavior, family and peer context, risk behavior (tobacco use, alcohol and drugs consumption, sexual activity), and perceptions of school and the school's influence. Descriptive statistics, Chi-square test and logistic regression were applied for statistical analyzes.

Results

Thirteen percent of adolescent reported that they had sexual intercourse before age 15 years. Average age of first sexual intercourse was 13.88. Average number of sexual partners they had was 3.10. One out of three never used condom. Eight percent reported multiple sex partners, and fourteen percent alcohol use before intercourse. Factors associated with adolescent sexual risk behavior include other form of risk behaviors, family and peer context, and school environment.

Conclusion

Adolescent relationships are complex and future research should consider not only causality of adolescent sexual risk behavior, but also the etiology of the satellite behaviors.

Key Words: adolescence, sexual risk behavior, family, peers, school

INTRODUCTION

In bringing medicine to the community the provision of health services for children of school age should have a high priority. The requirements of children are basically similar everywhere, and a study of the historical growth and geographical pattern of school health services reveals that they have developed on very similar lines in most parts of the world.

Historical

It was not until the nineteenth century that serious study was given to the health of children at school.

In 1812 James Ware reported on the eyesight of school children in London and of students at Oxford University. In 1840 several doctors were appointed in a number of training colleges in Sweden. In 1866 Herman Cohn investigated the eyesight of over 10 000 children in Breslau; by 1883 he was urging the appointment of school doctors and had the eminent support of Virchow. The first school doctor in Germany was, in fact, appointed that year in Frankfurt-am-Main. Two years later one was appointed in Lausanne. In 1888 the Swedish Government inquired into the physical condition of over 11 000 Swedish children. At about the same time school medical inspection was started in all the Departments of France. In 1895 six school physicians were appointed to supervise the elementary schools in Moscow [1].

Adolescence

Adolescents are important! Throughout the world, they constitute a large proportion of any population, and their absolute numbers are increasing. Financially, they are the most expensive group of any age with regard to the investment of the community in their training and education, and socially they are the most commercially powerful, exploited and important since patterns of behavior established in adolescence inevitably continue into adulthood [2]. Adolescents are also politically important, but despite their enormous power to influence the community of the present day and the future, society has not yet learned to provide its adolescents with a structure of normal care during the period of their transition from child to adult [2].

Indeed, adolescence is a critical age for the development of coping behaviors and responses. This period is characterized by rapid physical, psychological, sociocultural and cognitive changes, and is unfortunately fraught with many threats to health. Much of the adverse health consequences experienced by adolescents are, to a large extent, the result of "risk behaviors". The initiation of risky behavior is occurring at a progressively younger age [3,4]. As a result of these trends, many adolescents may be vulnerable to experiment and initiate risk behaviors that have deleterious consequences during adolescence and later.

Risk behaviors and their associated adverse health outcomes represent a serious threat to life time health [5,6].

Reproductive Health in Adolescence

The health and well-being of adolescents is closely intertwined with their physical, psychological and social development, but this is put at risk by sexual and reproductive health hazards which are increasing a much of the world. Changes in population growth and distribution, the rise of telecommunications, the increase in travel and a decline in the family, as well as a generally earlier start of menarche and later age of marriage are contributing to an increase in unprotected sexual relations before marriage. This combined with risks from early marriage, result in early or unwanted pregnancy and childbirth, induced abortion in hazardous circumstances, and sexually transmitted diseases, including HIV infection leading to AIDS [7].

Sexuality is a fundamental quality of human life, important for health, happiness, individual development, and indeed for the preservation of the human race. During the dynamic period of adolescence in which the passage from childhood to maturity takes place, sexuality takes on new dimensions; feelings become more intense, relations become more complex, and the consequences of sexual behavior are radically altered. This not only affects the behavior of young people but also of those who interact with them, their families and peers, and those who work in health, education, youth, social welfare, and other sectors [8].

Adolescent sex has become a complex phenomenon among the researches, due to high sensitivity of this area. During the last two to three decades, the importance of this issue has increased because, its association with teenage pregnancies, sexual abuse such as rape and molestation, illegal birth, illegal and unsafe abortion and risk of STD and HIV-AIDS among adolescent. The basic problems of such studies are gathering of reliable information [9].

Unfortunately, there are still large numbers of misconceptions among adolescents towards sexual behavior. Some of them include that all teens are having sex, having sex makes you an adult, something is wrong with an older teen (17-19) who is not having sex, a girl can't get pregnant if she's menstruating, or a girl can't get pregnant if it's her first time [10].

Which Factors Influence Adolescents' Decisions about Sex?

Relevant factors include both risk factors and protective factors, which may be equally important in terms of their relevance. Risk factors are those that encourage behavior that could result in a pregnancy or sexually transmitted disease (STD) or, conversely, that discourage behavior that could prevent them. Protective factors are those that discourage behavior that could lead to a pregnancy or STD or that encourage behavior that can help prevent them. Put another way, as the number of risk factors in a adolescent's life increases and/or the number of protective factors decreases, the likelihood that he/she will have sex, become pregnant/cause a pregnancy, or contract an STD increases [11].

More than 400 factors are identified that affect one or more sexual behaviors (the initiation of sex, frequency of sex, number of sexual partners, use of condoms, and use of other contraceptives) or consequences of those behaviors (pregnancy, childbearing or STD).

Important risk and protective factors include characteristics of the adolescents' states, communities, families, friends and peers, romantic partners, and the adolescents themselves. Factors also involve adolescents' relationships with these important individuals or organizations in their environment. Some factors directly involve sexuality, while others do not [11,12].

These risk and protective factors may be grouped into four key themes:

1. Individual biological factors (e.g. age, physical maturity and gender)
2. Disadvantage, disorganization and dysfunction in the lives of the adolescents themselves and their environments (e.g. rates of substance abuse, violence, and divorce; also levels of education)
3. Sexual values, attitudes, and modeled behavior (e.g. adolescents' own values about sexual behavior as well as those expressed by parents, peers, and romantic partners)
4. Connection to adults and organizations that discourage sex, unprotected sex, or early childbearing. (e.g. attachment to parents and other adults in their schools and places of worship) [11].

METHODS

A survey was conducted applying the WHO research protocol for a cross-national survey "Health behavior in school aged children" (HBSC), as a cross-sectional study among Belgrade adolescents. It was a research project that aimed to gain new insight into and increased understanding of health and risk behavior, lifestyles and their context regarding young people.

Sample

A total of 64 public schools, and school classes at the appropriate grade levels were randomly selected. Thus, cluster sample design was used; and once the first level of sampling occurred at the school or school class level, then all adolescents in an appropriate age group were surveyed. Minimum sample size derived from HBSC recommended protocol was 1536 adolescents. This sample size assumes 95% confidence interval and a design effect of 1.44 [5]. A total of 1540 adolescents, aged 15 years, were included in this study.

Instrument

The multiple choice questionnaire for adolescents includes 119 items, covering topics such as: demographic characteristics, psychosocial determinants of health, leisure time behavior, family and peer context, risk behavior (tobacco use, alcohol and drugs consumption, sexual activity), and perceptions of school and the school's influence.

Measures

The data collection was performed by specialized staff, trained to address issues related to risk behavior, and to approach children in schools. These research assistants documented the process of data collection in a classroom report. The completion of the questionnaire by the participants took ca. 45 minutes. Teachers were absent from the classroom during this process. The project team guarantees anonymity of the answers provided by students.

Risk behavior was estimated through questions regarding sexual activity, smoking, alcohol and drug consumption. Adolescents were asked whether they had ever had sexual intercourse. Sexually active adolescents were asked how many times in lifetime they had engaged in sexual intercourse, how many partners they had, consistency of contraceptive use, and practice of other risk behavior. To determinate the prevalence of current tobacco use adolescents were asked, "how often do you smoke at present?" Only those who reported smoking at least once a week were referred to as current smokers. In addition the adolescents participating in the survey were asked about their use of alcohol. Specifically, they were asked how frequently they took alcoholic drinks, and whether they had ever been drunk. Current consumption of alcohol was defined as drinking some kind of alcoholic beverage at least every week. The term "illicit drugs" includes substances like: marijuana, a combination of alcohol and pills, inhalants and cocaine. Any frequency of the use of drugs above mentioned in a life time were taken into account and analyzed. Questions regarding family context included family structure, communications with parents, and family support. Questions addressed peer context included number of close friends, communication and spending time with friends, and attitudes towards classmates. School environment was estimated through questions about attitudes towards school and teachers.

Statistical Analysis

Data were analyzed by methods of descriptive statistics, chi-square test regarding differences by sex, and multivariate logistic regression. Associations between variables were initially tested using Chi-square tests. Logistic regression was used to identify the odds ratios for adolescent early onset of sexual behavior. Independent variables were related to other form of risk behavior, family and peer context and school environment. The odds ratio (OR) and 95% confidence intervals were obtained, and p value <0,05 was taken as the minimum level of significance.

Results

A study included a total of 1540 15-year old adolescents, 822 female and 718 male. Overall questionnaire was successfully conducted in 89.16% of the study population.

School as a Setting

Girls reported better school performance compared to their boys classmates. Asked how they feel about school at present seventy per cent of adolescents answered that they like school a bit, with no statistical difference by gender. Almost half of adolescents agree that their school is nice place to be, and that they belong at that school. Asked about their teachers, 10.3% of adolescents strongly agree that they are encouraged to express their own views in classes by teachers, and 10.4% that teachers treated them fairly. If they need extra help at school, 52.4% of respondents believe that they can get it by teachers. One out of three adolescent feel that their teachers expect too much of them at school, and 19.2% of them feel a lot pressured by the schoolwork they have to do. Almost half of adolescent neither agree nor disagree that their teachers are interested in them as a person. Less than 4% strongly agree with this statement. One out of five of respondents never or rarely feel tired when go to school in the morning, and 15.9% feel tired every day. Great number of boys had opinion (33.6%) that going to school is boring. Eleven per cent of girls had opposite opinion that going to school is never boring. Differences between boys and girls were also found in skipping classes or school. Twelve per cent of boys did it at least once, and 5% four or more times. Most of adolescent (78.7%) feel safe at school (Table 1).

Parent Relationships

Most of adolescent (84.2%) live with both biological parents. Boys reported better communication with father compare with girls who reported better communication with mother.

One out of three girls has difficult communication with father about things that really bother her, and 11.4% of boys recognized the same problem in communication with mother. Most of respondents (84.4%) think if they have problems at school, their parents are always

Table 1. School environment - gender differences

variable	gender		total	X²	p
	boys n (%)	girls n (%)			
Good school performance	315 (43.9)	512 (62.4)	827 (53.8)	89.09	0.000
Like school a bit	510 (71.9)	563 (68.9)	1073 (70.3)	2.41	0.492
School is a nice place to be	337 (48.0)	420 (51.3)	757 (49.8)	1.68	0.194
I feel I belong at this school	404 (57.2)	464 (56.9)	868 (57.1)	0.01	0.909
I am encouraged to express my own views in my class(es)	84 (11.9)	73 (9.0)	157 (10.3)	16.99	0.002
Teachers treat us fairly	96 (13.5)	62 (7.6)	158 (10.4)	31.60	0.000
When I need extra help, I can get it	347 (49.2)	450 (55.3)	797 (52.4)	5.70	0.017
My teachers are interested in me as a person	33 (4.7)	24 (3.0)	57 (3.8)	12.52	0.014
Rarely or never feel tired when they go to school in the morning	169 (23.6)	162 (19.7)	331 (21.5)	7.96	0.047
Feel safe at school	559 (78.3)	650 (79.1)	1209 (78.7)	4.08	0.395
Going to school is often boring	240 (33.6)	171 (20.9)	411 (26.7)	40.79	0.000
Skipping classes at least once	85 (11.9)	79 (9.7)	164 (10.7)	22.12	0.000

Table 2. Family context – gender differences

variable	gender		total	X²	p
	boys n (%)	girls n (%)			
I live with both parents	602 (84.1)	691 (84.4)	1293 (84.2)	5.97	0.202
Easy communication with father	487 (70.0)	410 (50.6)	897 (59.6)	58.22	0.000
Easy communication with mother	569 (81.3)	694 (85.4)	1263 (83.5)	4.53	0.033
If I have problems at school, my parents are ready to help	605 (85.2)	685 (83.6)	1290 (84.4)	5.18	0.159
Parents are willing to come to school to talk to teachers	519 (72.9)	572 (69.7)	1091 (71.2)	3.32	0.345
Parents encourage me to do well at school	599 (84.0)	707 (86.2)	1306 (85.2)	1.55	0.671
Parents expect too much of me at school	245 (34.6)	210 (25.6)	455 (29.8)	14.56	0.000

ready to help, 71.2% have parents who are willing to come to school to talk with teachers, and 85.2% are encouraged to do well at school by their parents. That their parents expect too much of them at school believe 29.8% of adolescents (Table 2).

Table 3. Peer context – gender differences

variable	gender		total	X^2	p
	boys n (%)	girls n (%)			
Three or more close friends	580 (81.2)	522 (63.6)	1102 (71.8)	61.39	0.000
Easy to make new friendship	656 (91.9)	731 (89.3)	1387 (90.5)	3.04	0.081
Easy communication with friends of the same sex	254 (37.4)	385 (47.5)	639 (42.9)	45.52	0.000
Easy communication with friends of the opposite sex	183 (27.0)	182 (22.8)	365 (24.7)	11.49	0.022
Spending time with friends after school 4-5 days a week	185 (26.3)	111 (14.0)	296 (19.8)	57.31	0.000
Students enjoy always being together	300 (42.6)	252 (31.1)	552 (36.5)	27.19	0.000
Most of the students are kind and helpful	569 (80.5)	687 (84.4)	1256 (82.6)	4.04	0.045
Students accept me as I am	659 (93.3)	760 (93.3)	1419 (93.3)	0.01	0.943
Take part in bullying other students even once	56 (7.9)	25 (3.0)	81 (5.3)	49.28	0.000

Peer Relationships

Seventy two per cent of adolescents have three or more close friends. Being withdrawn by classmates was present in 1.6% of adolescents. Making new friendships was easy for 90% of both girls and boys. Girls reported better communication with friends of the same sex. Almost half of them (47.5%), can very easy to talk about things that really bother them with friends of the same sex. One out of four of respondents have very easy communication with friends of the opposite sex with no statistical difference according to gender. There was a significant difference according to sex noted in the way students spent time with friends right after school. 26.3% of boys and 14% of girls went out with friends four to five times a week. Forty three per cent of boys believe that the students in their class(es) always enjoy being together compare to thirty per cent of girls. Twenty five per cent of girls think that is possible only sometimes. Good opinion about their classmates was noticed among adolescents, with no difference according to sex. That most of the students in their class(es) are kind and helpful reported 82.6% of adolescents, and 93.3% that other students accept them as they are. Eight per cent of boys have taken part in bullying other adolescents in school at least once in that term in comparison to 3.0% of girls (Table 3).

Substance Use

The current prevalence of cigarette smoking was 14,8% with non significant difference according to sex observed (129 female and 99 male smokers).

5,6% of students consumed alcohol regularly. The percentage of students reported to having "been drunk" were 34,9% of males and 13,2% of females, with significant difference by sex. Having five or more drinks in a row was found commonly among students who use alcohol with 25% of males, regularly drinking alcohol, in particular on weekends.

Table 4. Adolescent substance use and sexual behavior - gender differences

variable	gender		total	X²	p
	boys n (%)	girls n (%)			
Substance use					
cigarette smoking	99 (13.8)	129 (15.7)	228 (14.8)	1.10	0.294
regular alcohol consumption	41 (8.1)	15 (3.1)	56 (5.6)	11.71	0.001
been drunk	189 (34.9)	70 (13.2)	259 (24.2)	68.63	0.000
have five or more drinks in row	132 (24.2)	44 (8.2)	176 (16.3)	84.51	0.000
drug use	98 (13.6)	69 (8.5)	167 (10.8)	10.95	0.001
Sexual behavior					
sexual intercourse before age 15 years	160 (23.8)	19 (2.5)	179 (12.6)	146.21	0.000
first sexual intercourse was wished by both partners	117 (84.2)	12 (92.3)	129 (84.9)	1.66	0.647
had a relationship with their partners in the moment of first sexual intercourse	122 (81.3)	8(61.5)	130 (79.8)	2.90	0.088
main reason for the first sexual intercourse - curiosity	61 (40.9)	5 (38.5)	66 (40.7)	1.28	0.973
main outcome that bothers adolescents- pregnancy	91 (62.3)	10 (76.9)	101 (63.5)	4.54	0.338
condom use	95 (64.2)	12 (100)	107 (66.9)	6.43	0.011
multiple sex partners	13 (8.8)	0 (0)	13 (8.1)	1.24	0.265
alcohol use before intercourse	20 (13.4)	2 (15.4)	22 (13.6)	0.14	0.932

Lifetime experience of illicit drug use was 14% for boys and 8,5% for girls, with significant difference according to sex. The most prevalent illicit drug was marijuana. Half of the students who had experience with drugs used marijuana, 11,3% used a combination of drugs (alcohol and pills), 9,4% used inhalants and 4% used cocaine (Table 4).

Sexual Behavior

Thirteen percent of adolescent reported that they had sexual intercourse before age 15 years, more boys (23.8%) than girls (2.5%). Average age of first sexual intercourse was 13.88. Average number of sexual partners they ever had was 3.20 for boys, and 1.50 for girls. Most of adolescents (84.9%) reported that their first sexual intercourse was wished by both partners, and 79.8% that they had a relationship with their partners in the moment of first sexual intercourse. For the majority of respondents main reasons for the first sexual intercourse were curiosity (40.7%), passion (19.1%), and to stay in relationship with partner (19.8%). Five percent did it because it was peer expectation, and ten per cent of adolescents out of love. Other reasons were physical attraction (3.7%) and under alcohol or other drugs (1.9%). Pregnancy was the main concern for most of adolescents (63.5%). One third was afraid of AIDS, 1.9% of parents' disapproval, 2.5 reported other reasons, and less than one per cent was concerning other sexually transmitted diseases. Despite these facts, use of contraceptive methods during each sexual intercourse was inconsistent and sporadic. Condom was the most used contraceptive method by adolescents. Girls always use condoms, and one out of three boys did not use it at all. Other methods were contraceptive pills (5.6%), and interrupted coitus (5.6%). Rest of the adolescent reported some other methods. Eight percent of boys and none of the girls reported multiple sex partners. Fourteen percent of respondents admitted alcohol use before intercourse, more girls than boys (Table 5).

Table 5. Odds ratios of adolescent early sexual intercourse, according to factors from family, peer, school setting and other form of risky behavior

variable	OR*	95% CI**	p
I live without both parents	1.54	1.04-2.26	0.033
Difficult communication with mother	1.75	1.20-2.55	0.004
Parents don't encourage me	2.16	1.23-3.80	0.008
Difficult communication with friends of the opposite sex	0.49	0.34-0.71	0.000
Three or more close friends	1.56	1.07-2.29	0.022
Difficult to make new friendship	0.36	0.16-0.78	0.010
Spending time with friends after school	1.39	1.28-1.54	0.000
School is not a nice place to be	1.41	1.02-1.94	0.037
I don't feel that I belong at this school	1.45	1.06-1.99	0.022
Cigarette smoking	2.74	1.91-3.94	0.000
Regular alcohol consumption	6.43	3.61-11.45	0.000
Been drunk	7.45	5.15-10.79	0.000
Drug use	3.46	2.34-5.13	0.000

* Odds ratio from multiple logistic regression models.
** Confidence Interval.

Associations with Adolescent Sexual Risk Behavior

Using logistic regression analysis we found that factors associated with early onset of adolescent sexual behavior include other form of risk behaviors, family and peer context, and school environment. Boys and girls who live in families without both biological parents [odds ratio (OR)=1.53, 95% confidence interval (CI)=1.04-2.26] and in families without support (OR=2.16, 95%CI=1.23-3.80) often have firs sexual intercourse before age 15 years compare with others. Difficult communication with mother (OR=1.75, 95%CI=1.20-2.55) and easy communication with friends of the opposite sex (OR=0.49, 95%CI=0.34-0.71) were found to be associated with early sexual activity. Other factors regarding peer context were large number of close friends (OR=1.65, 95%CI=1.07-2.29), easy way of making new friendships (OR=0.36, 95%CI=0.16-0.78), and spending a lot of time with friends after school (OR=1.39, 95%CI=1.28-1.54). Attitudes towards school also influence sexual activity among adolescents. Those who did not think that school is nice place to be (OR=1.41, 95%CI=1.02-1.94), and that they don't belong at that school (OR=1.45, 95%CI=1.06-1.99) experienced with sexual behavior earlier. Other forms of risk behavior, such as smoking cigarettes (OR=2.74, 95%CI=1.91-3.94), alcohol (6.43, 95%CI=3.61-11.45) and drug consumption

(OR=3.46, 95%CI=2.34-5.13) are related to a younger age at the onset of sexual activity (Table 5).

CONCLUSION

Sexual and reproductive ill-health mostly affects women and adolescents. Women are disempowered in much of the developing world and adolescents, arguably, are disempowered everywhere. Sexual and reproductive health services are absent or very often of poor quality and underused in many countries because discussion of issues such as sexual intercourse and sexuality make people feel uncomfortable. The increasing influence of conservative political, religious, and cultural forces around the world threatens to undermine progress made since 1994, and arguably provides the best example of the detrimental intrusion of politics into public health [13].

According to a growing body of research, most young people begin having sexual intercourse during their teenage years. Current data suggest that slightly more than half of females and nearly two-thirds of males have had intercourse by their 18th birthday. In the last several decades there have been substantial increases in the proportion of adolescents who report sexual activity at each year of age. Increases have been greatest among females, especially among young females. Thus, more than twice as many females ages 14, 15, and 16 are sexually active now, compared with young women of the same ages just 15 years ago. Moreover, on average, there are seven years for women and ten years for men between first intercourse and first marriage [14]. Our findings show that thirteen percent of adolescent had sexual intercourse before age 15 years, more boys (23.8%) than girls (2.5%), and average age of first sexual intercourse was 13.88. Average number of sexual partners among adolescents in our study was 3.20 for boys, and 1.50 for girls. Data from Center for disease control and prevention suggest that in 2005, 47% of high school students had ever had sexual intercourse, and 14% of high school students had had four or more sex partners during their life [15]. In addition, young people use alcohol and other drugs at high rates. Adolescents are more likely to engage in high-risk behaviors, such as unprotected sex, when they are under the influence of drugs or alcohol [16]. In 2005, 23% of high school students who had sexual intercourse during the past three months drank alcohol or used drugs before last sexual intercourse. 34% of currently sexually active high school students did not use a condom during last sexual intercourse [15]. In our study fourteen percent of adolescents admitted alcohol use before sexual intercourse, more girls than boys. One out of three boys did not use condom at all.

Many variables are related to the timing of first sexual intercourse. On average, males begin having sex at younger ages than females. In addition families and schools, provide an environment within which adolescents make decisions related to sexual activity. Unconventional psychosocial attitudes and behaviors--as reflected by early use of alcohol, tobacco and other drugs, school problems, delinquency, and physical aggression--are associated with earlier onset of adolescent sexual intercourse. Parents' marital disruption and living with a single parent have been found to be associated with earlier onset of adolescent sexual behavior. Similarly, having sexually active siblings and friends is strongly related to a younger age at the onset of sexual activity [14, 17].

Our findings are consistent with other studies [14,17,18]. We found that factors associated with early onset of adolescent sexual behavior include other form of risk behaviors, family and peer context, and school environment. Adolescents who live in families without both biological parents, in families without support, and who have difficult communication with mother often have firs sexual intercourse before age 15 years compare with others. Other factors regarding peer context were easy communication with friends of the opposite sex, large number of close friends, easy way of making new friendships, and spending a lot of time with friends after school. Attitudes towards school also influence sexual activity among adolescents. Those who did not think that school is nice place to be, and that they don't belong at that school experienced with sexual behavior earlier. Other form of risk behavior, such as smoking cigarettes, alcohol, and drug consumption are related to a younger age at the onset of sexual activity.

When interpreting the findings of this study, a number of limitations should be considered. When responding to questions about risk behaviors, some adolescents might have felt uncomfortable and untrusfull and had the need to give responses that were socially acceptable. Moreover, the cross-sectional study design does not allow us to establish causal relationships among variables. Despite these limitations, we believe that there are several important trends in the data. Our data are consistent with other studies, and our results may stimulate further research, and provide valuable reference point for future studies of this issue.

To prevent problems before they happen, we must identify the factors that put adolescents at risk and either eliminate, reduce, or somehow buffer the effect of exposure to the risk. Risk for adolescent problem behavior exists in many domains of life. However, it is important to remember that exposure to a single risk factor does not condemn an individual to problem behavior [19]. The findings summarized above have important implications for parents, teachers, clinicians and others responsible for the well-being of adolescents. There is an urgency to develop and implement behavioral interventions that motivate adolescents to adopt and/or maintain risk taking behavior prevention practices. Behavioral change interventions have attempted to reduce or eliminate the consequences of adolescents risk behavior. Interventions have been attempted to delay the initiation of sexual activity, to improve contraceptive use among sexually active adolescents, to (in some cases) influence pregnancy resolution decisions among those who become pregnant, and to eliminate or reduce sexual transmitted diseases. Adolescents who begin having sexual intercourse need to understand the importance of using an effective contraceptive every time they have sex. This requires convincing sexually active adolescents who have never used contraception to do so. In addition, sexually active adolescents who sometimes use contraceptives need to use them more consistently (every time they have sex) and use them correctly. Finally, sexually active adolescents need to take actions to prevent sexually transmitted infections, as well as unintended pregnancy.

REFERENCES

[1]   Henderson P. The health of the school child. *Public health* 1971; 85 (2): 58-66.
[2]   Bennett LD. Worldwide problems in the delivery of adolescent health care. *Publ Hlth Lond* 1982; 96: 334-340.

[3]   Office of Disease Prevention and Health Promotion. Intervention for adolescents at risk. *Prevention Report*, 1993 February/March (pp. 1-2). Washington, DC: United States Department of Health and Human Services, U.S. Public health Service.

[4]   DiClemente R, Hansen BW, Ponton EL. Adolescent at Risk, a Generation in Jeopardy. In: *Handbook of Adolescent Health Risk Behaviour*, New York; Planum Press; 1996: 1-52.

[5]   Currie C. Health Behavior in School-Aged Children: Research Protocol for the 1997-98 Survey. Edinburgh: Edinburgh University; 1998.

[6]   Jovic Vranes A, Vranes B, Marinkovic J, Cucic V. Adolescent substance abuse, the importance of family, school and peers: data from the health behavior in school children. *Soz Praventivmed*. 2005; 50(2):119-24.

[7]   Friedman HL. Reproductive health in adolescence. *World Health Stat Q*. 1994; 47 (1): 31-5.

[8]   Friedman HL. Changing patterns of adolescent sexual behavior: consequences for health and development. *J Adolesc Health* 1992; 13(5): 345-50.

[9]   Nainakwal R, Nainakwal M. *Adolescent sexual behavior, contraception, and unsafe abortion* (A study on the college student in Mumbai, India). University of Mumbai 2001. Available from: URL: http.//www.iussp.org/Brazil2001/s80/s85_p06_nainakwal.

[10]   Focus Adolescent Services. *Teen Sexual Behaviors: Issues and Concerns.* 1999. Available from: URL: http.//www.focusas.com/SexualBehavior.html.

[11]   Kirby D, Lepore G, Rayan J. *Sexual Risk and Protective Factors.* Factors affecting teen sexual behavior, pregnancy, childbearing and sexual transmitted disease: Which are important? Which can you change. ETR Associates, Washington 2005.

[12]   Sallis JF, Nader PR. Family determinants of health behavior. In: D.S. Gochman, *Health Behaviour: Emerging Research Perspectives*, Plenum Press, New York ;1988.

[13]   Glasier A, Gulmezoglu AM, Schmid GP, Moreno CG, Van Look PF. Sexual and reproductive health: a matter of life and death. *Lancet*. 2006 Nov 4; 368(9547):1595-607.

[14]   Moore AK, Miller CB, Sugland WB, Morrison RD, Glei AD, Blumenthal C. Adolescent sexual behavior, pregnancy and parenthood. *U.S. Department of Health and Human Services*. 2006. Available from: URL: http.//www. aspe.os.dhhs.gov/hsp/cyp/xsteesex. htm.

[15]   CDC. Youth Risk Behavior Surveillance—United States, 2005. *Morbidity & Mortality Weekly Report* 2006; 55(SS-5):1–108.

[16]   Leigh B, Stall R. Substance use and risky sexual behavior for exposure to HIV: issues in methodology, interpretation, and prevention. *American Psychologist* 1993; 48:1035–1043.

[17]   Klingon YS, O Sullivan AL. The family as a protective asset in adolescent development. *J holist Nurs* 2001; 19(2): 102-21.

[18]   Jacar J, Dittus JP, Gordon VV. Maternal Correlates of Adolescent Sexual and Contraceptive Behavior. *Family Planning Perspectives* 1996; 28: 159-165.

[19]   Hawkins JD. *Risk for Health and Behavior Problems.* Fifteenth Annual Gsela Lectureship, University of Minnesota 1993.

In: Psychology of Decision Making in Risk Taking …   ISBN 978-1-60021-854-5
Editor: Rachel N. Kelian   © 2008 Nova Science Publishers, Inc.

Chapter 4

SEXUAL AGGRESSIONS AMONGST UNDERAGED: VULNERABILITIES, RISK FACTORS, SIGNS OF CALLING FOR HELP

Philippe Bessoles
"Victimology and Criminology"
University Pierre Mendés France, Grenoble II, France
In collaboration with Myriam Linnell-Boutaud

Keywords: Victimology, traumatism, criminology, sexuality, resilience.

VULNERABILITY AND TRAUMA

Post-trauma notion of vulnerability, following a sexual aggression, appears too general in infantile clinical psychopathology to be sufficiently operating. Differences regarding criteria for symptomatological assessments, differential diagnosis with post-trauma disorders, personality changes inherent to child development, specificity (or not) of a post-traumatic semiology inherent to under fifteen, etc. add to the complexity of the question. According to research, vulnerability can be, at once, synonym of psycho-social factors of risk, signs of victimarius call for help or badly circumscribed psychological vulnerabilities. International studies often diverge as investigation methodologies are so contradictory and epidemiological data not consensual enough… Notions of abuse, touching, incest, remain blur and badly defined despite a number of publications in which categorizations are suggested by searchers like M. Montés de Oca, C. Yohant and A. Markowitz (1990), who differentiate:

- *Sexual abuse without body contact*: public or private exhibitionism, pornographic pictures, verbal incitation towards sexual activity, and erotic talk on sex in front of children.

- *Sexual abuse with body contact*: erotic caresses or kisses, touching, calls for masturbation.
- *Sexual abuse with penetration*: rape attempt or rape with anal, vaginal or oral penetration (the French penal code completes this definition of rape *"with the use of any object"*.

Legal, clinical or medical definitions overlap or oppose themselves. Inside a research field, contradictions add to the complexity of psychopathological and therapeutic aims such as *"compliant hymen"* regarding medico-legal expertise or the statute of limitation after 10 years in the case of rape. Legal expertise is paradigmatic of these difficulties.

In this relatively complex context and based on our clinical victimology consultations in the ward of clinical forensic (CHU Montpellier, France – University Hospital Center), we have taken an interest (over a period of three years; 1998-2000) in two major questions on ill-treatments inflicted to underage:

1st question: *by differentiating sexual and non-sexual ill-treatments, what is the proportion of girls or boys who are affected?*
2nd question: *amongst observed disorders, do vulnerabilities, specific to under 15, exist that could lead to the hypothesis of a post-sexual-abuse syndrome?*

SYNTHETIC REVIEW OF THE QUESTION (CLINICAL ASPECTS)

The main epidemiological problem comes from the fact that some works are carried out based on retrospective sociological data gathered from adults, surveys from significant adult samples or studies limited to notional territory. These simple references demonstrate a disparity of assessment and methodological referential. These referential have no epistemological consensus and lead to bias in analysis.

We limit out research to a clinical approach of the phenomenon and the main publications on the subject.

The decade 70 – 80 can be called phenomenological to the extent that epidemiological data are statistically not very numerous. They are essentially, testimonies from female adults victim of incest during their childhood. The interest resides in the fact that research community has becoming aware of the need for granting this phenomenon with fundamental and applied research it deserves. Y.H.L. Haesevoets in 1997 and in 2004 emphasized that an important step has been taken in 1976 in K. Meiselman's study. This study, carried out between 1973 and 1976, on a sample of 58 adults abused in their childhood, observed chronic traumatic pathologies i.e. persisting 15 years after the trauma occurred. From this observation, analyses diverge. This divergence is partly due to the absence of comparative studies using either a control group or a clinical group of reference, the non-existence of standardized instruments in order to diagnose, the size of samples or the scarce anamnesistic studies prior to sexual trauma. This group of methodological approximations generates impassable bias for a rigorous research.

From the years 1980, researchers attempted to harmonize their investigation protocols even if the undertaken notions appear more phenomenological than clinical or psychopathological. H. Van Gijseghem demonstrates the irreversibility of psychological wounds; S. Groi, of symptoms of anxiety and exacerbated fright (insomnia, nightmares, sleeping disorders, somatic disorders,...). Other research report after-effects such as food disorders, depression or phobia,...

In the years 1990, J. Kieser et al. show, with a sample of 10 children between 2 and 6, the development of symptoms in connection with Post Traumatic Stress Disorder criteria with reference to the DSM III R. Other studies balance these works [26]. We can retain:

- Loss of self-confidence (Mac Leer, 1998).
- Loss of self-esteem (shame and culpability) (Herman, 1981; S. Groi, 1982).
- Symptoms of depression, sometimes severe.
- Significant correlations between sexual brutalities and delinquent or criminal behaviors (David and Earls, 1987).
- Intellectual development disorders and sociability disorders (Gomes-Swartz; Horowitz, 1985).
- Depressions and suicidal thoughts (Wozencraft, 1991).
- Alteration in identity structure (Hunter; Childers, 1988).
- Typically psychiatric severe disorders (Cole; Putman, 1992).

In 1997, Y.H. L. Haesevoets suggests a grid of the principle psychopathological disorders connected with incest. This grid analyses somatic, physical and physiological, psychosomatic, cognitive, behavioral and relational, familial and social factors. The author yet specifies that the consequences of an abusive situation appear to depend on uncontrollable variables such as precocity of detection, the beginning of therapeutical treatment, designation of the sexual trauma (touching, rape, incest, sexual brutality, etc...) as well as the individual experience of the trauma by the underage.

The unpredictability of symptoms is not synonymous of their inexistence. From an empirical point of view, we observe symptomatic *"silences"* becoming loud, months – if not decades – later (as in peri- menopausic psychological changes, for example), symptomatic *"over-determinations"* revealed during subsequent minor trauma, for example. Some clinical constants appear and most theoretical models take them into account:

- Some symptoms seem inseparable from pre-existing symptoms. Post-trauma disorders intervene as an accentuation of the previous psychopathology.
- The clinical picture tends to put into relation some symptoms, with the real coercions of traumatic break-in, particularly coercions of humiliation as in collective rapes or torture.
- The recurrence of sexual violence during childhood seems to correlate with the severity of ulterior disorders, from a psychiatric point of view as much as a somatic decompensation one.
- With the exception of some sexual conduct disorders in the underage, there does not seem to be any evidence of causality between sexual abuse and symptom production.

Methodological *"weaknesses"* observed in different studies temporarily lead, not to postulate for a post sexual abuse answering to precise diagnostic assessment, specific diagnosis and sufficient anamnesistic backgrounds (research involving control groups).

Although, some of these bias appear in our works, considering the complexity of interactions whether psychological, pathological or inherent to child or teenage development, they seem to aim towards an opposite conclusion, which is the existence of such pathology.

STUDY 1

Method

The repartition according to sex of the victim and nature of sexual/non sexual ill-treatment has been studied in a first longitudinal research over three years (1999, 2000 and 2001). The data collection is from consultations in victimology in forensic ward (University Hospital Centre – Montpellier – France) during the first appointment.

Non-sexual ill-treatment: assaults, injuries, scratches, tortures, moral harassment, brutalities, punishments, deprivations.

Sexual ill-treatments: rape, incest, exhibitionism, voyeurism, sexual touching, sexual brutality, sexual tortures.

Results

Table 1. Study 1999- number of consultations: 61

Type of aggression	% girls	% boys
Non-sexual ill-treatments	17.6	29.4
Sexual ill-treatments	44.1	14.7
All ill-treatments overcome	61.7	38.2

Table 2. Study 2000- number of consultations: 111

Type of aggression	% girls	% boys
Non-sexual ill-treatments	3.6	25.2
Sexual ill-treatments	52.2	18.9
All ill-treatments overcome	55.8	44.1

Table 3. Study 2001- number of consultations: 160

Type of aggression	% girls	% boys
Non-sexual ill-treatments	6.5	23.7
Sexual ill-treatments	64.75	5.3
All ill-treatments overcome	71	29

Table 4. Average of the studies 1999, 2000,2001- number of consultations: 332

Type of aggression	% girls	% boys
Non-sexual ill-treatments	9.15	26.1
Sexual ill-treatments	53.6	12.9
All ill-treatments overcome	62.8	37.1

STUDY 2

Method

The data collection is for the year 2000 from 160 consultations. The semiology is identical to the one observed during the first interview. The interview's technique is semi-directive and aims towards a diagnosis. We do not use the repartition by age slice.

Data analysis was done in two parts. The first part was a generic draft of types of syndromes, of disorders encountered amongst underage, in order to, in a second part, specifies items susceptible to help us towards the creation of a symptomatic analysis grid. The aim of our research was the creation of a clinical assessment tool for sexually abused underage or underage suspected of having been sexually abused. This study was part of a HPCR (Hospital Project in Clinical Research) in relation to the French legal context – June 1998 law on audio-visual recording of interviewed of underage who are suspected to have been sexually abused, and the effects of "*over victimization*".

Results

Table 5. Frequency of the clinical signs expressed in % - year 2001- Number of people: 160- Clinical picture after the first consultation- Sex and age overcome.

Oral sphere disorders	26.5
Sphincterian functioning disorders	18.9
Disorders of the cognitive sphere	94.9
Behavior and conduct disorders	60.7
Sleeping and falling asleep disorders	22.7
Genital sphere disorders	20.25
Social link disorders	20.25

Table 6. Repartition per item. Oral sphere disorders.

Disorder of the oral sphere	Percentage
Anorexia	5.06
Bulimia	11.3
Weight loss	6.3
Weight gain	3.7

Table 7. Repartition per item. Sphincterian functioning disorders

Sphincterian functioning disorders	Percentage
Enuresis	2.53
Encopresis	2.53
Diarrhea	0.01
Constipation	5.06
Abdominal pains, stomach aches	8.96

Table 8. Repartition per item. Disorders of the cognitive sphere

Disorders of the cognitive sphere	Percentage
Sudden school failure	7.5
Scholastic drop	17.7
Scholastic non-implication	20.25
Mnemic disorders	10.12
Learning disorders	8.86
Concentration disorders	7.59
Language and communication disorders	11.3
Graphics and writing disorders	11.3

Table 9. Repartition per item. Behavior and conduct disorders

Behavior and conduct disorders	Percentage
Self-aggressive conducts	5.06
Aggressive behaviors	7.55
Passivity-depression- submission	13.8
Repetitive activities	5.6
Psycho-motor activities agitation	6.86
Psychosocial instability, within the group	8.75
Behavioral impulsivity	11.3

Table 10. Repartition per item. Sleeping and falling asleep disorders

Sleeping and falling asleep disorders	Percentage
Nightmares	7.6
Falling asleep disorders	11.5
weariness	3.8

Table 11. Repartition per item. Genital sphere disorders.

Genital sphere disorders	Percentage
Masturbation – touching	5.06
Exaggerated modesty	14.65
Frigidity	9.82
Anorgasmia	11.5
Definitive interruption of sexual intercourse	20.56
Gynecological problems	8.87
Compulsive washing disorders	19.86

Table 12. Repartition per item. Social link disorders.

Social link disorders	Percentage
Aggressiveness	6.32
Isolation-withdraw	12.08
Inhibition	7.34

Results' Synthesis

General data show a strong incidence of sexual trauma on the cognitive sphere for the quasi majority (94.9%) of the population examined. The study of individual items tends to confirm that troubles are not of an instrumental nature. It is the relation with didactic content and implication towards learning, which are being disturbed. The post-traumatic effect seems to interfere with concentration, representations and memorization. Scholastic drop (17.7%) and non-implication (20.25%) underline this *"leech off"* in the attitude towards learning like tools for appropriation of knowledge (language in particular).

Symptoms in relation to oral sphere disorders are feeding disorders of a bulimic nature (11.3%). Bulimic behavior emphasizes (based on the number of people we observed) the alterations of the body image especially the upheaval of body topography (inside, outside, bottom, top front, back…).

Sphychterian function disorders are not directly linked with mastering of sphincter -anal or urethral, for example- intestinal transit causing colonopathy or abdominal pain (8.96%). Sleeping disorders occur mainly in the form of difficulties to go to sleep (11.5%).

Behavior and conduct disorders (BCD) appear contradictory, when only reading on quantitative level. The item "passivity-depression- submission" (13.8%) is apparently in opposition with the item "behavioral impulsiveness" (11.3%). It seems that this opposition shows a double aspect of the BCD meaning predominance of passivity from which facial expressions–often anxious- of behavioral impulsiveness emerge. This aspect can be corroborated by social links disorders in which the item "isolation-withdrawal" is at 12.08%. The behavioral propensity would be a propensity towards withdrawal and isolation more than a post-traumatic pathology loud manifestation.

Finally, disorders of the genital sphere can appear surprising in particular the item related to the definitive interruption of sexual intercourse, considering our study is on under 15. This interruption regards the eldest underage we observed (20.56%). The item "compulsive disorders" (19.86%) qualifies compulsive washing behaviors (of an obsessional type), frequent change of underwear with cleaning control, etc.

Comments and Analyses

The qualitative analyses of the above quantitative data permit to better assess psychological and psychical mechanisms striving, even though our preliminary study calls for other complementary and deepened researches. It still corroborates the 20 indicators of sexual exploitation defined by S. Groi as early as 1986 (cited by Y.H. Haesevoets).

On the level of cognitive process analysis, it seems that post-traumatic effects do not invalidate the efficiency of the cognition mechanisms (language, memory, perception, etc…). We, essentially, observe phenomenon of "interference" and inhibition more of less important, which, indeed, have some serious and durable consequences. This seriousness of sexual trauma tends to be correlated with the sensitive phases in the development (for example, the pubertal phase and its identity changes) or their duration (recurrent incest over many years).

Although, longitudinal studies are essential, when studying sexually abused underage, in order to avoid anamnesistic reconstructions or the after effect, it appears that phenomenon of anxiety consecutive to trauma pervert (literally) learning processes. H. Van Gijseghem (1975, 1985) underlines intellectual development deficiencies particularly of symbolic and Piagetian thought. Scholastic symptomatology shows a disharmony of learning processes generated by "*fright, inhibition of thought and relational passivity*". For school children, sexual trauma disturbs learning process even if that learning can help towards a better control of the sustained event as well as helping towards it verbalization.

A research consensus agrees that the earlier the abuse occurs in life, the more risks that wounds become irreversible at all levels; "*particularly on identity level*" adds H. Van Gijseghem. At more advanced ages, observed phenomenon on cognition level are identical to those observed amongst younger children. On the other hand, behavioral and conduct disorders (depression, dysthymia, running away, suicidal ideation, etc…) generate, for the essential, these cognitive disturbances.

Pathogenic components that touch the oral sphere, such as sphyncterian or functional (stomach ache) malfunctioning appear as somatic symptoms for want of sufficient psychical elaboration (alteration of representational mechanisms, in general). Bulimic behaviors, for example, emphasize alterations of processes of identity construction, in particular, the progressive construction of the body image. Bulimia appears during clinical examination like a reactional formation when facing the breaking of primary psychic sheaths. It acts like "*a lipidic protection*" for want of "*protective shield*" efficiency.

The "*psychosomatic*" aspect of psychical investments tends to accreditate the hypotheses of impossibilities in the representation of sexual trauma, such as pain affects, mentioned by M. Bertrand (cited by L. Crocq and P. Bessoles). This aspect of a symptomatology of the psychic body and the skin-Ego (D. Anzieu, 1987) attests of the victimarius destruction in the underage. All recent works confirm this double aspect of psychosomatic symptoms and disturbance in the image of the body. These same research corroborate others, more ancients, such as the model of D. Finkelhor and D. Browne in 1985, published in the American Journal of Orthopsychiatry.

Disturbances in falling asleep reveal the failures of the work of thought and dream. Abused underage appear to be fighting against the decline of the level of vigilante consciousness to which, falling asleep, lead, being too scared to be invaded with anxieties and traumatic reviviscence. This attitude, highly phobic, that can take the clinical shape of diurnal and nocturnal terrors is typical of post-traumatic syndromes amongst children as well as adults. We wish to underline this phobic aspect, which is at the source, it seems, of dysmorphophobia which particularly pathogenic amongst female teenagers.

The visible contradiction in our study, due to passivity ……. Withdrawal, isolation or inhibitions coexist through aggressive behaviors –sometimes violent-. Hyper-vigilance and hypersensitivity translate psycho-affective insecurity of the underage. It is expressed by constant submission and passivity. Violence appears like the manifest expression of anxious faces, facing paroxystic anxieties of an anaclitic type. This behavioral *"dyschrony"* attests of the underage internal disturbances, of which, acting out behaviors –auto or hetero aggressive – are the mirror of post-traumatic suffering.

Genital sphere disorders are, for the essential, psychosomatic (dermatosis, cystitis, prurit, inflammatory process, vaginal herpes attacks...). These phenomena, well known by medical corps, can be treated by using psychotherapeutic processes and without any medicine apart from comfort. On the other hand, it is true, particularly for female teenagers that, rituals of washing rituals of the uro-genital zone, particularly their frequency and intensity, have a tendency to modify the self-immune balance of the pelvic belt. Sexuality and sexual conducts disorders, in its different components according to the age of the underage, are constant. They lead to sexual prematureness, compulsive conducts of masturbation or important inhibitions (notably nudity) often observed by pediatricians or doctors (in the context of school medical).

With the exception of very few particularly suggestive mimes of coitus using a doll (which does not necessarily express the reality of the sexual trauma), a majority of underage patients did not show any seductive or provocative attitude, as it is often stated in literature. On the contrary, underage children show important inhibitions which require some form of talk prior to any somatic examination.

In an attempt to summarize clinical and psychopathological forms of vulnerabilities amongst sexually abused underage children, we can divide them into four main domains:

- A symptomatology of school learning. It is about learning process which become disturbed, inhibited and leeched off by post-traumatic effects. It is, therefore, the relationship with knowledge and knowledge which is at cause and not the cognitive efficiency.

- A symptomatology on behavior and conduct disorders centered on a dominating inhibition of the psychical link and social link. This domination sometimes turns into anxious acmes in the form of auto or hetero-aggressive raptus.

- A more or less invalidating phobic symptomatology, with obsessional behaviors mainly centered on rituals of washing.

- A somatoform symptomatology which indicates the alterations of representational processes and the effects of psychical staggering due to sexual trauma.

DISCUSSION

The evaluation of post-traumatic vulnerabilities amongst sexually abused underage children emphasizes, independently from clinical characteristics, the main – and durable – traumatogenic impact on the process of identity construction.

Ancient Freudian's works (1920) and Férenczian's (1927-1933) have broadly described post-traumatic psychopathologies for the same reasons as those more recent from L. Crocq, F. Lebigot, L. Daligand, etc... Our research confirms the presence of a psychopathological entity of trauma neurosis independent from psychopathological backgrounds, amongst underage children (as also observed amongst adults).

This traumatic neurosis adds to pre-existing pathologies but appears specific, even if the interactions with post-traumatic pathologies complexify the differential analyses of the clinical picture.

Our arguments rest on the above study as well as the therapeutic treatment of the underage children. We would like to specify that the hospital conditions for admitting patients (clinical victimology ward CHU Montpellier), were purposely limited to post-immediate sharp states. Underage children were addressed to partners of the network we collaborated with (specialized institution, CMPP -Medico Psycho Pedagogic Center-, child psychiatry…).

- A direct incidence exists between the event sustained and the emergence of a specific psychopathology described above (even if this incidence, still today, calls for more in depth research in order to specify their characteristics).
- Post-traumatic psychopathology observed cannot be limited to a reading of co-morbidity or accentuation factors in previous disorders. Even if it can be the case, for some of the examined underage children (like boarders in an institution for mentally deficient children), it is wrong to assert (from an empirical point of view to this date) that sexual trauma only produces a quantitative and qualitative surcharge of previous disorders.
- The specificity of a post-traumatic syndrome is argued in the differential diagnosis, i.e. significant correlations between sexual trauma characteristics and generated disorders. Thus, the "unfavorable" diagnosis has been confirmed for those, victim of sexual aggression with penetration, humiliation, repetition and torture.
- At an adult age, traumatic pathologies are even more persistent when the person has not been able to undertake any treatment, independently from therapeutical fields of reference.
- Sexual trauma generates real "*cataclysms*" in the underage child's psychic organization, not only in his psychical system of economy but above all in his structural organization. This aspect seems more pathogenic at time of phases of psychical organizations such as Oedipus, puberty or adolescence phase.
- The alteration of identity process is apparent in the clinical picture's somatoform expressions. This expression does not just reveal the difficulties in psychically elaborating the trauma but also the breaking of primary psychical sheaths ("*secure base*").
- Finally, "*we have to take into account*" the fact that most sexual abuses are committed by a member of family (or a relative) in 85 to 90% of cases (according to our panel). These epidemiological data confirm the idea of pervertion of affective, familial, social,… bond, even if the degree of relativity between the underage child and his abuser remains to be specified.

CONCLUSION

We wish to emphasize the phobic dimension of post-traumatic states amongst the underage. On the semiological level, phobic symptoms observed in our study are not only due to classical description of child and teenager psychopathology. The intensity of anxiety does not only answer to phobic situations, it is often close to states of panic, notably in the difficulties in going to sleep. Likewise, dysmorphobia, observed in our research, do not appear to be phobia in the "strict" meaning, but disorders in the construction of body image, independently from corporal mutations inherent to the development of the young subject.

Anxiety is not only related to a potential traumatic situation as in traumatic reviviscences (notion of "anxiety warning"). It generates a constant and chronic feeling of anxiety, as well as an extremely invalidating subjacent depression of a neglected or anaclitic type, for most observed underage children.

The phobic aspect appear to evocate some border-line psychic functioning, as these phobia are atypical because of the context in which they appear, their content and the fact that they have no impact on anxiety. On the contrary, it soaks-in the entire underage mental function, and compromises relationships with others. The whole of the subject is threatened as anxiety is so massive and intrusive.

If, as stated by D. Marcelli, on the subject of phobic psychopathologies amongst the under aged and teenagers, "*it is a phobic neurosis from a clinical point of view, [...] there is a reason to look for anxiety of a paranoid type*". Empirically, we agree with the term of paranoid anxiety, for some of the patients, during the sexual trauma post-immediate phase. It is characterized by the following aspects:

- The formulation of the trauma sustained, sometimes, appears incoherent, badly systemized, if not incomprehensible, independently from the syntactic or semantic level of the under-aged. This formulation appears terrifying and incommunicable, sometimes completed with invasions of interfering coenesthesia (twitches, shivers, spasms, interfering actions, mimes,...).

- The under-aged sometimes feel, spied on, observed or threatened and uses strategies such as para-verbal or psychomotor allusions (scribbles in dolls crotch done by young children, for example) or whispers in the doctor or psychologist ear "*but, you know...*".

- The threat of psychic dismantling can often be spotted in the form of persecutions, notably in graphic productions realized during the clinical interview. The people drawn are often being attacked, aggressed; sometimes, a whole has been made in the paper with the felted-pen. The intensity of anxiety is such that in some cases, dolls are literally destroyed, as if the esthetic experience was close to that feeling of having one's body cut into pieces.

- The way the body is apprehended, amongst the most dramatic cases (collective rapes perpetrated on female teenagers), is close to real processes of depersonalization with, a feeling of body dispossession, ideas of body transformation and for two clinical cases conducts of self-mutilations and autolysis.

These productive moments can be transitory, but we cannot, due to the absence of longitudinal follow-up, specify the evolution of chronicity. On the other side, retrospective studies on adults tend to confirm long lasting psychopathological after-effects as well as pathogenic reviviscences decades after the infantile trauma. It seems, in an empirical at this point in time, that specific phases of vulnerability, which are not related to life psychical hazard, exist. These phases are the one when identity changes are directly "requested" like peri-partum or pre-menopause phases.

On the other side, we feel that it is important to emphasize, in the same way we have done it elsewhere, on the resilient capacities, sexually abused children and teenagers are capable of. Psychical and psychological "fragilities" underlined hereby appear as, as much plasticity in psychical changes and elaborations of the sexual trauma. Recent research by M. Lemay (1998, 1999) or B. Cyrulnick (199, 2001) show these under-aged can elaborate particularly terrible and destroying sexual traumatisms. Nevertheless, it would be a mistake to think that these psychical elaborations are definite.

REFERENCES

Anzieu D. *Les enveloppes psychiques*. Paris : Ed. Dunod ; 1987

Baccino E, Bessoles P. *Le traumatisme sexuel et ses devenirs*. Lecques : Ed. Le Champ Social ; 2001.

Baccino E, Bessoles P. *Traumatisme et résilience : lien psychique, lien social*. Lecques : Ed. Le Champ Social, 2003.

Bessoles P. *Torture et temporalité : contribution à une sémiologie de psychose post traumatique.* In : *Les cahiers de psychologie clinique*. Bruxelles : Ed. De Boëck University ; 2004.

Bessoles P. 2000, Le *meurtre au féminin, clinique du viol*. Saint Maximin : Théétète Editions, 1997.

Bessoles P. *La psychose post-traumatique*. In : L'encéphale. Paris : Elsevier Editions ; 2005.

Brusset B. *Etats anxieux et névroses* : critique des concepts. In : Marcelli D, Braconnier A, editors. Adolescence et psychopathologie, 4. Paris : Ed. Masson ; 1999. p. 203-38.

Coutenceau R. *Vivre après l'inceste*. Paris : Ed. Desclée de Brouver ; 2004.

Crocq L. *Névrose traumatique et élaboration résiliente*. In : *Victime-Agresseur*, Tome 4. Lecques : Ed. Le Champ Social ; 2003. p. 27-41.

Crocq L. Bessoles P. *Récidive, réitération, répétition : lien d'emprise et loi des séries*. Lecques : Ed. Le Champ Social ; 2004.

Cyrulnik B. *Un merveilleux malheur*. Paris : Ed. Odile Jacob ; 1999.

Cyrulnik B. *Les vilains petits canards*. Paris : Ed. Odile Jacob ; 2001.

Dalignand L, Gonin D. *Violence et victimes*. Lyon : Ed. Méditions ; 2004.

Damiani C. *Les Victimes : violences publiques et crimes privés*. Paris : Ed. Bayard ; 1997.

Defrancis V. *Protecting the child victim of sex crimes committed by adults*. Denver, CO : American Human Association, Children's division ; 1976.

Fattah EA. *Le rôle de la victime dans le passage à l'acte : vers une approche dynamique du comportement délictuel*. Rev Int Criminol Police Tech 1973 ; XXVI(2) : 173-88.

Ferenczi S. 1927-1933, *Confusion de la langue entre l'adulte et l'enfant*, in : *Œuvres complètes*, Psychanalyse IV, Paris, Payot, 1968.

Finkelhor D. *Sexuality victimized children*. New-York : Free Press ; 1979.

Finkelhor D. Browne A. *The traumatic impact of child sexual abuse : a conceptualization*. Am J Orthopsychiatry 1989 ; 55 :530-41.

Gabel M. *Les enfants victimes d'abus sexuels*. Paris : PUF ; 1994.

Gabel M. *Le traumatisme de l'inceste.* Psychiatrie de l'enfant. Paris : PUF ; 2000.

Gutton P. *Adolescens.* Paris : PUF ; 1996.

Haesevoets YH. *L'enfant victime d'inceste.* Bruxelles : Ed. De Boëck Université ; 1997.

Haesevoets YH. *L'enfant en question. De la parole à l'épreuve du doute dans les allégations d'abus sexuels.* Bruxelles : Ed. De Boëck Université ; 2003.

Lebigot F. Bessoles P. *Situation d'urgence, situation de crise : clinique du psychotraumatisme immédiat.* Lecques : Ed. Le Champ Social ; 2004.

Lemay M. *Résilience devant la violence.* J Psychologues 1999 ; 164 :36-47.

Lighezzolo J, de Tyché C. *La résilience : se (re)construire après le traumatisme.* Paris : Ed. In Press ; 2004.

Marcelli D, Braconnier A. *Adolescence et psychopathologie.* Paris : Masson ; 1995.

Marcelli D. *Enfance et psychopathologie.* Paris : Ed. Masson, 1996.

Mazet P, Stoléru S. *Psychopathologie du nourrisson et du jeune enfant.* Paris : Masson ; 1993.

Montes de Oca M, Yohant C, Markowitz A. *Revue critique des travaux épidémiologiques anglo saxons récents sur l'abus sexuel à l'égard des enfants.* In : *Les abus sexuels à l'égard des enfants,* CTNERHI. Paris : PUF ; 1990. p. 7-70.

Van Gijseghem H. *L'enfant mis à nu. L'allégation d'abus sexuel : la recherche de vérité.* Québec : Méridien ; 1992.

Van Gijseghem H. *Autre regard sur les conséquences de l'inceste père-fille.* Revue canadienne de psycho-éducation ; 1985 ;14(2) :138-45.

Van Gijseghem H. *Facteurs interférents avec la qualité du témoignage de l'enfant au tribunal dans les causes d'abus sexuels.* Québec : Revue canadienne de Psycho-éducation 19.1.11.22 ;1975.

In: Psychology of Decision Making in Risk Taking ...   ISBN 978-1-60021-854-5
Editor: Rachel N. Kelian   © 2008 Nova Science Publishers, Inc.

Chapter 5

PREDICTORS OF MIDDLE SCHOOL YOUTH EDUCATIONAL ASPIRATIONS: HEALTH RISK ATTITUDES, PARENTAL INTERACTIONS, AND PARENTAL DISAPPROVAL OF RISK

Regina P Lederman[*], *Wenyaw Chan*[**] *and Cynthia Roberts-Gray*[***]

[*]University of Texas Medical Branch;
[**]University of Texas School of Public Health
[***]Resource Network

ABSTRACT

School-wide surveys in five middle schools were used to measure educational aspirations, attitudes toward sexual health risk behaviors and drug use, and perceptions of parental interactions and disapproval of risk behavior at baseline and one year later. Participants were male and female students of Black ($n = 222$), Hispanic ($n = 317$), White ($n = 216$), and Asian or other heritage ($n = 85$), ages 11 to 14. Analyses were performed for three factors with Cronbach's alpha coefficients ≥ 0.65 (youth's attitudes, discourse with parents, and parents' disapproval of risk behavior), and three single items inquiring about use of alcohol, use of marijuana, and sexual behavior. Generalized Linear Model (GLM) with logit link was used to evaluate the contribution of these measures at baseline as predictors of educational aspirations at the one-year follow-up. Results showed race/heritage ($p < .001$), attitudes toward health risk behaviors ($p < .01$), extent to which youth talked with parents about use of drugs and other health risk behaviors ($p < .05$), and perceptions of their parents' disapproval of risk behavior ($p < .05$) each made significant contributions in predicting educational aspirations. Gender did not contribute to the prediction of educational aspiration nor did self-report of actual risk behavior. These results indicate that youth interactions with parents regarding health risk behaviors is

[*] Contact Author: Regina P Lederman, PhD, University of Texas Medical Branch, 301 University Blvd. Galveston, TX 77555-1029. Phone: 713 666 0172. 409 772 6570. email: rlederma@utmb.edu

worthy of further exploration to develop interventions to reduce adolescent health risks and increase educational aspirations.

INTRODUCTION

Parent-child relations occupy important positions in pathways linking education and health. Parental encouragement for educational attainment is, for example, closely linked to youth educational aspirations (Looker and Thiessen, 2004; Goyette and Xie, 1999). Educational aspirations of youth (Trusty and Harris, 1999) and parental involvement in their children's education (Trusty, 1999) are linked to educational attainment. Lack of educational attainment and low educational aspirations in turn are associated with a variety of health and health behavior problems, including substance abuse (Caetano, 2002) and rates of teenage birth (Pamuk, Makuc, Heck, Reuben, and Lochner, 1998). The association of poor education and poor health is a consistent finding from domestic and international research in economics, epidemiology, and sociology (Blane, 2003; Morowsky and Ross, 2003).

In some formulations of the pathways linking education and health, education is identified as a health-protecting factor (see Hannum and Buchman, 2003). Because of the abundant empirical evidence that better educated people lead longer, healthier lives, those who espouse the health protection formulation recommend investment in programs and practices that promote educational attainment as a means for improving health and reducing health inequalities. At a local program level, such an initiative might include parenting education and supportive services to assist families in encouraging their children to aspire to and achieve higher educational attainments, anticipating that positive health outcomes will accrue.

Other analyses demonstrate that good health in adolescence predicts both higher educational attainment and better adult health (Chandola, Clarke, Blane and Morris, 2003). Recommendations for action from this perspective focus on interventions to help families encourage healthy behaviors in childhood and adolescence with the expectation that better educational and adult health outcomes will follow.

In this chapter we examine a secondary analysis of data from a prevention research project exploring relationships among the educational aspiration of middle school youth, their health risk attitudes and behaviors, and interactions with their parents regarding risk behavior. The data, originally obtained to test the effectiveness of an innovative parent-child program for the prevention of sexual health risk behaviors (see Lederman, Chan, and Roberts-Gray, 2004; Lederman and Mian, 2003), were collected in school-wide surveys at five middle schools during a baseline period and again the next school year. The purpose of this secondary analysis of the data is to explore the possibility that, in addition to putting the health of youth at risk, negative health attitudes and behaviors distract youth from the pursuit of educational goals and thereby constrain educational aspirations, while appropriate parental involvement in discouraging negative health behaviors in youth can contribute to higher educational aspirations. We hypothesized that middle school youth involvement in and attitudes toward health risk behaviors, and their perceptions of interactions with their parents/guardians regarding health risk behaviors would be predictive of educational aspiration measured during the subsequent school year.

RESEARCH DESIGN AND METHODS

This study analyzed data collected in school-wide surveys over two successive school years from students in five middle schools in two school districts in coastal Texas. The written survey questionnaire provided self-report measures of: (1) sexual involvement and the use of alcohol and other drugs; (2) attitudes toward sexual health risk behavior; (3) the frequency and breadth of discourse with parents about sexual health topics; (4) perceptions of parents' disapproval of the youth's involvement in sexual and other health risk behaviors; and (5) educational aspiration. The protocol was approved by the Institutional Review Board of the University of Texas Medical Branch at Galveston. Active assent of students and consent of parents was obtained and documented.

Participant Recruitment

Participants were recruited in four steps. First, we sent invitations through the mail and through presentations at conferences to all urban school districts located in and near Galveston, Texas. Leaders in two school districts indicated willingness to have their schools participate in the prevention intervention research project. The next step was meeting with principals and counselors at middle schools in the consenting districts. Two out of the three middle schools in one district and three of the four middle schools in the second district agreed to participate. The third step was partnership with the consenting schools to invite families to participate. A cover letter, consent form, and informational flyer were sent to parents via the students and through the mail informing them about the program and providing details regarding the research protocol. The school principals at each of the participating schools endorsed the program and signed the letters to parents, which were written in both English and Spanish.

The participating schools represented diversity in school size, ethnic heritage of the student body, and performance characteristics. Two of the schools had approximately 500 students, two had between 700 and 1,000 students, and one had more than 1,200 students. Across the five schools, the percent of students of different heritage ranged from 0.0 to 3.4 Asian, 7.0 to 54.3 African American, 32.8 to 85.8 Hispanic, and 5.2 to 52.1 White. Three of the schools had more than two-thirds of the student body identified as economically disadvantaged. The percent of students with special circumstances ranged from 3.7 to 23.6 with limited English proficiency, 4.5 to 13.6 participating in gifted and talented programs, and 2.2 to 4.3 percent with disciplinary placement. Total enrollment across the five schools was 3,881. Informed consent and actual participation in the survey was obtained for 848 youth.

Demographic Characteristics of the Participating Youth

More than half of the students were in sixth grade at the time they completed the baseline survey. There were approximately equal numbers of females and males. The majority was youth of color with nearly 40% indicating Hispanic/Latino/Mexican ethnicity. These data are displayed in Table 1.

Table 1. Demographic Characteristics of Survey Participants

Youth characteristics	Number of Youth	Percent
GENDER		
Male	383	45%
Female	465	55%
RACE/ETHNICITY		
Hispanic/Latino/Mexican	317	38%
Black/African American	222	26%
White – not Hispanic	216	26%
Asian or Mixed or Other	85	10%
GRADE LEVEL		
Sixth	480	60%
Seventh	249	31%
Eighth	76	9%

Survey Administration

Students completed the survey questionnaire during a special assembly at the school. The survey items originally were selected to be relevant in evaluating outcomes of prevention education interventions to reduce sexual health risk behaviors and prevent teen pregnancy and the spread of HIV and other sexually transmitted infections (STI). Adapted from the National Youth Survey (Elliot, Huizinga, and Ageton, 1985) and a middle school survey developed by ETR Associates (Kirby et al, 1997), the 9-page, 94-item survey questionnaire was divided into sections asking: "What do your parents think?," "What do you think?," "What do you do?," and "Do you talk with your parents?" Students typically completed the survey in 30 to 45 minutes. Unique identifying codes were marked on the survey forms so that records could be matched from year to year without disclosing individual identifying information.

Measures

Survey items addressing a common content domain (e.g., youth attitudes toward risk behaviors) and having similar response options (e.g., strongly agree to strongly disagree) were combined to produce domain scales which then were tested for internal consistency. Those obtaining a Cronbach alpha of 0.65 or greater were retained as scales. The scales and survey items used in the current analyses are described as follows.

- *Educational Aspiration* was measured with a single item asking, "How far do you think you will go in school?" Response options were assigned ordinal codes of 1 = "Won't graduate from high school," 2 = "Will finish high school," 3 = "Will go to trade, vocational, or business school after high school," 4 = "Will attend college."

Youth involvement in and attitudes toward risk behaviors were measured with two sets of survey items, one that counted the number of self-reported risk behaviors and the other a scale measuring perceived acceptability of "someone my age" having sex.

- *Health Risk Behaviors* was measured with three single items: (1) "In the last 30 days, did you drink alcohol such as beer, wine, wine coolers or hard liquor?," (2) "In the last 30 days, did you use marijuana?," and (3) "In the last 6 months, did you try to get someone to have sex with you?" Response options were coded 1 = No and 0 = Yes.

- *Attitude Toward Sexual Health Risk Behavior* was measured with a 14-item domain scale asking about conditions under which it is acceptable to have sex. Sample items are: "I believe it's OK for someone my age to have sex with someone they like, but don't know well," "I believe people my age should always use a condom if they have sex," and "If my boyfriend or girlfriend wanted to have sex and I didn't, it would be OK to say 'no'." Response alternatives were "Strongly agree," "Agree," "Disagree," and "Strongly Disagree," coded 1 through 4 with more desirable responses receiving a higher numerical score. Cronbach's alpha for the baseline sample was 0.76.

Interactions with parents regarding risk behaviors was assessed with two domain scales, one measuring the frequency and breadth of youth discourse with parents about sexual health topics and the other measuring youths' perceptions of whether or not parents or guardians would disapprove of youth engaging in risk behaviors.

- *Discourse with Parents about Sexual Risk Behavior* measured how often in the last three months youth had talked with their parents about five topical items: menstruation, the risk of getting pregnancy or getting someone pregnant, being a teenage parent, different kinds of birth control, and sexually transmitted diseases (STDs) or AIDS. Response options were coded 0 = "Never," 1 = "1-3 times;" and 2 = "More than 3 times." Cronbach's alpha for this domain scale at baseline was 0.73.

- *Parental Disapproval of Risk Behavior* was measured by asking if the parent or guardian would "approve" or "disapprove" if the youth engaged in six types of risk behavior: used alcohol; sniffed paint or glue or used marijuana; used hard drugs such as heroin, cocaine or crack; had sex (made love, went 'all the way'); got pregnant or got someone pregnant; and failed a grade in school. Responses were coded 1 and 0. The Cronbach alpha for this scale at baseline was 0.65.

A study reported elsewhere (Lederman, Chan, and Roberts-Gray, 2004) showed the domain scales selected for the predictive model tested in the current study were independent of one another. The obtained inter-domain correlations were low with Pearson correlation coefficients of $r = 0.10$ for Discourse and youth Attitude, $r = 0.04$ for Discourse and perceived Parental Disapproval, and $r = 0.29$ for youth Attitude and perceived Parental Disapproval.

Data Analyses

Generalized Linear Model with logit link was applied to evaluate the contribution of the baseline measures of interactions with parents and youth involvement in and attitudes toward risk behaviors as predictors of youths' educational aspirations measured in the subsequent school year. Additional variables included in the statistical models were students' age (11 and 12 versus 13 and 14), self-reported ethnic heritage, and gender. A limitation of this study is that all analyses assume the data are taken from random samples. Like many studies reported in the research literature, this study cannot verify this assumption. Generalization of the results should be cautious.

RESULTS

Educational Aspirations. Virtually all (99%) of the middle school students that participated in the survey indicated they plan to finish high school. Ten percent indicated completion of high school is the highest level of education they expect to attain. The vast majority of the students (86%), however, indicated they plan to attend college.

Predictors of Educational Aspirations. Race/heritage ($p < .001$), youth attitudes toward sexual health risk behaviors ($p < .01$), discourse with parents about health risk behavior ($p <.05$), and perception of parental disapproval of youth involvement in risk behavior ($p < .05$) each made significant contributions in predicting educational aspirations. The full model is displayed in Table 2. Neither age nor gender made significant contributions in predicting educational aspirations, nor did actual risk behaviors. Excepting the exclusion of actual risk behavior, the hypothesized model fit the data well (Chi-Square = 735.19, $df = 740$).

Table 2. Generalized Linear Model with PREDICTORS Measured at Baseline and the Criterion Variable EDUCATIONAL ASPIRATION Measured the Subsequent School Year

Predictors	Beta Weight	SE	Chi Square	*p*-value
Gender	0.1835	0.2376	0.60	NS
Age (11-12 versus 13-14)	0.4917	0.3779	1.69	NS
Race/Ethnicity				
Hispanic / Latino, including Mexican	-1.3867	0.4196	10.92	<.01
Black / African American	0.1924	0.4792	0.16	NS
White – not Hispanic	-0.0617	0.4722	0.02	NS
Asian or Mixed or Other	0		.	
Health Risk Behaviors				
Use alcohol	-0.1672	0.2894	0.33	NS
Use marijuana	0.1890	0.4317	0.19	NS
Try to get someone to have sex	-0.3618	0.4139	0.76	NS
Parental disapproval of risk behaviors	2.0630	1.0186	4.10	<.05
Discourse with parents about risk behaviors	-0.7926	0.3454	5.27	<.05
Attitudes about acceptability of having sex	2.0928	0.6970	9.02	<.05

Lower educational aspiration was predicted by higher levels of discourse with parents about sexual health risk behaviors and with being Hispanic/Latino/Mexican. Higher educational aspiration was predicted by youth holding attitudes less accepting of sexual activity and perceiving that their parents/guardians disapprove of their being involved in risk behaviors.

CONCLUSION

This analysis demonstrates that the attitudes of middle school youth toward health risk behaviors and their perceptions of interactions with their parents/guardians regarding health risk behavior are useful in predicting educational aspiration measured during the subsequent school year. Youth who are at baseline less accepting of involvement in sexual activity and who perceive that their parents disapprove of their involvement in risky behaviors are more likely than those with more tolerant attitudes and perceptions to continue into the next school year with high educational aspirations. The finding that perceived parental disapproval of health risk behavior predicts youths' educational aspiration is consistent with other research indicating that maternal connectedness may facilitate the development of a positive future time perspective by young adolescents (Aronowitz and Morrison-Breedy, 2004).

An unexpected finding in the current analyses was that frequency and breadth of youths' discourse with their parents about sexual health topics showed a negative relationship with youths' educational aspirations. Youth who reported more discourse with parents about sexual health topics were significantly more likely than their peers to report lower educational aspirations. This finding underscores conclusions presented in Healthy People 2010 (U S Department of Health and Human Services, 2000, Chapter 25) regarding the need to give further attention toward helping parents impart information about sexual health risks. The research literature suggests there is no simple, robust relationship between parent-adolescent communication about sexuality and subsequent adolescent sexual health behaviors (Miller, 1998; Dittus and Jaccard, 2000). A hypothesis for exploration in future research is the possibility that young adolescents talk with their parents about risk behavior only when their behavior has created a predicament that forces discussion between parent and child. Another possibility is that more discussion about risks and protection may have a normalizing effect on the youth's perceptions of risk behavior. Yet another possibility is that more discourse about risk behavior occurs in families where parental control experienced as excessive or coercive, and impels the youth toward acting out and/or toward a more negative future time perspective (Tiongson, 1997).

The current study indicates that the interactions of youth with parents regarding health risk behaviors is worthy of further exploration and the development of interventions to improve adolescent health, and educational and adult health outcomes. There is a clear need for additional research to identify ways to marshal, nurture, and work in concert with parental efforts to reduce adolescent health risks and encourage educational attainment.

REFERENCES

Aronowitz, T., and Morrison-Breedy, D. (2004). Comparison of the maternal role in resilience among impoverished and non-impoverished early adolescent African American girls. *Adolescent and Family Health*, 3(4), 155-163.

Blane, D. (2003). Commentary: Explanations of the difference in mortality risk between different educational groups. *International Journal of Epidemiology*, 32, 355-356.

Caetano, R. (2002). *Education, psychiatric diseases and substance use/abuse.* Presentation made at conference on Education and Health: Building a Research Agenda. National Institutes of Health. Available to read online: www.wws.princeton.edu/chw conferences/conf1002/session/Caetanofiles/frame.html

Chandola, T., Clarke, P., Blane, D., and Morris, J. (2003). *Pathways between education and health: A causal modeling approach.* University College London (UCL). Published online: www.ucl.ac.uk/epidemiology/Chandola/healtheducation.htm

Dittus, P., and Jaccard, J. (2000). The relationship of adolescent perceptions of maternal disapproval of sex and of the mother-adolescent relationship in sexual outcomes. *Journal of Adolescent Health*, 26, 268-278.

Elliot, D., Huizinga, D., and Ageton, S. (1985). *Explaining delinquency and drug use.* Beverly Hills, CA: Sage.

Goyette, K., and Xie, Y. (1999). Educational expectations of Asian-American youth: Determinants and ethnic differences. *Sociology of Education*, 71, 24-38.

Hannum, E., and Buchman, C. (2003). *The consequences of global educational expansion: Social science perspectives.* Cambridge, MA: American Academy of Arts and Sciences. Available to read online: www.amacad.org

Kirby, D., Korpi, M., Adivi, C., and Weissman, J. (1997). An impact evaluation of SNAPP, a pregnancy- and AIDS-prevention middle school curriculum. *AIDS Education Prevention*, 9(Suppl A), 44-67.

Lederman, R., Chan, W., and Roberts-Gray, C. (2004). Sexual risk attitudes and intentions of youth age 12-14 years: Survey comparison of parent-teen prevention and control groups. *Behavioral Medicine*, 29(4), 155-163. Available to read online: www.findarticles.com/p/articles/mi_m0GDQ/is_4_29/ai_n6192603

Lederman, R., and Mian, T., (2003). The Parent-Adolescent Relationship Education (PARE) Program: A curriculum for prevention of STDs and pregnancy in middle school youth. *Behavioral Medicine*, 29, 33-41.

Looker, D., and Thiessen, V. (2004). *Aspirations of Canadian youth for higher education.* Learning Policy Directorate, Strategic Policy and Planning, Canada. Available to read on-line: www.pisa.gc.ca/SP-600-05-04E.pdf

Miller, B. (1998). *Families matter: A research synthesis of family influences on adolescent pregnancy.* Washington, DC: National Campaign to Prevent Teen Pregnancy.

Morowsky, J., and Ross, C. (2003). *Education, Social status, and Health.* New York: Aldine de Gruyter.

Pamuk, E., Makuc, D., Heck, K., Reuben, C., and Lochner, K. (1998). *Socioeconomic Status and Health Chartbook. Health, United States, 1998.* Hyattsville, MD: National Center for Health Statistics, Table 9, page 185 of 464. Available to read online: www.cdc/nchs/data/hus/hus98.pdf

Tiongson, A. (1997). Throwing the baby out with the bathwater: Situating young Filipino mothers and fathers beyond the dominant discourse on adolescent pregnancy. In: M. Root (Ed), *Filipino Americans: Transformation and Identity*, Thousand Oaks, CA: Sage.

Trusty, J. (1999). Effects of eighth-grade parental involvement on late adolescents' educational expectations. *Journal of Research and Development in Education*, 32, 224-233.

Trusty, J., and Harris, M. (1999). Lost talent: Predictors of the stability of educational aspirations across adolescence. *Journal of Adolescent Research*, 14, 359-382.

U S Department of Health and Human Services. (2000). *Healthy People 2010: Understanding and Improving Health* (2nd ed). Washington DC: US Government Printing Office.

In: Psychology of Decision Making in Risk Taking ...   ISBN 978-1-60021-854-5
Editor: Rachel N. Kelian   © 2008 Nova Science Publishers, Inc.

Chapter 6

RISK MITIGATION:
INDIVIDUAL AND MARKET BEHAVIOR

Jamie Brown Kruse[1] and Kevin M. Simmons[2]

[1] Wind Science and Engineering Research Center, Texas Tech University, Lubbock, TX,
and Center for Natural Hazards Mitigation, East Carolina University,
Greenville, NC
[2] Department of Business and Economics, Austin College, Sherman, TX

INTRODUCTION

Wind research has focused mainly on the meterological aspects of storms and the engineering challenges to construct resistant structures. Over the last several years, however, an effort has been launched to understand the behavior of people living in areas threatened by violent windstorms. The aftermath of a significant windstorm event brings instant media attention to the affected area and government aid is usually forthcoming to lessen the financial blow to residents and businesses. It is rare, but some storms produce damage so severe that it alters the economic conditions, not only of those living and working in the path of the storm but third party insurers as well. Hurricane Andrew is a relatively recent example. As losses from these events mount, several questions continue to arise. What can be done to lessen the effect of a tornado or hurricane? And second, will people adopt mitigation measures that may be available to them?

The second question has been of interest to economists and there is some debate on the potential response of people living in vulnerable areas. These events are rare and it is possible that people simply ignore the risk. If this tendency prevails, then storm resistant construction will not be adopted due to the increased cost. Essentially, the safety offered by the storm resistant engineered structures is a form of insurance and the value placed on that insurance may or may not correspond to the perceived risk of an event. This paper uses experimental economics techniques to examine the human response to changes in risk and how this response aggregates to become market demand for risk mitigation measures.

We will examine the relationship between individual bidding behavior and the aggregative properties of a market for full insurance. We utilize a Vickrey auction to sell from one to six policies. A Vickrey auction is a sealed-bid auction in which participants each simultaneously submit bids. The auctioneer discloses the identity of the highest bidder(s) who is declared the winner. The price paid by the winning bidders is equal to the highest bid that does not win the object(s). This format is named after William Vickrey who first described it and pointed out that bidders have a dominant strategy to bid their true values. Participants in the laboratory experiment reported here either acquire one of the available insurance policies in the auction or face exposure to the risk of a two-dollar loss. There is a rich literature in Psychology and Economics that has contributed to our current understanding about decision under risk. We describe a few of the important papers in the next section. This is followed by our experimental design, results and conclusions.

REVIEW OF RELATED LITERATURE

An early lab experiment performed by Slovic, Fischhoff, Lichtenstein, and Corrigan (1977) tested the attractiveness of insurance to consumers at various probability levels. The subjects were given an amount of money, which was put at risk through the drawing of a ball from an urn filled with red and blue balls. If a blue ball was drawn the subject lost his/her money. A red ball would signal that there would be no penalty. Full insurance was available for purchase at a fixed premium equal to the expected value of the loss. The results of this experiment indicated that as the probability of loss increased, the percentage of subjects purchasing the insurance increased. At low probabilities, only about 20% of the subjects purchased the insurance. When the probability of loss increased to over 0.2, the percentage of subjects purchasing insurance increased to over 80%. A second treatment studied was the level of the premium. It was found that as the premium was lowered, through a subsidy, the percentages purchasing insurance at all probability levels increased. Finally, the authors tested the effect of compound lotteries. A compound lottery has nested probabilities. The subjects were told that the probability of loss on each draw was the same, for instance 5%, but the number of draws increased thus increasing their overall probability of loss. An interesting finding resulted from this manipulation of the experiment. At a probability level of 0.01, little change was observed in the percentage purchasing insurance. However, beginning at the .05 level, almost all subjects purchased the insurance. The general conclusion of the study was that as probabilities increased either directly or through a compounding effect, consumer's willingness to purchase insurance also increased.

Shoemaker (1979) reports the results of an experiment that explored several issues regarding insurance. First, the experiment was designed to measure the level of aversion to a high-probability-low-loss event versus a low-probability-high-loss event. Second, the willingness to pay for varying premium/deductible combinations was elicited and finally, the willingness to pay for comprehensive insurance was measured. Subjects for the experiment came from two sources. One group was undergraduate students at the University of Pennsylvania. The other group was solicited by mail from the client list of a Philadelphia insurance agency.

To test differences concerning risk aversion, the subjects were asked to choose between a 60% chance of losing $100 or a 1% chance of losing $6,000. Losses to the subjects were hypothetical in contrast to the first experiment, which used real money losses. The expected value of both choices is the same. The majority of students chose the low probability, high loss option. The majority of insurance clients, mostly adults, chose the high probability, low loss option. A possible explanation for this difference, offered by the authors, was that the adults had a larger accumulated wealth. This increased wealth influenced their decision in that they had more to lose than young college students.

The second group of questions tested various premium/cost combinations of insurance policies. It is interesting to note that for both groups, there was a clear preference for very low deductible and very high deductible policies. The least preferred policies were those in between the two extremes. One possible explanation for this result is the inability to process choices rationally with two variables, premiums and deductibles.

Regarding the willingness to pay for comprehensive insurance, the subjects were asked the amount they were willing to pay for insurance to cover each of three losses. They were then asked how much they would be willing to pay for a policy to cover all losses. Of the student group, 49% indicated that they would pay less for the comprehensive policy. Similarly, 53% of the client group also said they would pay less.

A final set of questions tests preferences for policies where the only difference is in scale. Two choices are offered to the subjects: a premium of $100 to mitigate a 25% chance of a $500 loss or a premium of $1 to mitigate a 25% chance of losing $5. The expected value of the two choices is the same but 49% of the clients and 47% of the student subjects preferred the $1 premium. Only 13% of the students and 7% of the clients indicated consistent choices.

More recently, an experiment performed by McClelland, Schulze, and Coursey (1993) used a Vickrey auction to allocate four insurance policies that protect the subject from a negative result in a lottery. Similar to the urn experiments of Slovic et al., the subjects could earn monetary awards based on the results of the lottery. This differed from the Slovic et al. (1977) study in that the price of the insurance policy could vary whereas in the earlier study the price was fixed. Once the four policies were allocated to the highest bidders, the lottery was held. If a red chip was drawn, all subjects without a policy lost $4. The draw of a white chip resulted in a gain of $1 for all subjects. Six levels of probabilities were used ranging from .01 to .9. Ten rounds for each probability level were conducted.

A bid to EV ratio was calculated for each individual in each round. These ratios were then compared at the different levels of loss probability. One result of the study was that mean Bid/EV declined as the probability of loss increased. Further, in low probabilities (less than 0.10) a bi-modal distribution was observed with a zero bid forming one node and Bid to EV ratios greater than 1 forming the other extreme. At low probabilities, subjects either ignored the risk and bid zero, or focused predominately on the loss and submitted a bid in excess of the expected value of the loss. As probabilities increased the distribution of Bid/EV began to take the shape of a normal distribution.

A second experiment was used to test differences in bids as the subjects gained experience with the lottery. Fifty rounds, all at a probability of 0.01, were conducted. On round 33, a red chip was deliberately drawn from the jar. The authors observed that as the subjects gained experience with the process, the bids began to drop. Subsequent to the drawing of a red chip in round 33, bids began to increase. Decreased bids prior to round 33 were attributed to the subjects lowering their perception of the risk until a loss occurred. The increase in the bids after the loss was attributed to a fear that once a loss has occurred, it seems more likely to happen again.

Ganderton, Thurston, Brookshire, Stewart, and McKee (1997) used lab experiments to test consumers' willingness to purchase insurance protection from a disaster such as a flood. The authors created three possibilities in the lottery. One possibility was no event, the second was a periodic flood and the third was an episodic flood that results in severe damage. Further, in many disasters, some homes are destroyed while neighboring structures suffered little damage. To model this possibility, once the nature of the event was determined by the lottery, a second drawing was held to determine if the damage was slight or severe.

Prior to each treatment, the subjects were told the possibilities for each event, potential losses and the cost of the insurance to protect them from the losses. A total of eighteen treatments were tested with different combinations of probabilities, losses, and cost of insurance. The authors found that as the level of expected loss increased, subjects purchased more insurance. Also, at a given level of loss, insurance was more likely to be purchased as the cost of the policy decreased.

One of the benefits of experimental research is the ability to identify individual behavior that determines the characteristics of a market. Market data aggregates the many decisions made by market participants. It is quite possible, that individual decisions may violate rational decision rules while the market does not. A study by Evans (1997) constructs a set of experiments where participants bid on a set of choices with the same expected value. If their choices exhibit inconsistency the author calculates the deviation of the individual bid from the expected value. These deviations are violations of a form of rationality known as the "betweenness property" of the *independence axiom* of Expected Utility Theory. The study concluded that betweenness violations were high for individuals.

Evans (1997) examined market behavior using a fifth price Vickrey auction. A fifth price auction is a device, which assigns the fifth highest bid as the market price in an auction. In the market setting, while betweenness violations continued to exist, the magnitude of the violations dropped dramatically. One of the reasons, suggested by the author, for the improved market behavior was the mechanism to set the market price. A fifth price auction selects a price from the middle of the bid distribution. This ignores the tails of the distribution that yield most violations. Evans states that it may be that research on individual bidding behavior is less relevant to market behavior than previously thought. Market mechanisms, which target the middle of the bid distribution, perform well. By this logic, other mechanisms which choose extreme bids, for instance a first price auction, may not perform as well.

Camerer (1987) examines the role of probability bias in setting market prices. In this experiment, participants were allowed to bid on lottery tickets that paid a state dependent dividend. The expected value of the dividend could be determined by multiplying the payoff by the state probability. Bids for the tickets were compared to the expected values to determine individual bias. Several competing theories were tested to determine which theory did the best job of predicting market price. The first theory uses Bayes Rule to determine the probability. The probability was determined by a compound lottery. Participants using Bayes Rule to determine the probability needed to correctly assess the state probability in the initial drawing. Competing theories assume participants either overestimate or underestimate the probability in the initial drawing.

Results indicated that while individual bias was prevalent, generally market prices converged to Bayesian expected values. This convergence occurred more quickly with experienced subjects than with inexperienced subjects. As each type of subject participated in additional rounds, bids more closely tracked expected values. This result suggests that participants learn from the market.

METHODOLOGY

The experiment we report was divided into five sessions with 8 to 12 participants in each session. Subjects were recruited from undergraduate and graduate courses at Texas Tech University as well as the local community. A total of 50 volunteers participated in the three sessions. There were 17 women and 34 men who participated in the experiments. All subjects were offered the same incentives. The length of each session ranged from 1½ to 2 hours. Payment per subject ranged from $18 to $25.

Each session began with volunteers signing an alphabetical participant list for the session. Volunteers were then given a copy of the Consent Form to read and sign. When all subjects had arrived and signed the consent form they were assigned a seat and given an envelope containing the experiment instructions, bid forms and their individual record sheet. The instructions were explained and a time for questions regarding those instructions was allowed prior to the session.

Each session contained 11 rounds, 1 practice and 10 actual rounds. After the practice round, each participant received $2.00 at the beginning of each round. Before they could claim the money, a lottery was held in which 1 ball was drawn from a bingo cage containing 100 balls numbered sequentially 1-100. Every participant was assigned a range of numbers on his/her record. If the ball drawn was within the assigned range, the subject must forfeit the $2.00. The probability for loss was the same for all participants in each round, however, the range of numbers was different for each individual. Five different loss probabilities were used in the experiment, 1%, 5%, 10%, 15%, and 20%. These probabilities were not explicitly given on the record sheets, but could be calculated by examining the range of numbers assigned. Each probability level was used in one of the first five rounds and the last five rounds. The sequence of probabilities in each half of the experiment was randomly determined prior to the experiment.

Prior to the lottery, all participants were given an opportunity to purchase a license (an insurance policy), which would protect their $2.00, regardless of the outcome of the lottery. A Vickrey auction mechanism was used to allocate 1, 2, 3, 4, 5, or 6 licenses. Bids were posted from highest to lowest. All bids were public knowledge but the identity of the bidder was not. After the bids were posted, a six-sided die was rolled to determine the number of licenses available in that round. With the protocol we used, subjects did not know the number of available licenses at the time they submitted their bids. The license price was the bid whose rank was one more than the number of available licenses in that round. For example, if the roll of the die was 3, three licenses were sold to the highest bidders. The price of the license was equal to the fourth bid. In the event of a tie, tied bids were randomly queued for license allocation purposes.

Once the number, price and allocation of licenses were determined, the bid forms were returned with an indication of whether the participant had purchased a license. A ball was then drawn from the bingo cage, its number announced, displayed, and then returned to the bingo cage. For those with a license, the earnings for that round were $2.00 minus the price of the license. All other participants were exposed to the results of the lottery and thus had earnings of $2.00 or zero depending on the draw from the bingo cage. At the conclusion of the round, the participants were asked to total their earnings, update their accumulated balance and prepare their bid form for the next round. After all ten rounds were complete, the participant earnings were verified and paid in cash.

RESULTS

In a previous study, McClelland et al. (1996) demonstrated that Bid/EV at low probabilities exhibited a bi-modal distribution. One node was at zero Bid/EV and the second node was a Bid/EV ratio well in excess of 1. Our study corroborates this finding. As is shown in Figure 1, there is a large cluster of bids at zero, few bids at middle ranges and a second cluster at Bid/EV in excess of 5. In fact at a probability of 1%, three quarters of the bids were zero. This confirms the observation made by McClelland et al. (1996) that at very low levels of probability, subjects either ignore or exaggerate the risk. The effect of subjects who exaggerate the risk is particularly noteworthy at these very low levels of probability. Since the expected value of the loss is minimal, it takes a small increase in the bid to increase dramatically the Bid/EV ratio at low probabilities. This fact is illustrated in Figure 2. The average Bid/EV at a probability of 1% is almost 3 while the percentage of zero bids was 75%. Some of the participants submitted bids in which the Bid/EV ratio was over 40. There are actually two forces at work here. First, as noted in McClelland et al. (1996), subjects who value mitigation at low probabilities exaggerate the risk. A second reason for the high Bid/EV ratio is the fact that the Bid/EV measure at low probability levels is extremely sensitive to very small changes in the bids. As the probability increases, the bid distribution begins to take a more normal shape. Again, two reasons account for this. First, the number of subjects bidding zero declines and second, the sensitivity of the Bid/EV ratio to small changes in the bids is lower. As Figure 2 indicates, beginning at a 5% probability, average Bid/EV tracks closer to one. In fact, at 20% probability, average Bid/EV is not significantly different from 1 [t-statistic = 1.35589 assuming unequal variance. P(T<=t) = .08911 (one tail test)].

To address the question of whether the subject bidding behavior responds to increases in probability we performed a regression with bid as the dependent variable and probability as the independent variable.

$$\text{Bid} = \beta_0 + \beta_1 \text{Prob} + \beta_{2-51} \text{Subject} + \text{Error}$$

Even though our database contains 500 bid decisions by the experiment participants, the sample contains only 50 individuals. To control for the small number of participants we used a fixed effects regression model. This model controls for possible error correlation within the observations for a given individual by adding a dummy variable for each individual in the experiment. As can be seen in Table 1 the regression is significant. The intercept is very close to zero, although it is not significant. Probability is highly significant. The 2.196 coefficient of Probability indicates a Bid/EV ratio of 1.098 over the entire distribution, since EV = $2.00 x Probability. This corresponds to the observation seen in the graph in Figure 2. Clearly, an increase in probability motivates subjects to increase their bid for the license.

Figure 1. (Continues on next page.)

Bid Distribution at 1% Probability

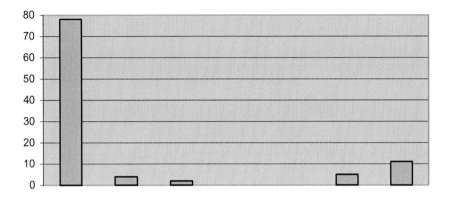

Bid Distribution at 5% Probability

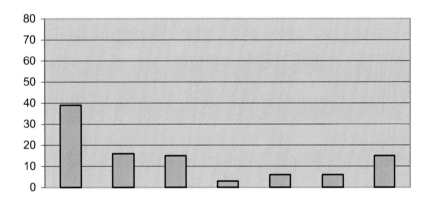

Bid Distribution at 10% Probability

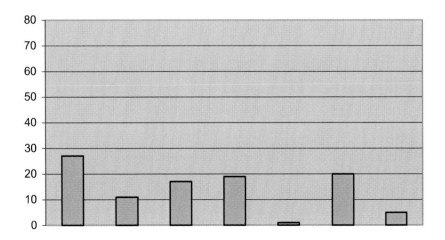

Bid Distribution at 15% Probability

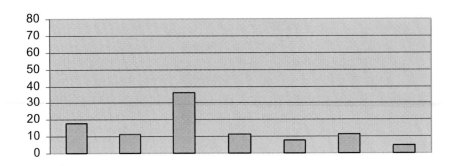

Bid Distribution at 20% Probability

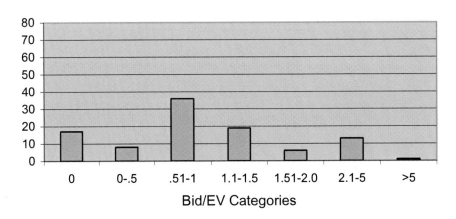

Bid/EV Categories

Figure 1.

Avg Bid/EV

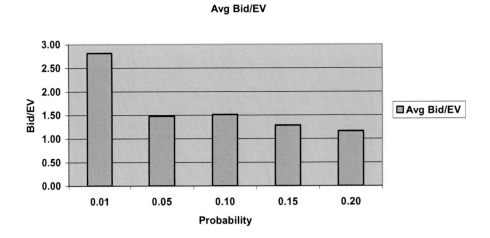

Figure 2.

Since the zero bids are prominent in this analysis, we plotted the changes in the percentage of subjects bidding zero at increasing probabilities. McClelland et al. (1996) noted that the number of zero bids declined as probability increased but never disappeared entirely. This observation is consistent with the results of our study. As shown in Figure 3, zero bids at 1% probability are 78% of the total bids. The percentage of zero bids decreases as probability increases but never completely disappears. Small increases in subjects bids translate to large increases in Bid/EV. A similar effect is created by the zero bids. Since negative bids were not an option the bid distribution has a floor, which at low probabilities creates a distribution that is asymmetrical. As probability increases, the effect of the floor diminishes.

Table 1. Regression Results

	Parameter Estimate	Std Error	T Value	Prob>T	R-Sq	Adj.R-Sq
Bid/Probability Model (All Participants)						
Intercept	0.0470	.0999	0.475	.6353	.5003	.4446
Probability	2.1961	.2016	10.892	.0001		
Bid/Hit Model (All Participants)						
Intercept	0.0752	.1018	0.739	.4606	.4818	.4220
Probability	2.3550	.2438	9.661	.0001		
Bid/Hit Model (Participants which Experienced a Hit)						
Intercept	0.0860	.1056	0.815	.4157	.5016	.4448
Probability	2.2206	.2029	10.944	.0001		

EV = 2.00 X
.01 = .02

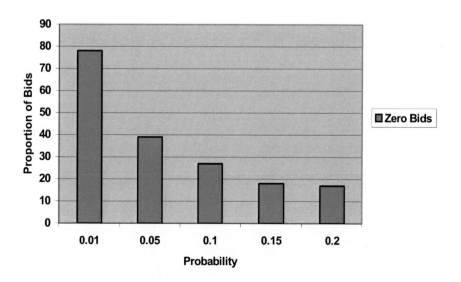

Figure 3.

This experiment used a Vickrey auction to allocate licenses. A unique feature of the study was to withhold information about the allocation of the licenses. Subjects did not know the number of available licenses until their bids were submitted. As a result, we can examine the behavior of prices at each probability for six possible allocations. Figure 4 shows the behavior of the prevailing price, averaged across sessions, for each of six allocation possibilities. As expected, prevailing price declines as allocation increases. This models the effect of the scarcity of the license. When only 1 license is allocated, price begins and remains high. As the probability increases, price rises, although for 1 license the relationship is more erratic than when 2, 3, 4, or 5 licenses are available. When six licenses are available, the price increase across probabilities begins to lose some stability. This is an interesting result and it reflects the effect of bids on price at the upper and lower end of the bid distribution. As noted by Evans (1997), individual bids do not always track expected value. However, the market price is remarkably consistent. Her study used a fifth price auction to determine market price. The design of our study allows for analysis of six different prices and confirms her result at the middle of the bid distribution. As allocation of licenses increases, the price function approaches a linear function. But when allocation exceeds 4 licenses, the instability seen in the 1 license allocation reappears. At these high levels of available licenses, price is largely determined by the low and sometimes zero bids. To examine this effect further, we performed regressions on each allocation using price as the dependent variable and probability as the independent variable. (Table 2) These regressions contain few observations, so only the general behavior of the relationship between price and probability can be examined. Each of the six regressions indicated that probability was highly significant and the value of the intercept was very close to zero. The difference seen in the graph, however, is reaffirmed by differences in the value of the adjusted R-Square, for each regression. R-Square for the 1 license and 6 license allocation was .31 and .32. The middle allocations, 2 through 5 licenses, had adjusted R-Square values ranging from .41 to .48. These middle allocations minimize the effect of the high and low bidders on price and indicate that market price responds well to increases in the probability of a loss.

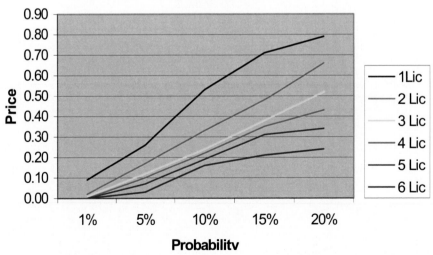

Figure 4.

**Table 2. Regression Results: Market Price/Probability Model
for Different License Allocations**

	Parameter Estimate	Std. Error	T Value	Prob>T	R-Sq	Adj. R-Sq
One License Allocation						
Intercept	0.0866	.0974	0.889	.3786	.3244	.3103
Probability	3.8176	.7951	4.801	.0001		
Two License Allocation						
Intercept	-0.0079	.0682	-0.117	.9075	.4261	.4140
Probability	3.3232	.5567	5.96	.0001		
Three License Allocation						
Intercept	-0.0186	.0541	-0.310	.7577	.4313	.4194
Probability	2.6626	.4413	6.033	.0001		
Four License Allocation						
Intercept	-0.0186	.0446	-0.416	.6790	.4596	.4483
Probability	2.3231	.3636	6.389	.0001		
Five License Allocation						
Intercept	-0.0167	.0346	-0.482	.6321	.4933	.4827
Probability	1.9302	.2824	6.836	.0001		
Six License Allocation						
Intercept	-0.0109	.0342	-0.320	.7502	.3370	.3232
Probability	1.3801	.2794	4.939	.0001		
Total Regression						
Intercept	0.0026	.0274	0.095	.9241	.3083	.3060
Probability	2.5728	.2232	11.525	.0001		

While the main focus of this study was the response of subjects to increases in the probability of loss, two side issues were examined. First, does experiencing a "hit" from the lottery have an effect on subsequent bidding behavior? McClelland et al. (1996) devised a scheme to test this effect by contriving a hit to all subjects on the 33rd round of a 50-round experiment. Their observation was that bids increased after the loss. Our study tests the effect of a loss, but the hit is allowed to occur naturally from the lottery itself. For all subjects, we create a variable whose value is zero if no loss occurs in the previous round and has a value of 1 if a loss does occur in the previous round. We also created a variable that had a value of 1 in every round subsequent to a loss. This variable is analogous to the method used by McClelland et al. (1996). A graph comparing the Bid/EV ratio for subjects experiencing a hit and those who did not is shown in Figure 5. We used a fixed effects regression model similar to the one described earlier to test the effect of a hit on bidding behavior.

$$Bid = \beta_0 + \beta_1 Prob + \beta_2 Hit + \beta_{3-53} Subject + Error$$

Gender Comparison - Average Bid

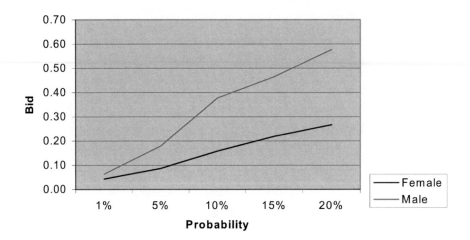

Figure 5.

The first model regressed bid against hit for all participants in the study, regardless of whether they experienced a hit. Secondly, we regressed bid against hit for only the participants who experienced a hit. As can be seen in Table 1, HIT is not a significant explanatory variable for bidding behavior in either model. We therefore conclude, that experience with a hit in the lottery has no effect on subsequent bidding behavior.

A second issue was the effect of gender on bidding behavior. We assigned a value to each subject indicating whether the subject was male or female. It was then possible to compare the bids by gender. Figure 6 shows average bids by women and by men at increasing probability levels. At every probability, bids by women were lower than the bids submitted by men. To test the strength of this observation, we ran a regression where bid was the dependent variable and the independent variables were probability and whether or not the subject was female.

$$\text{Bid} = \beta_0 + \beta_1 \text{Prob} + \beta_2 \text{Gender} + \text{Error}$$

The variable for female was highly significant and the sign of the coefficient was negative. We also conducted a t-test on the bids of men and women. As Figure 6 shows, the bids submitted by men generally increased as probability increased. However, the increase was large between 5% and 10%, declined at 15% and then increased again at a probability of 20%. Compared to the pattern for women, these increases were more erratic. Some of this difference can be seen in the variances for bids from women and bids for men. The variance for women's bids was under $0.03 whereas the variance for men's bids exceeded $0.23. Further, men submitted bids that were consistent with higher risk aversion (Figure 7). This result is consistent with other experimental results and gives an instance where men appear to be more conservative toward risk than women. Our conclusion is that there is a significant difference in the bidding behavior between men and women.

Comparison of Bid/EV by Hit and No Hit

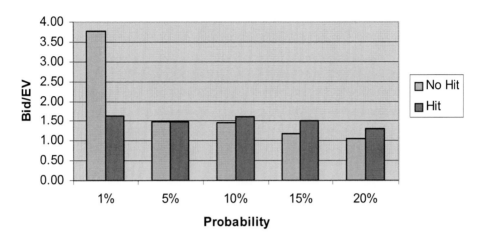

Figure 6.

Gender Comparison - Average Bid/EV

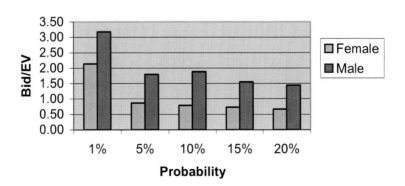

Figure 7.

CONCLUSION

This study generated three important results. First, individual bids and consequently market price are affected by probability of loss. As shown in the McClelland et al., subjects do respond to increasing loss probabilities in their willingness to buy protection. This behavior, at low probabilities, indicates a bimodal response to risk with most subjects ignoring the risk and a minority over-valuing the risk. At higher probabilities, the distribution appears to take a shape similar to a normal distribution. Further, bid/EV ratios correspond closely to the expected value of the loss.

Second, in contrast to the McClelland et al. study, we find that experience with a hit in the lottery has no discernible effect on subsequent bidding behavior. This may be due to the contrast in the way that a loss was implemented in the two studies. Although the probabilities for an individual were the same for the two studies, in McClelland et al., when a loss occurred, it hit everyone whereas a hit was isolated to only one or two individuals in our study. This could be likened to when a single property is damaged by a tornado versus an entire community that could be damaged by a hurricane. Finally, we find a difference in the bidding behavior of men and women. Men tend to bid higher than women indicating that men value the protection of the license more highly than women do.

Extreme wind events such as hurricanes and tornadoes are low-probability-high-consequence events. The annual probability that a tornado will touch down at a given location is less than 1% even in the states in "tornado alley." The annual probability that a hurricane force storm will strike a location is 10% or less even in hurricane-prone regions. The results of this study give us insight on mitigation investment behavior when the probability of loss is low. Admittedly, a two dollar loss in the laboratory is not a high consequence event. However, the preponderance of zero bids at low probabilities match up with the syndrome the Kunreuther calls "it can't happen to me." Likewise, those individuals that overweight the probability are likely to be the first to adopt mitigation measures that otherwise fail cost effectiveness tests. Individuals that overweight the probability are likely to unnecessarily evacuate when a hurricane threatens and contribute to congestion on evacuation routes. Public policy that takes into account individual biases will be more effective in managing mitigation efforts and protecting the population when a disaster occurs.

ACKNOWLEDGEMENTS

This work was performed under the Department of Commerce NIST/TTU Cooperative Agreement Award 70NANB8H0059.

REFERENCES

Camerer, Colin F. (1987). "Do Bias in Probability Judgment Matter in Markets? Experimental Evidence," *American Economic Review*, Vol. 77, No. 5, pp. 981-977.

Evans, Darla A.(1997). "The Role of Markets in Reducing Expected utility Violations," *Journal of Political Economy*, Vol. 105, No. 3, pp. 622-636.

Ganderton, P., Thurston, H., Brookshire, D., Stewart, S., and McKee, M. (1997). *"Buying Insurance for Disaster-Type Risks: Experimental Evidence,"* Manuscript. Albuquerque: University of New Mexico.

McClelland, Gary H., Schulze, William D., and Coursey, Don L. (1993)."InsuranceFor Low-Probability Hazards: A Bi-Modal Response to Unlikely Events," *Journal of Risk and Uncertainty*, Vol. 7, pp. 95-116.

Schoemaker, Paul J. H., and Kunreuther, Howard (1979). "An Experimental Study of Insurance Decisions," *The Journal of Risk and Insurance*, Vol. 46, No. 4, pp. 603-618.

Slovic, P., Fischhoff, B., and Lichtenstein, S. (1977). "Behavioral Decision Theory," *Annual Review of Psychology*, Vol. 28, pp. 1-39.

In: Psychology of Decision Making in Risk Taking …   ISBN 978-1-60021-854-5
Editor: Rachel N. Kelian   © 2008 Nova Science Publishers, Inc.

Chapter 7

FREQUENCY-DOMAIN VERSUS TIME-DOMAIN ESTIMATES OF RISK AVERSION FROM THE C-CAPM: THE CASE OF LATIN AMERICAN EMERGING MARKETS

Ekaterini Panopoulou[*]

University of Piraeus, Greece and Trinity College Dublin

ABSTRACT

Campbell (2003) confirms the equity premium puzzle in an international context based on the Consumption-CAPM and cross-country evidence on implausibly large coefficients of relative risk aversion. In this paper we adopt a spectral approach to re-estimate the values of risk aversion over the frequency domain for six Latin American emerging markets. We complement our analysis with the traditional time series approach and confirm the results of existing literature of large coefficients of relative risk aversion. Our frequency domain findings, however, indicate that at lower frequencies risk aversion falls substantially across countries, thus yielding in many cases reasonable values of the implied coefficient of risk aversion.

Keywords: Equity premium puzzle; Consumption-CAPM; risk aversion; frequency domain; emerging markets.

JEL Classification: G10; C13

---

[*] Correspondence to: Ekaterini Panopoulou, Department of Statistics and Insurance Science, University of Piraeus, 80 Karaoli & Dimitriou str., 18534, Piraeus, Greece. Email: apano@unipi.gr. Tel: 0030 210 4142728. Fax: 0030 210 4142340.

1. INTRODUCTION

Economists accept as a stylized fact that average stock returns are substantially higher than average returns on short-term debt instruments. The failure of financial theory to explain the magnitude of these excess returns has led to this phenomenon being labeled as the "equity premium puzzle" by Mehra and Prescott (1985). Standard asset pricing models can only match the data if investors are extremely risk averse. In particular, the coefficient of relative risk aversion must be implausibly large for traditional models to reconcile the large differential between real equity returns and real returns available on short-term debt instruments.[1] Of course, we expect different financial assets to deliver large variations in returns, but typically financial economists have explained such differentials by attributing them to differences among the covariances of asset returns and investors consumption, e.g. the Consumption Capital Asset Pricing Model (C-CAPM) of Lucas (1978) and Breeden (1979). The more traditional version of CAPM assumes a perfect correlation between the stock market return and the consumption path of the typical investor. This allows us to measure asset risk as its covariance with the market return. However, in their path breaking work, Mehra and Prescott (1985), using annual US data from 1889 to 1978, showed that the covariance of equity returns with consumption growth was insufficient to explain the observed equity premium of over 6%. In fact, they could only account for a premium of approximately 0.35%.

Much of the resulting empirical literature has focused on the US markets where longer data series exist, but Campbell (1996, 2003) focuses on some smaller stock markets and finds evidence that an equity premium is also a feature of these markets. Specifically, Cambpell (2003) reports evidence from 11 countries that imply extremely high values of risk aversion, which usually exceed many times the value of 10 considered plausible by Mehra and Prescott (1985), and claims "...that the equity premium puzzle is a robust phenomenon in international data". Using the same theoretical setup as in Campbell (2003) and a dataset from six Latin America emerging markets, we adopt both a time series and a spectral approach to re-estimate the values of risk aversion over the frequency domain.[2]

Our approach allows for long-term consumption dynamics by performing a dynamic analysis of the link between consumption and returns at several frequencies rather than over the time domain. As pointed out by Granger and Hatanaka back in 1964, according to the spectral representation theorem a time series can be seen as the sum of waves of different periodicity and, hence, there is no reason to believe that economic variables should present the same lead/lag cross-correlation at all frequencies. We incorporate this rationale into the context of the single-factor C-CAPM by using well-developed techniques to estimate the coherency (the analog of the correlation coefficient in the time domain) between returns and consumption over the frequency domain along with the related spectra of the series (the analog of variance).[3] In this way, we can separate different layers of dynamic behavior of consumption and returns by distinguishing between the short run (fluctuations of 2 to 6

---

[1] Kocherlakota (1996) provides an excellent survey of the topic.

[2] Some studies have investigated the implications of spectral analysis within economic applications, mostly by interpreting (high) low-frequency estimates as the (short) long-run component of the relationship under scrutiny; see, for instance, Engle (1974, 1978).

[3] See Hamilton (1994) for a general overview of spectral analysis.

quarters), the medium run or business cycle (lasting from 8 to 32 quarters), and the long run (oscillations of duration above 32 quarters). Our findings indicate that at lower frequencies risk aversion falls substantially across countries, thus yielding in many cases reasonable values of the implied coefficient of risk aversion.

The paper is structured as follows. Section 2 presents the theoretical model, while our frequency domain technique is developed in Section 3. Section 4 discusses our data and its properties, while Section 5 presents the empirical results. Concluding remarks are contained in Section 6.

2. MEASURING RISK AVERSION AND THE EQUITY PREMIUM

The equity premium puzzle can be presented in different ways. We adopt the approach of Campbell (1996, 2003) which follows the seminal papers of Lucas (1978), Mehra and Prescott (1985) on the equity premium puzzle. Specifically, we assume that there is a representative agent who maximizes a time-separable utility function:

$$MaxE_t \sum_{j=0}^{\infty} \delta^j U(C_{t+j}) \tag{1}$$

where δ is the discount factor, C_{t+j} is the investor's future consumption stream and $u(C_{t+j})$ is the period utility derived from such consumption. This problem yields the following Euler equation to describe the optimal consumption and investment path of the investor;

$$U'(C_t) = \delta E_t[(1 + R_{i,t+1})U'(C_{t+1})] \tag{2}$$

with $1 + R_{i,t+1}$ representing the gross rate of return available on asset i. The investor equates the loss in current consumption with the expected gain in discounted consumption next period.

Consistent with other studies, we employ a time-separable power utility function:

$$Max \sum_{j=0}^{\infty} \delta^j \frac{C_{t+j}^{1-\gamma}}{1-\gamma} \tag{3}$$

where γ is the coefficient of relative risk aversion. The features of this utility function are well known and have had their validity questioned in the literature.

Specifically, this utility allows risk premia to remain stable over time even if both aggregate wealth and the economy increase. In this respect, aggregation of different investors with different wealth levels but the same power utility function into a single representative investor can be performed. On the downside, however, the tight link between the elasticity of intertemporal substitution which is equal to the reciprocal of the coefficient of relative risk aversion is preserved. Epstein and Zin (1991) and Weil (1989) introduced a more general utility function that breaks the aforementioned link.

Despite some shortcomings of the power utility specification, we retain this specification in this study for two reasons. Firstly, it facilitates comparison with other studies. Secondly, Kocherlakota (1996) reports that modifications to preferences such as those proposed by Epstein and Zin (1991), habit formation due to Constantinides (1990) or "keeping up with the Joneses" as proposed by Abel (1990) fail to resolve the puzzle.

Combining equations (2) and (3), we get the familiar expression,

$$
1 = E_t \left[(1 + R_{i,t+1}) \delta \left(\frac{C_{t+1}}{C_t} \right)^{-\gamma} \right]. \tag{4}
$$

Following Hansen and Singleton (1983) and Campbell (1996), we assume that the joint conditional distribution of asset returns and consumption is lognormal, with time-varying volatility. Taking logs of equation (4), we get

$$
0 = E_t r_{i,t+1} + \log \delta - \gamma E_t [\Delta c_{t+1}] + 0.5(\sigma_{it}^2 + \gamma^2 \sigma_{ct}^2 - 2\gamma \sigma_{i,ct}) \tag{5}
$$

where $r_{i,t} = \log(1 + R_{i,t})$, $c_t = \log(C_t)$, σ_{it}^2 and σ_{ct}^2 denote the conditional variance of log returns and log consumption growth respectively, and $\sigma_{i,ct}$ represents their conditional covariance. The log risk premium is

$$
E_t \left[r_{i,t+1} - r_{f,t+1} \right] + \frac{\sigma_{it}^2}{2} = \gamma \sigma_{ict} \tag{6}
$$

where the variance term on the left-hand side of equation (6) is Jensen's Inequality adjustment term due to using expectations of log returns. Therefore the log risk premium is a function of the coefficient of relative risk aversion multiplied by the covariance of stock returns with consumption growth. In this respect, riskier assets get a larger risk premium as these assets are the ones that have a high covariance with consumption and produce low returns when consumption is low.

Letting then $e_{i,t+1} \equiv E_t[r_{i,t+1} - r_{f,t+1}]$ denote the excess return over the risk free rate, we get that the excess return on any asset over the riskless rate is constant and therefore the risk premium on all assets is linear in expected consumption growth with the slope coefficient, γ, given by:

$$
\gamma = \frac{e_{i,t+1} + 0.5\sigma_i^2}{\sigma_{i,c}} \tag{7}
$$

Equation (7) provides a working formula for the estimation of the coefficient of relative risk aversion by simply calculating the sample moments of excess returns and consumption growth. This type of calculation is refereed to as the 'time-domain' estimate of relative risk aversion.

3. ECONOMETRIC METHODOLOGY

In this section, we present an alternative econometric methodology employed to study the behavior of the equity premium and the coefficient of relative risk aversion over the frequency domain.

Departing from the time domain to the frequency domain we can rewrite (7) for each frequency.[4] After dropping the time subscript for simplicity, we get that the coefficient of risk aversion over the whole band of frequencies ω, where ω is a real variable in the range $0 \leq \omega \leq \pi$, is given by:

$$\gamma_\omega = \frac{e + 0.5 f_{ee}(\omega)}{f_{ec}(\omega)} \tag{8}$$

where e denotes the excess log return of the stock market over the risk-free rate. As is well known, the cross-spectrum, $f_{ec}(\omega)$, between e and c is complex-valued and can be decomposed into its real and imaginary components, given here by:

$$f_{ec}(\omega) = C_{ec}(\omega) - iQ_{ec}(\omega),$$

where $C_{ec}(\omega)$ denotes the *co-spectrum* and $Q_{ec}(\omega)$ the *quadrature spectrum*. The measure of comovement between returns and consumption over the frequency domain is then given by:

---

[4] In general, the spectrum of a process, say x_t, can be written as $f_{xx}(\omega) = \rho_0 + 2 \sum_{k=1}^{\infty} \rho_k \cos(k\omega)$, where ρ_k is the k-order autocovariance function of the series. In turn, we can consider the multivariate spectrum, $F_{yx}(\omega)$, for a bivariate zero mean covariance stationary process $Z_t = [y_t, x_t]^T$ with covariance matrix $\Gamma(\cdot)$, which is the frequency domain analog of the autocovariance matrix. The diagonal elements of $F_{yx}(\omega)$ are the spectra of the individual processes, $f_{yy}(\omega)$ and $f_{xx}(\omega)$, while the off-diagonal ones refer to the cross-spectrum or cross spectral density matrix of y_t and x_t. In detail, $F_{yx}(\omega) = \frac{1}{2\pi} \sum_{k=-\infty}^{\infty} \Gamma(k)e^{-ik\omega} = \begin{bmatrix} f_{xx}(\omega) & f_{yx}(\omega) \\ f_{xy}(\omega) & f_{yy}(\omega) \end{bmatrix}$, where $F_{yx}(\omega)$ is an Hermitian, non-negative definite matrix, i.e. $F_{yx}(\omega) = F_{yx}^*(\omega)$, with * denoting the complex conjugate transpose since $f_{yx}(\omega) = \overline{f_{xy}(\omega)}$. See Hamilton (1994) for a more detailed presentation of spectral analysis.

$$c_{ec}^2(\omega) \equiv \frac{|f_{ec}(\omega)|^2}{f_{ex}(\omega)f_{cc}(\omega)} = \frac{C_{ee}^2 + Q_{cc}^2}{f_{ee}(\omega)f_{cc}(\omega)} \tag{9}$$

where $0 \le c_{ec}^2(\omega) \le 1$ is the squared *coherency*, which provides a measure of the correlation between the two series at each frequency and can be interpreted intuitively as the frequency-domain analog of the correlation coefficient.[5]

The spectra and co-spectra of a vector of time-series for a sample of T observations can be estimated for a set of frequencies $\omega_n = 2\pi n/T$, $n = 1, 2, ..., T/2$. The relevant quantities are estimated through the periodogram, which is based on a representation of the observed time-series as a superposition of sinusoidal waves of various frequencies; a frequency of π corresponds to a time period of two quarters, while a zero frequency corresponds to infinity.[6]

4. TIME-DOMAIN AND FREQUENCY DOMAIN PROPERTIES OF THE DATA

4.1. Data

Our dataset comprises quarterly equity and macroeconomic data for the Latin American emerging markets, namely Argentina, Brasil, Chile, Colombia, Mexico and Peru. The source for equity data is the Morgan Stanley Capital International (MSCI) indices adjusted for dividends for emerging markets. The indices are denominated in local currency and the domestic money market rate is employed. In this respect, we calculate the equity premium that a domestic investor faces in contrast to calculating returns in a foreign currency, for example in US dollars and adjusting them for the US risk free rate.[7] Data on population, household consumption, GDP deflator, and a short-term interest rate, mainly a 3-month T-bill rate are available at the IFS Statistics Database (International Monetary Fund). Real personal consumption per capita was calculated by dividing personal consumption with the population and adjusting it for price changes utilizing the GDP deflator.[8] Additionally, seasonal adjustment of the consumption series was also undertaken for the cases that consumption data were unadjusted. Our dataset is the longest available for each country at hand. Specifically, the samples employed are as follows: Argentina (1988:Q1- 2005:Q4), Brasil (1988:Q1-

---

[5] Engle (1976) gives an early treatment on the frequency-domain analysis and its time-domain counterpart.

[6] Consistent estimates of the spectral matrix can be obtained by either smoothing the periodogram, or by employing a lag window approach that both weighs and limits the autocovariances and cross-covariances used. We use here the Bartlett window, which assigns linearly decreasing weights to the autocovariances and cross-covariances in the neighborhood of the frequencies considered and zero weight thereafter, with the lag, k, set using the rule $k = 2\sqrt{T}$, as suggested by Chatfield (1989).

[7] The approach of calculating US denominated excess returns would signal the equity premium faced by an international investor investing in the emerging markets. Such an approach is taken by Salomons and Grootveld (2003).

[8] Population data are reported annually. The series were converted to quarterly by means of linear interpolation.

2005:Q4), Chile (1988:Q1- 2005:Q4), Colombia (1993:Q1-2005:Q4), Mexico (1988:Q1-2005:Q4) and Peru (1993:Q1-2005:Q4).

4.2. Descriptive Statistics

Table 1 reports summary statistics for stock market excess returns and consumption growth. Excess returns are calculated by subtracting the return on the relevant short-term risk-free asset from the return in the stock market index and consumption growth is the difference in the logarithm of seasonally adjusted personal consumption per capita GDP deflated. For each country we report the mean and standard deviation in annualized percentage points of the series and countries under scrutiny.[9] The table shows that Latin American countries share the same stylized facts with developed countries (Campbell, 2003).

First, Latin American stock markets have delivered average returns of 7% or more in excess of the risk free rate. Specifically, Chile, Colombia and Peru just exceed 7%, whereas the excess return in Mexico is 17%. These figures are roughly equivalent to the figures for the developed markets examined by Campbell (2003). In his dataset, excess returns range between 3% and 14%. Quite interestingly, the respective figures for Argentina and Brasil reach the impressive 170% and 146% for the period under examination.

Second, the annualized volatility of stock returns ranges from 25% to 35% for Chile, Colombia, Mexico and Peru. As expected, the higher Argentinean and Brasilian excess returns are followed by higher risk as depicted in their volatility that reaches 461%. Comparing the volatility of these emerging markets with the developed ones, we have to note that the volatility of the former is on the upper part of the latter which experience a volatility of 15% to 27%.

Table 1. Descriptive Statistics

Country	Excess return (mean)	Excess return (standard deviation)	Consumption Growth (mean)	Consumption Growth (standard deviation)
Argentina	170.44	461.01	7.50	13.31
Brasil	146.45	131.78	18.04	21.40
Chile	7.75	24.99	14.46	4.48
Colombia	7.22	35.25	14.85	3.51
Mexico	16.60	29.58	22.09	9.42
Peru	7.06	29.30	12.63	5.97

Notes: Means and standard deviations are given in annualized percentage points. Means are multiplied by 400 and standard deviations by 200.

---

[9] To annualize the raw quarterly data, means are multiplied by 400 and standard deviations by 200 given that in serially uncorrelated data standard deviations increase with the square root of the interval.

Third, consumption growth is rather elevated and depicts higher volatility compared to developed countries. This is expected since developing countries normally experience faster growth that undergoes larger swings. The fastest growth in consumption is for Mexico (22%), followed by Brasil (18%), while the lowest one is the Argentinean one with annualized growth of almost 8%. In any case these figures are 4 to ten times greater than the growth in developed countries. The least volatile economy in our dataset is Colombia, while the ones with the greater volatility are Argentina and Brasil.

5. EMPIRICAL RESULTS

5.1. Time-domain Techniques

We follow Campbell (2003) and present two measures of risk aversion. The first one termed RRA1 is calculated directly from (7), while the second one, denoted by RRA2 assumes a unitary correlation of excess returns and consumption growth. Although this is a counterfactual exercise, we follow closely Campbell (2003) and postulate a unitary elasticity between returns and consumption growth to account for the sensitivity of the implied risk aversion on the smoothness of consumption rather than its low correlation with excess returns. Table 2 reports the average equity premium, the unconditional correlation between excess returns and consumption along with the two estimates of relative risk aversion for the countries at hand.

In detail, the second column reports the mean equity premium given by the left part of equation (6)[10] (i.e. adjusted with the respective variance term).[11] Quite interestingly, there is a great dispersion among the values of the equity premia for the Latin American countries. The higher one is the one of the Argentinean market that exceeds 1200% per, followed by Brasil which is over 200% with the lowest one being the one that corresponds to Peru of just over 10%. The huge numbers for Argentina and Brasil combine two effects, both the increased mean of average excess returns and the respective increased volatility. The correlation between the returns and consumption also exhibits great variation among countries. The lowest is reported in Argentina and Mexico (4%) and the highest one in Brasil (51%). The lower correlations should normally correspond to higher estimates of risk aversion while the higher ones to the lower estimates. This is true as column 3 (Table 2) suggests that reports these estimates.

Specifically, this traditional approach yields the usual finding (see also Campbell 1996, 2003). The estimated coefficients of relative risk aversion of 502 for Argentina, 175 for Mexico and 81 for Peru are much larger than suggested by economic theory.[12] This is often interpreted as an equity premium puzzle. While still outside the economically accepted range,

---

[10] This approach has been advocated by Jobson and Korkie (1981), amongst others, in relation to the application of Modern Portfolio Theory.

[11] The equity premium is given in annualized percentage points. The calculations, however, are done in natural units.

[12] Mehra and Prescott (1985) impose an upper limit of 10 on 'reasonable' values of the coefficient of RRA. However, others such as Kandel and Stambaugh (1991) argue that this parameter could be much higher (up to 30) in financial markets and still imply reasonable economic behaviour.

the estimates of 36 and 16 for Chile and Brasil, respectively certainly move the relative risk parameter in the right direction.[13]

We repeat the analysis for the hypothetical situation where the correlation between stock returns and consumption growth is unity. This case gives the model the best chance of explaining the premium. Indeed, the estimated coefficients are reduced. With the exception of Argentina (RRA= 20) and Colombia (RRA=11), the remaining estimates of risk aversion are all within the economically acceptable values. What it shows is that the extreme risk aversion displayed in the actual data is driven mainly by an almost complete dis-connect between stock returns and consumption.

5.2. Frequency-domain Techniques

Before moving on with the estimates of relative risk aversion, we report some evidence on the comovement between returns and consumption growth in the frequency domain along with the estimated spectra of the series at hand. Tables 3A-3F report the coherency and the variance decomposition of excess returns and consumption growth over the frequency domain (columns 3-5). Column 1 states the respective frequency as a fraction of π, while column 2 reports the time-domain analogue of the frequency in quarters. Zero frequency corresponds to an infinite horizon, while a frequency of π corresponds to a 2-quarter horizon.

Overall our estimates suggest that the correlation (measured by coherency) between returns and consumption growth exhibits an upward trend as we move from high to low frequencies with the exception of Colombia. More in detail, coherency in the long-run is around 99% for Argentina, Brasil and Chile, 67% for Mexico, 32% for Peru and just 9% for Colombia. The Colombian co-spectrum is rather inverse exhibiting higher correlation in the short-run rather than the long-run. On the whole, the short-run correlation (2 to 6 quarters) between returns and consumption growth ranges from 13% in Peru to 90% in Argentina, while the business-cycle correlation (8 to 32 quarters) fluctuates between 8% in Colombia to 78% in Argentina and Brasil.[14]

Table 2. Time Domain Estimates of Relative Risk Aversion

Country	Equity premium (mean)	Correlation	RRA1	RRA2
Argentina	1233.11	0.04	502.01	20.10
Brasil	233.29	0.51	16.12	8.27
Chile	10.87	0.27	35.51	9.71
Colombia	13.43	<0	---	10.87
Mexico	20.97	0.04	175.48	7.53
Peru	11.36	0.08	81.43	6.49

Notes: Equity premium is given in annualized percentage points. RRA1 is calculated from (7) and RRA2 by imposing a unitary correlation between excess returns and consumption growth.

---

[13] The negative correlation between excess returns and consumption for Colombia does not allow us to calculate the RRA coefficient.

[14] The respective figures are calculated by averaging their frequency domain counterparts over the relevant frequencies.

Table 3A. Frequency Domain Estimates of Relative Risk Aversion (Argentina)

Frequency	(Quarters)	Coherency $f_{ec}(\omega)$	Returns Variance $f_{ee}(\omega)$	Consumption Variance $f_{cc}(\omega)$	RRA1	RRA2
0	(inf)	0.995	1.663	0.610	1.25	1.25
1/16	(32.000)	0.987	1.437	0.476	1.39	1.38
1/8	(16.000)	0.940	1.067	0.233	1.99	1.92
3/16	(10.667)	0.776	0.895	0.070	3.95	3.48
1/4	(8.000)	0.448	0.834	0.025	8.74	5.85
3/8	(5.333)	0.792	0.733	0.056	4.39	3.90
1/2	(4.000)	0.936	0.706	0.144	2.52	2.44
5/8	(3.200)	0.981	0.794	0.245	1.88	1.87
3/4	(2.667)	0.986	0.925	0.290	1.73	1.71
13/16	(2.462)	0.976	1.007	0.243	1.90	1.88
7/8	(2.286)	0.953	0.938	0.139	2.53	2.47
15/16	(2.133)	0.876	0.755	0.053	4.28	4.01
1	(2.000)	0.651	0.640	0.023	7.67	6.19

Notes: Frequency is expressed as a fraction of π. RRA1 is calculated from (8) and RRA2 by imposing a unitary correlation between excess returns and consumption growth.

Table 3B. Frequency Domain Estimates of Relative Risk Aversion (Brasil)

Frequency	(Quarters)	Coherency	Returns Variance	Consumption Variance	RRA1	RRA2
0	(inf)	0.989	0.634	1.294	0.76	0.75
1/16	(32.000)	0.969	0.413	0.852	0.98	0.97
1/8	(16.000)	0.826	0.150	0.318	2.22	2.02
3/16	(10.667)	0.606	0.085	0.170	4.37	3.40
1/4	(8.000)	0.740	0.067	0.149	4.65	4.00
3/8	(5.333)	0.799	0.043	0.164	5.14	4.59
1/2	(4.000)	0.646	0.030	0.200	6.14	4.93
5/8	(3.200)	0.637	0.035	0.404	4.05	3.23
3/4	(2.667)	0.602	0.032	0.591	3.60	2.79
13/16	(2.462)	0.209	0.027	0.434	7.72	3.53
7/8	(2.286)	0.587	0.044	0.220	5.17	3.96
15/16	(2.133)	0.548	0.051	0.146	6.16	4.56
1	(2.000)	0.270	0.025	0.121	13.34	6.93

Notes: See Table 3A.

Table 3C. Frequency Domain Estimates of Relative Risk Aversion (Chile)

Frequency	(Quarters)	Coherency	Returns Variance	Consumption Variance	RRA1	RRA2
0	(inf)	0.976	0.003	0.012	3.51	3.47
1/16	(32.000)	0.943	0.001	0.000	45.37	44.07
1/8	(16.000)	0.993	0.003	0.000	48.73	48.54
3/16	(10.667)	0.593	0.006	0.000	85.63	65.96
1/4	(8.000)	0.354	0.008	0.000	185.63	110.38
3/8	(5.333)	0.864	0.001	0.000	218.04	202.72
1/2	(4.000)	0.964	0.003	0.000	119.81	117.66
5/8	(3.200)	0.846	0.002	0.000	215.19	197.92
3/4	(2.667)	0.943	0.004	0.000	77.07	74.86
13/16	(2.462)	0.668	0.006	0.000	179.88	146.98
7/8	(2.286)	0.987	0.003	0.000	177.33	176.20
15/16	(2.133)	0.868	0.001	0.000	411.44	383.23
1	(2.000)	0.331	0.000	0.000	1696.00	975.16

Notes: See Table 3A.

Table 3D. Frequency Domain Estimates of Relative Risk Aversion (Colombia)

Frequency	(Quarters)	Coherency	Returns Variance	Consumption Variance	RRA1	RRA2
0	(inf)	0.093	0.010	0.001	22.34	6.81
1/16	(32.000)	0.061	0.009	0.001	30.71	7.61
1/8	(16.000)	0.035	0.008	0.001	51.13	9.53
3/16	(10.667)	0.059	0.007	0.000	55.82	13.60
1/4	(8.000)	0.170	0.006	0.000	62.59	25.79
3/8	(5.333)	0.304	0.005	0.000	83.65	46.10
1/2	(4.000)	0.371	0.004	0.000	103.01	62.70
5/8	(3.200)	0.268	0.003	0.000	155.69	80.63
3/4	(2.667)	0.178	0.003	0.000	244.71	103.19
13/16	(2.462)	0.119	0.002	0.000	356.00	123.03
7/8	(2.286)	0.089	0.002	0.000	441.08	131.25
15/16	(2.133)	0.039	0.003	0.000	643.67	127.02
1	(2.000)	0.053	0.004	0.000	531.75	122.52

Notes: See Table 3A.

Table 3E. Frequency Domain Estimates of Relative Risk Aversion (Mexico)

Frequency	(Quarters)	Coherency	Returns Variance	Consumption Variance	RRA1	RRA2
0	(inf)	0.674	0.006	0.006	8.60	7.06
1/16	(32.000)	0.618	0.005	0.004	12.90	10.15
1/8	(16.000)	0.389	0.003	0.001	36.69	22.88
3/16	(10.667)	0.188	0.004	0.001	60.99	26.43
1/4	(8.000)	0.345	0.005	0.001	45.56	26.76

Table 3E. Continued

Frequency	(Quarters)	Coherency	Returns Variance	Consumption Variance	RRA1	RRA2
3/8	(5.333)	0.504	0.003	0.000	56.87	40.36
1/2	(4.000)	0.588	0.002	0.000	93.57	71.75
5/8	(3.200)	0.477	0.002	0.000	107.61	74.33
3/4	(2.667)	0.242	0.006	0.000	114.33	56.23
13/16	(2.462)	0.233	0.008	0.000	108.09	52.20
7/8	(2.286)	0.030	0.006	0.000	334.33	58.33
15/16	(2.133)	0.310	0.004	0.000	116.19	64.68
1	(2.000)	0.285	0.003	0.000	136.24	72.68

Notes: See Table 3A.

Table 3F. Frequency Domain Estimates of Relative Risk Aversion (Peru)

Frequency	(Quarters)	Coherency	Returns Variance	Consumption Variance	RRA1	RRA2
0	(inf)	0.324	0.003	0.001	15.51	8.83
1/16	(32.000)	0.320	0.004	0.001	16.51	9.34
1/8	(16.000)	0.258	0.003	0.001	22.68	11.53
3/16	(10.667)	0.174	0.003	0.000	38.08	15.89
1/4	(8.000)	0.116	0.003	0.000	72.84	24.80
3/8	(5.333)	0.150	0.002	0.000	102.77	39.79
1/2	(4.000)	0.156	0.003	0.000	120.48	47.57
5/8	(3.200)	0.141	0.003	0.000	137.56	51.66
3/4	(2.667)	0.126	0.004	0.000	152.96	54.22
13/16	(2.462)	0.126	0.004	0.000	159.15	56.48
7/8	(2.286)	0.090	0.004	0.000	207.61	62.26
15/16	(2.133)	0.081	0.004	0.000	237.79	67.71
1	(2.000)	0.112	0.004	0.000	216.75	72.47

Notes: See Table 3A.

As aforementioned the spectra of the series under scrutiny (reported in columns 4-5 of Tables 3A-3F) can be interpreted as the variance decompositions over various frequency bands (stated as a fraction of π). As can be readily observed, the variability of returns and consumption growth exhibit substantial changes over the frequency domain. Specifically, the variability of consumption is generally muted for 2 to 16 quarters; however, for horizons exceeding 16 quarters a steep increase is prevalent. As the time horizon approaches infinity, the variance of consumption is thirty times greater than its short-run value in Brasil for example.[15] Similar patterns are observed in all the countries under scrutiny. Turning to the spectra of returns, we have to note that in general the variance of returns increase as we move to the end of spectrum (long-run) but these increases are milder compared with the ones prevailing the consumption growth.

---

[15] The concentration of variance in low frequencies is an indication of short-term correlation in consumption growth, such as an AR(1) with a positive coefficient, rather than an indication of non-stationarity of the process, which can be ruled out for the series at hand.

These findings have direct implications for the subsequent analysis, i.e. the estimation of the coefficient of risk aversion, since the variance of consumption growth and returns are inversely related to the coefficient of risk aversion and coherence is positively related to relative risk aversion. Consequently, we expect that as the lower frequencies are taken into account, risk aversion will decrease.

Column 6 (Tables 3A-3F) reports the coefficient of relative risk aversion calculated from (8) (RRA1) while column 7 reports the respective coefficient after imposing a unitary correlation coefficient between returns and consumption (RRA2). Starting with Argentina, we have to note that both RRA1 and RRA2 are sufficiently reduced even at high frequencies. Specifically RRA1 reduces to 1.25 in the long run from 7.67 in the short run. Marginal reductions prevail when RRA2 is considered. This stems from the high coherency between returns and consumption growth over roughly the entire spectrum.

Turning to Brasil, a similar pattern is observed with RRA1 decreasing from 13.34 to 0.76 over the spectrum, while the respective figures are 6.93 and 0.75 for RRA2. Our results for Chile are more impressive as the short-term RRA1 is estimated at the enormous value of 1696 in the short-run and falls to 3.51 in the infinite horizon with similar reductions prevailing RRA2 as well. With respect to Colombia, the low correlation between consumption and returns in the short-run leads to high relative risk aversion of 531.75, whereas in the low frequency a somewhat increased coherency and increased variability in returns and consumption leads to a reduced estimate of 22.34. These gains are further amplified when the unitary coefficient is imposed and as such RRA2 reduces to 6.81. Our results for Mexico and Peru paint a similar picture suggesting that risk aversion at high frequencies is found to be extremely large while it considerably reduces at the low frequencies with estimates at 8.60 and 15.51 respectively. This picture continues to hold under the assumption of a unitary elasticity between excess returns and consumption growth that leads to further reductions to 7.06 and 8.83, respectively.

On the whole, the estimates of relative risk aversion improve substantially at low frequencies and range from 0.76 (Argentina) to 22.34 (Colombia). When a unitary correlation coefficient is imposed, these estimates are slightly reduced for all the countries at hand and range from 0.75 to 8.83. This improvement in the estimates of relative risk aversion for the lowest frequency is driven by the spectral properties of the data at hand. As we move to lower frequencies, the variability of consumption growth increases significantly matching the variability of excess returns and as such the covariance of returns and consumption increases. This property is coupled for most of the countries at hand with a rise in the estimated coherency (i.e. the correlation in the frequency domain) between consumption and returns.

6. CONCLUSION

We re-investigate the presence of an equity premium puzzle in six Latin America emerging stock markets. We attempt to re-address the empirical issue of implausibly high risk aversion within the context of the C-CAPM by looking at the pattern of risk aversion over the frequency domain. Our results show that as lower frequencies are taken into account, risk aversion falls substantially across countries and, in many cases, is consistent with more reasonable values of the coefficient of risk aversion.

Specifically, the traditional time series approach yields the usual finding of high risk aversion with estimates of relative risk aversion of 502 for Argentina, 175 for Mexico and 81 for Peru. However, the estimates of 36 and 16 for Chile and Brasil, respectively certainly move the relative risk parameter in the right direction. When repeating the analysis by imposing a unit coefficient between stock returns and consumption growth, the estimated coefficients are reduced. With the exception of Argentina (RRA= 20) and Colombia (RRA=11), the remaining estimates of risk aversion are all within the economically acceptable values.

Turning to our frequency domain estimates, we get substantially improved estimates of relative risk aversion at low frequencies that range from 0.76 (Argentina) to 22.34 (Colombia). Our findings mainly stem from the fact that the variability of consumption growth increases significantly matching the variability of excess returns and as such the covariance of returns and consumption increases, as we move to lower frequencies. This property is coupled for most of the countries at hand with a rise in the estimated coherency (i.e. the correlation in the frequency domain) between consumption and returns. Furthermore, when a unitary correlation coefficient is imposed, these estimates are slightly reduced for all the countries at hand and range from 0.75 to 8.83.

This evidence shows some improvement towards understanding the dynamics of the C-CAPM in the Latin America countries by reconciling its standard single-factor version with lower values of risk aversion and thus the equity premium over the frequency domain appears to be less of a puzzle.

REFERENCES

Abel, A.B. (1990). Asset Prices under Habit Formation and Catching up with the Joneses. *American Economic Review*, 80, 38-42.

Breeden, D.T. (1979). An Intertemporal Asset Pricing Model with Stochastic Consumption and Investment Opportunities. *Journal of Financial Economics*, 7, 265-296.

Campbell, J.Y. (1996). Consumption and the Stock Market: Interpreting International Experience. *Swedish Economic Policy Review*, 3, 251-299.

Campbell, J.Y. (2003). Consumption-Based Asset Pricing, *Handbook of the Economics of Finance*, George Constantinides, Milton Harris, and Rene Stulz eds., North-Holland, Amsterdam, Vol 1B, 803-887.

Cochrane J. (2005) `Financial markets and the real economy', *Foundations and Trends in Finance*, 1, 1, 1-101.

Constantinides, G. (1990). Habit Formation: A Resolution to the Equity Premium Puzzle. *Journal of Political Economy*, 98, 519-543.

Chatfield C. (1989). *The Analysis of Time Series*, London: Chapman and Hall.

Engle R.F. (1974). Band spectrum regression, *International Economic Review*, 15, 1, 1-11.

Engle R.F. (1976). Interpreting spectral analysis in terms of time-domain models, *Annals of Economic and Social Measurement*, 5, 89-109.

Engle R.F. (1978). Testing price equations for stability across spectral frequency bands, *Econometrica*, 46, 4, 869-881.

Epstein, L. and S.E. Zin (1991). Substitution, Risk Aversion and the Temporal Behaviour of Consumption Growth and Asset Returns: An Empirical Investigation. *Journal of Political Economy*, 99, 263-286.

Granger C.W.J. and M. Hatanaka (1964). *Spectral Analysis of Economic Time Series*, Princeton: Princeton University Press.

Hamilton, J.D. (1989). A new approach to the economic analysis of nonstationary time series and the business cycle, *Econometrica*, 57, 357-384.

Hamilton J.D. (1994) *Time Series Analysis*, Princeton: Princeton University Press.

Hansen, L.P. and K.J. Singleton (1983). Stochastic Consumption, Risk Aversion and the Temporal Behavior of Asset Returns. *Journal of Political Economy*, 91, 249-268.

Jobson, J.D. and B. Korkie (1981). Putting Markowitz Theory to Work. *Journal of Portfolio Management*, 70-74.

Kandel, S., and R.F.Stambaugh (1991). Asset returns and intertemporal preferences. *Journal of Monetary Economics*, 27, 39-71.

Kocherlakota, N.R. (1996). The Equity Premium: It's still a Puzzle. *Journal of Economic Literature*, 34, 42-71.

Lucas, R. (1978). Asset Prices in an Exchange Economy. *Econometrica*, 46, 1429-1445.

Mehra, R. and E. Prescott (1985). The Equity Premium: A Puzzle. *Journal of Monetary Economics*, 15, 145-161.

Salomons, R. and H. Grootveld (2003). The equity risk premium: emerging vs developed markets. *Emerging Markets Review*, 4, 121-144.

Weil, P. (1989). The equity premium puzzle and the risk-free rate puzzle. *Journal of Monetary Economics*, 24, 401-421.

In: Psychology of Decision Making in Risk Taking …   ISBN 978-1-60021-854-5
Editor: Rachel N. Kelian   © 2008 Nova Science Publishers, Inc.

Chapter 8

HURRICANE RISK PERCEPTIONS AND PREPAREDNESS

John C. Whitehead

Department of Economics, Appalachian State University, Boone, NC

INTRODUCTION

Preparedness is one component of effective hurricane risk mitigation. Emergency managers attempt to persuade residents of coastal zones to watch weather reports closely, develop and rehearse evacuation plans, store necessary supplies, and prepare property when storms threaten. Many coastal zone residents do not follow these recommended guidelines, even when recent experience suggests that the benefits of preparation exceed the costs. Understanding the factors that encourage these behaviors is an important step toward motivating coastal zone residents to become better prepared and minimize the losses from hurricanes. Toward this end we explore the relationship between wind and flood risk perceptions and hurricane preparedness.

Measures of objective and subjective risk factors are among the most important predictors of evacuation and other mitigating behavior during hurricanes (Baker, 1991). Those who do not feel safe staying home tend to evacuate (Dow and Cutter, 1997). Mobile home residents are more likely to evacuate than other housing residents (Baker, 1991; Whitehead et al., 2000). Storm intensity (Whitehead et al., 2000) and actual damages (Riad, Norris, and Ruback, 1999) are also factors in evacuation behavior. The purchase of mitigating goods is another type of mitigating behavior. Simmons and Kruse (2000) find that coastal residents value houses with hurricane shutters greater than inland residents. Ozdemir and Kruse (2000) find that the purchase of tornado shelters is based on risk perceptions.

In this paper we measure wind and flood risk perceptions and five determinants of hurricane preparedness in surveys of North Carolina coastal residents conducted after hurricane Bonnie (1998) and hurricanes Dennis and Floyd (1999). These data allow an analysis of changes in risk perceptions and preparedness and their interrelationship. We explore a two-stage model. In the first stage, objective risk factors, hurricane experience, and demographics are determinants of risk perceptions. In the second stage, risk perceptions, hurricane experience, and demographics are the determinants of hurricane preparedness.

In the rest of the paper we describe the surveys and data. Then we use multivariate regression models to analyze the determinants of risk perception and preparedness. Finally we discuss our results and offer some conclusions.

THE SURVEYS

During August of 1998 hurricane Bonnie approached the North Carolina coast prompting evacuations of all eight coastal counties. Hurricane Bonnie made landfall on the coast of North Carolina, near Cape Fear, 20 miles south of Wilmington (Avila, 1998). At landfall hurricane Bonnie was a low category 3 storm and quickly diminished to a category 1 storm on the Saffir-Simpson Hurricane Scale (Tropical Prediction Center, 1999). During the next two days a weakening hurricane Bonnie made its way up the entire North Carolina coast. Much of coastal North Carolina experienced hurricane Bonnie as a tropical storm.

During January 1999 we conducted a telephone survey of North Carolina residents who were affected by hurricane Bonnie in the summer of 1998. The survey used a random digit dial sample of households in the eight North Carolina ocean counties: Brunswick, Carteret, Currituck, Dare, Hyde, New Hanover, Onslow, and Pender. Of the households contacted, 76% completed the interview. The data has 1063 complete and partially complete cases.

During August of 1999, hurricane Dennis approached the North Carolina coast as a category 1 storm, missed the coast, stalled off the Outer Banks for two days, and then landed on the northeast North Carolina coast and quickly lost hurricane intensity (Beven, 2000). Again, portions of the entire North Carolina coast received evacuation orders. Less than one month later, hurricane Floyd traveled north along the Atlantic coast as a strong category 4 storm, weakened as it reached North Carolina, landed near Wilmington as a category 3 storm, and left the state the next day (Pasch, Kimberlain, and Stewart, 2000).

During January 2000 we attempted to contact the same member of the household that we contacted after hurricane Bonnie. Of the 1063 survey respondents, 66 had moved out of the sample counties, 20 had a non-working number, 99 had disconnected numbers, 16 had changed their number, and 29 numbers had become either a business, government, organization, or institute number. Subtracting these unavailable respondents from the total leaves 826 potential contacts. Of the potential contacts, 542 interviews were completed with another 23 interviews partially completed. These 565 contacts represent a response rate of 68% from the hurricane Bonnie survey respondents and an overall 49% response rate from the hurricane Bonnie sample. We focus on respondents to both surveys (n = 533).

We performed a multivariate regression analysis to determine who was more likely to respond to the follow-up survey. The major factor explaining whether recontacted respondents agreed to participate in the follow-up survey is whether the respondent evacuated for hurricane Bonnie (p = .01). The overall evacuation rate for hurricane Bonnie was 26%. The hurricane Bonnie evacuation rate for the subsample of resurvey respondents is 22% and 31% for the subsample of nonrespondents. Length of time at residence increases the probability of resurvey response (p = .01), a typical result for panel surveys. Non-respondents had lived at their residence an average of 9 years at the time of the Bonnie survey. Respondents had lived at their residence an average of 12 years.

DEPENDENT VARIABLES

Risk Perceptions

Following the conceptual model two sets of dependent variables are considered. In the first stage of the model the dependent variables are hurricane wind and risk perceptions. Hurricane wind risk perception is elicited with the question:

> "Now consider the risks from wind damage from a hurricane. In your opinion, was the home where you lived at the time of Hurricane [name] located in a high-risk site, a medium risk site, or a low-risk site?"

A similar question was asked to elicit flood risk perceptions:

> "Now consider the risks from coastal flooding from a hurricane. In your opinion, was the home where you lived at the time of Hurricane [name] located in a high-risk site, a medium risk site, or a low-risk site?"

Respondents were allowed to interpret the three-response categories, high, medium, and low, in their own way.

After hurricane Bonnie (1998), 46% and 34% of respondents perceived that they lived in a medium and high wind risk home. Following hurricanes Dennis and Floyd (1999), respondents revised their wind risk perceptions downward with 45% and 30% considering their home medium and high risk. The difference across surveys is statistically significant at the $p = .10$ level ($\chi^2=5.00[2$ df]). After hurricane Bonnie, 26% and 14% of respondents thought they lived in a medium and high flood risk home. Following hurricanes Dennis and Floyd, respondents revised their flood risk perceptions downward with 23% and 12% considering their home low, medium and high risk. However, the differences across surveys are not statistically significant ($\chi^2=2.55[2$ df]). Flood risk perceptions are significantly lower than wind risk perceptions in the first ($\chi^2=90.64[4$ df]) and second ($\chi^2=80.34[4$ df]) surveys.

Considering the interpersonal changes in risk perception, 49% and 41% of respondents changed their wind and flood risk perception from the first to the second survey. Nineteen percent of all respondents revised their wind risk perception up (i.e., from low to medium or high, from medium to high) and 29% revised their wind risk perception down. Seventeen percent of all respondents revised their flood risk perception up and 23% revised their flood risk perception down. When considering the interpersonal differences, changes in risk perceptions are significantly different at the $p = .01$ level for wind risk ($\chi^2=73.37[4$ df]) and flood risk ($\chi^2=85.85[4$ df]).

Hurricane Preparedness

In the second stage of the conceptual model the dependent variables are measures of hurricane preparedness. Preparedness is measured by whether the respondent follows the five steps of the North Carolina Division of Emergency Management's recommended steps of hurricane storm preparation: whether the household (1) has an evacuation plan, (2) rehearses the evacuation plan, (3) prepares their property in advance of a storm, (4) stores supplies, and (5) watches weather reports closely. The existence of an evacuation plan is elicited with the question:

> *"Which of the following recommended steps of Hurricane Storm Preparation does your household follow? Does your family have a Hurricane Evacuation Plan?"*

Respondents who answered yes were then asked: "Do you rehearse your Hurricane Evacuation Plan?" Other questions are "Do you prepare your property in advance of a storm?" "Do you store up to 2 weeks of supplies in your home?" and "Do you watch or listen to weather reports closely?"

Forty-six percent of the sample had an evacuation plan after hurricane Bonnie (1998) and 56% had an evacuation plan after hurricanes Dennis and Floyd (1999). The increase in evacuation plans is statistically significant at the $p = .01$ level ($\chi^2=10.94[1$ df]). Of those respondents who had an evacuation plan, 39% (1998) and 34% (1999) rehearsed their plan. For those who had an evacuation plan in both years (n = 172), 43% did not rehearse in either year, 20% rehearsed in both years, 19% rehearsed only after hurricane Bonnie (1998), and 17% rehearsed only after hurricanes Dennis and Floyd (1999).

Seventy-one respondents had an evacuation plan after hurricane Bonnie (1998) but not after hurricanes Dennis and Floyd (1999). One hundred twenty-five respondents had an evacuation plan in 1999 but not in 1998. Of those who had an evacuation plan in either year, 26% (1998) and 27% (1999) rehearsed the plan. There is no statistical difference in rehearsals across time ($\chi^2=0.34[1$ df]).

Most respondents store supplies and prepare their property in advance of a storm while almost all respondents watch weather reports closely. Sixty-nine percent (1998) and 61% (1999) store two weeks of supplies. This difference is statistically significant at the $p = .01$ level ($\chi^2=7.97[1$ df]). Ninety-two percent (1998) and 89% (1999) of respondents prepare their property. This difference is statistically significant at the $p = .10$ level ($\chi^2=2.83[1$ df]). Ninety-eight percent (1998) and 96% (1999) of respondents watch weather reports closely. This difference is not statistically significant ($\chi^2=2.53[1$ df]).

INDEPENDENT VARIABLES

Objective Risk

We consider several objective measures of risk as factors potentially affecting risk perceptions and hurricane preparedness. Variables that measure objective risk are *hurricane experience, property damage, mobile home, shutters, island residence, storm surge zone,* and *flood plain*. Property damage is equal to one if the respondent suffered property damage and zero otherwise. Property damage is expected to increase both wind and flood risk perceptions. Mobile home is equal to one if the respondent lived in a mobile home and zero otherwise. Mobile home is expected to increase wind risk perceptions.

Shutters is equal to one if the respondent had installed storm shutters on their home and zero otherwise. The shutters variable is expected to increase wind risk perception if the respondents in high-risk areas are those who install the shutters. However, shutters could have the opposite effect if respondents feel that shutters completely mitigate against risk. Storm surge zone is equal to one if the respondent lives in a storm surge zone and zero otherwise. Flood plain is equal to one if the respondent lives in the 100-year flood plain and zero otherwise. Storm surge zone and flood plain are expected to increase flood risk perception.

Hurricane experience is a measure of objective risk and is captured by a dummy variable equal to zero for the hurricane Bonnie (1998) data and one for the hurricanes Dennis and Floyd (1999) data. The effect of hurricane experience on perceived risk may be either positive or negative. If experience with hurricanes suggests that hurricanes are mild weather events, hurricane experience might lead respondents to adopt low perceptions of risk. If experience suggests that hurricanes are severe weather events, hurricane experience might increase risk perceptions.

Demographics

Demographic variables include *pets, homeowner, apartment, white, female, age, education*, and *income*. Pets is equal to one if the respondent owns at least one pet and zero otherwise. Similarly, homeowner is equal to one if the respondent owns their home, apartment is equal to one if the respondent lives in an apartment, townhouse, or condominium, white is equal to one if the respondent is white, and female is equal to one if the respondent is female. Age is the age of the respondent. Education is the number of years of schooling. Income is the 1998 household income of the respondent (in thousands).

County dummy variables are also included. *Brunswick, Carteret, Onslow*, and *Pender* are equal to one if the respondent lives in those counties and zero otherwise. *Outer Banks* is equal to one if the respondent lives in the "Outer Banks" counties of Currituck, Dare, or Hyde Counties and zero otherwise. New Hanover County is the omitted variable. We have no a priori expectations concerning the county dummy variables.

Data Summary

Most of the variables are similar in the two surveys (Table 1). Thirty-four percent of the sample suffered property damage during hurricane Bonnie (1998) and 33% suffered property damage during hurricanes Dennis and Floyd (1999). However, these numbers mask significant differences in the households that suffered property damage. Forty-eight percent of the sample did not suffer damage in either storm season. Eighteen percent suffered property damage in 1999 but not 1998. Nineteen percent suffered property damage in 1998 but not 1999. Only 15% suffered damage in both storms.

Table 1. Independent Variables

	Bonnie (1998)		Dennis/Floyd (1999)	
	Mean	**Std.Dev.**	**Mean**	**Std.Dev.**
Property Damage	0.34	0.47	0.33	0.47
Mobile Home	0.13	0.34	0.13	0.33
Shutters	0.17	0.38	0.16	0.36
Island	0.14	0.35	0.12	0.32
Storm surge zone	0.19	0.39	0.19	0.39
Pets	0.66	0.47	0.66	0.47
Homeowner	0.81	0.39	0.83	0.38
Apartment	0.08	0.27	0.08	0.26
White	0.85	0.35	0.85	0.35
Female	0.60	0.49	0.60	0.49
Age	47.85	16.45	47.85	16.45
Education	13.71	2.17	13.71	2.17
Income	42.91	30.53	42.91	30.53
Outer Banks	0.11	0.32	0.11	0.32
Brunswick	0.12	0.32	0.12	0.32
Carteret	0.15	0.36	0.16	0.36
Onslow	0.28	0.45	0.28	0.45
Pender	0.09	0.29	0.09	0.29

From the hurricane Bonnie (1998) survey, 13% of the sample lived in mobile homes, 17% have storm shutters, 14% lived on an island, 19% lived in a storm surge zone, and 22% lived on a flood plain. Each of these characteristics is slightly lower after hurricanes Dennis and Floyd (1999). Almost two-thirds of the sample owns a pet in both surveys. Eighty-one percent and 83% of the sample are homeowners in the first and second surveys. Eight percent of the sample lives in an apartment, townhouse, or condominium in both surveys.

Eighty-five percent of the sample is white and 60% is female. The average age is 48 years, the average education level is 14 years, and the average household income is $43 thousand.

EMPIRICAL MODEL

We estimate the factors that affect the wind and flood risk perceptions using the ordered probit model (Greene, 1999)

$$y_i^* = \beta' X_i + e_i \tag{1}$$

where y_i^* is the unobserved latent risk perception variables, $i = 1, \dots , n$, β is a vector of parameters, X_i is a vector of independent variables and the error term, e_i, is distributed normally with zero mean and variance equal to σ^2. The latent dependent variable is measured by the ordinal dependent variables. With $m = 3$ risk choices the dependent variables are coded $y = 0, \dots, m\text{-}1$. The ordered probit model uses the same structure as the basic probit model with a censoring parameter, μ,

$$y = 0 \quad if \ y^* \leq 0$$
$$y = 1 \quad if \ 0 < y^* \leq \mu \qquad\qquad (2)$$
$$y = 2 \quad if \ \mu \leq y^*$$

where $y = 0$ is low risk, $y = 1$ is medium risk, and $y = 2$ is high risk. The ordered probit model estimates the probability of the outcome variable using the normal distribution

$$\Pi(y = 0) = \Phi(-\beta' X_i)$$
$$\Pi(y = 1) = \Phi(\mu - \beta' X_i) - \Phi(-\beta' X_i) \qquad\qquad (3)$$
$$\Pi(y = 2) = 1 - \Phi(\mu - \beta' X_i)$$

where Φ is the standard normal distribution function.

Since we have multiple observations on both risk variables (i.e., measures of risk perceptions in the first and second surveys) we treat the data as a panel. The random effects ordered probit model is a panel data extension of the ordered probit model where the error term accounts for the correlation across respondents

$$y_{it}^* = \beta' X_{it} + e_{it} \qquad\qquad (4)$$

where $t = 1, 2$ time periods (i.e., observations for each respondent). The error term, e_{it}, is distributed normally and is composed of two parts, $v_{it} + u_i$, where v_{it} is the normally distributed random error with mean zero and variance, σ_v^2, u_i is the error common to each individual with mean zero and variance, σ_u^2, and $\sigma_e^2 = \sigma_v^2 + \sigma_u^2$. The correlation in error terms, $\rho = \sigma_u^2/\sigma_e^2$, is increasing in the contribution of the individual error to the total error and is a measure of the appropriateness of the random effects specification.

The determinants of hurricane preparedness are estimated with the binary probit model (Greene, 1999). The probit model is similar to the random effects probit, equation (1), except the latent dependent variable is measured by the dummy variable

$$y = 0 \quad if \ y^* \leq 0$$
$$y = 1 \quad if \ y^* > 0 \qquad\qquad (5)$$

where $y = 1$ if the respondent engaged in evacuation preparation and $y = 0$ otherwise. The probit model estimates the probability of the outcome variable with the normal distribution

$$\Pi(y = 1) = \Phi(\beta' X_i) \qquad\qquad (6)$$

The random effects probit model, which is similar to equation (4) but with only two outcomes, is used for the panel data. Each of the probit models is estimated with the LIMDEP statistical software (Greene, 1998).

EMPIRICAL RESULTS

Risk Perceptions

The hurricane Bonnie (1998) and hurricanes Dennis and Floyd (1999) wind risk models are statistically significant according to the model χ^2 value (Table 2). In the hurricane Bonnie model we find that property damage, mobile home and island residence have positive effects on perceived wind risk. Residents who live in a storm surge zone and the 100-year flood plain perceive higher wind risks. These variables likely distinguish between those who live near the water and are exposed to hurricane wind damage and those who live in the inland portions of each county. Those who live in the Outer Banks counties, Onslow and Pender counties perceive higher wind risks than New Hanover County residents.

Table 2. Ordered Probit Models of Wind Risk Perception

	Bonnie (1998)		Dennis/Floyd (1999)		Panel	
	Coeff.	t-ratio	Coeff.	t-ratio	Coeff.	t-ratio
Constant	-0.207	-0.47	0.009	0.02	-0.029	-0.07
Property Damage	0.392	3.67	0.259	2.34	0.344	4.04
Mobile Home	0.392	2.49	0.084	0.53	0.279	2.01
Shutters	-0.015	-0.12	-0.022	-0.16	-0.032	-0.28
Island	0.377	2.29	0.295	1.77	0.387	2.66
Storm surge zone	0.403	2.83	0.212	1.58	0.348	2.93
Flood Plain	0.222	1.75	0.234	1.87	0.217	2.12
Pets	-0.062	-0.54	0.186	1.66	0.089	0.85
Homeowner	0.147	0.97	-0.208	-1.35	0.011	0.08
Apartment	0.215	1.05	-0.163	-0.83	0.110	0.65
White	0.059	0.38	0.038	0.25	0.035	0.24
Female	-0.079	-0.76	-0.148	-1.45	-0.138	-1.41
Age	-0.002	-0.67	-0.000	-0.04	-0.001	-0.35
Education	0.032	1.23	0.025	1.02	0.033	1.33
Income	0.003	1.56	0.003	1.55	0.003	2.10
Outer Banks	0.380	1.89	0.176	0.93	0.337	1.74
Brunswick	0.154	0.88	0.190	1.08	0.239	1.53
Carteret	0.227	1.37	0.203	1.24	0.268	1.73
Onslow	0.301	2.13	0.021	0.15	0.187	1.42
Pender	0.430	2.32	0.398	2.00	0.497	2.54
Property Damage (1998)			0.077	0.71		
Hurricane Experience					-0.168	-2.29
μ	1.350	18.70	1.252	18.24	1.552	22.43
ρ					0.67	8.92
$\chi2$	65.18		46.25		135.58	
Sample Size	533		533		533	
Time Periods	1		1		2	

We find different determinants of wind risk perception in the hurricane Dennis and Floyd (1999) model. The determinants of risk are the property damages, island, flood plain, pets, and Pender County variables. We also include a lagged property damage variable, the coefficient of which is not statistically significant. Surprisingly, those who live in mobile homes perceive the same wind risks as those who live in a fixed structure. Closer inspection of the relationship between wind risk and mobile home supports this result. A significantly greater number of mobile home residents perceive high wind risks than others after hurricane Bonnie (χ^2=6.06[2 df]). However, there is no statistically significant difference in wind risk perceptions between the two groups after hurricanes Dennis and Floyd (χ^2=0.11[2 df]).

The random effects probit model constrains all coefficients to be equal across the years of the survey. The measure of correlation across time periods, ρ, is significantly different from zero, indicating that the random effects specification is appropriate. In this model all of the determinants of wind risk perception are the same as those in the hurricane Bonnie (1998) model except for the Onslow dummy variable. In addition, those with higher incomes and those in Carteret County perceive higher wind risks. The hurricane experience dummy variable measures the additional experience acquired from hurricanes Dennis and Floyd. The effect of hurricane experience is negative indicating that wind risk perceptions are significantly lower after hurricanes Dennis and Floyd when holding the other independent variables constant.

Each of the flood risk models are statistically significant according to the model χ^2 value (Table 3). In the hurricane Bonnie (1998) model we find that property damage, storm shutters, storm surge zone, flood plain residence, and Outer Banks variables have positive effects on perceived risk. Older respondents have lower perceived flood risks.

Table 3. Ordered Probit Models of Flood Risk Perception

	Bonnie (1998)		Dennis/Floyd (1999)		Panel	
	Coeff.	t-ratio	Coeff.	t-ratio	Coeff.	t-ratio
Constant	-0.003	-0.01	0.239	0.47	0.251	0.56
Property Damage	0.264	2.24	0.157	1.25	0.215	2.17
Mobile Home	-0.083	-0.51	-0.067	-0.36	-0.067	-0.43
Shutters	0.237	1.70	-0.169	-1.10	0.094	0.72
Island	0.242	1.46	0.440	2.39	0.360	2.49
Storm surge zone	0.906	6.31	0.766	5.20	0.914	7.38
Flood Plain	0.339	2.46	0.718	5.06	0.561	5.10
Homeowner	-0.075	-0.59	-0.231	-1.74	-0.110	-0.95
Apartment	-0.035	-0.21	-0.403	-2.19	-0.217	-1.44
Pets	0.099	0.40	-0.374	-1.30	-0.073	-0.35
White	-0.066	-0.41	0.163	1.00	0.018	0.12
Female	0.119	1.00	-0.003	-0.02	0.057	0.52
Age	-0.007	-2.13	-0.009	-2.38	-0.009	-2.63
Education	-0.020	-0.72	-0.020	-0.68	-0.024	-0.94
Income	-0.001	-0.40	-0.002	-1.07	-0.001	-0.83
Outer Banks	0.319	1.66	0.179	0.81	0.318	1.70
Brunswick	-0.157	-0.73	0.005	0.02	-0.119	-0.63
Carteret	0.209	1.10	0.085	0.44	0.151	0.87
Onslow	0.036	0.22	-0.034	-0.20	-0.013	-0.08
Pender	0.090	0.42	0.120	0.51	0.059	0.29
Property Damage (1998)			0.451	3.66		
Hurricane Experience					-0.127	-1.53
μ	0.963	12.31	0.981	12.06	1.141	14.99
ρ					0.67	6.45
χ^2	105.39		135.94		233.92	
Sample Size	533		533		533	
Periods	1		1		2	

In the hurricanes Dennis and Floyd (1999) model we find that lagged, but not current, property damage has a positive effect on flood risk. The current property damage coefficient is also insignificant in a model that does not include the lagged property damage variable. As in the hurricane Bonnie model, the storm surge zone, flood plain and age variables have statistically significant effects on flood risk. In addition, island residents perceive higher flood risks. Homeowners perceive lower flood risks than renters and apartment dwellers perceive lower flood risks than those in single-family homes.

In the panel data model, the correlation in errors across time periods is significantly different from zero, indicating that the random effects specification is appropriate. Property damage, island, storm surge zone, flood plain and Outer Banks residents perceive higher flood risks than others. Older respondents perceive lower risks. When the determinants of flood risks are held constant there is no difference in risk perceptions across time.

Hurricane Preparedness

The probit models for four of the hurricane preparedness activities are presented in Tables 4-7. Since almost all respondents watch weather reports closely, determinants of this measure of preparedness are not analyzed. In the individual models we test for whether perceived wind and flood risk are predictors of evacuation preparedness and include the demographic variables as control variables. In the random effects probit models we also test the effects of hurricane experience. Each of the probit models, except one, is statistically significant. In the random effects probit models the ρ statistics are statistically significant indicating that the panel data specification is appropriate.

In the hurricane Bonnie (1998) evacuation plan model, wind risk perception increases the likelihood that a household will have an evacuation plan (Table 4). Flood risk perception has no effect. Other results are that white and female respondents are more likely to have an evacuation plan. In the hurricanes Dennis and Floyd (1999) model, wind risk has a positive effect on whether the respondent has an evacuation plan. In the panel model, wind risk, white, female, and education each contribute to explaining whether the household has an evacuation plan. With hurricane experience, respondents are more likely to have an evacuation plan.

Table 4. Probit Models of Hurricane Preparedness: Evacuation Plan

	Bonnie (1998)		Dennis/Floyd (1999)		Panel	
	Coeff.	t-ratio	Coeff.	t-ratio	Coeff.	t-ratio
Constant	-1.348	-3.12	-0.710	-1.67	-1.469	-3.31
Wind Risk	0.162	1.96	0.222	2.78	0.223	3.09
Flood Risk	0.088	1.08	0.056	0.66	0.076	1.03
White	0.269	1.68	0.152	0.96	0.267	1.70
Female	0.220	1.93	0.156	1.36	0.238	2.03
Age	0.003	0.84	-0.005	-1.47	-0.001	-0.39
Education	0.032	1.18	0.044	1.62	0.049	1.77
Income	0.001	0.74	0.0002	0.09	0.001	0.57
Hurricane Experience					0.362	4.10
ρ					0.396	6.39
χ^2	17.71		19.40		78.74	
Sample Size	533		533		533	
Periods	1		1		2	

In the evacuation plan rehearsal models we include only respondents who had an evacuation plan in either year (Table 5). In the hurricane Bonnie model, flood risk perception increases the likelihood that a household will rehearse their evacuation plan and wind risk perception has no effect. Older respondents and those with more education are more likely to rehearse. None of the coefficients in the hurricanes Dennis and Floyd (1999) model are statistically significant. In the panel model, increasing perceived flood risk increases the likelihood that a household will rehearse their evacuation plan and wind risk has no effect. Other results are that older respondents are more likely to rehearse their evacuation plan. Those with greater income are less likely to rehearse their plan.

Table 5. Probit Models of Hurricane Preparedness: Rehearse the Plan

	Bonnie (1998)		Dennis/Floyd (1999)		Panel	
	Coeff.	t-ratio	Coeff.	t-ratio	Coeff.	t-ratio
Constant	-2.401	-3.94	-0.017	-0.03	-1.307	-2.50
Wind Risk	-0.013	-0.12	0.028	0.28	0.004	0.04
Flood Risk	0.190	1.84	0.084	0.82	0.147	1.71
White	-0.035	-0.16	-0.282	-1.38	-0.185	-1.04
Female	-0.094	-0.63	-0.113	-0.77	-0.114	-0.92
Age	0.015	3.17	0.001	0.23	0.008	2.07
Education	0.087	2.32	-0.013	-0.35	0.038	1.18
Income	-0.004	-1.59	-0.005	-1.90	-0.005	-2.19
Hurricane Experience					0.083	0.78
ρ					0.192	2.05
$\chi2$	18.78		8.30		22.20	
Sample Size	368		368		368	
Periods	1		1		2	

Wind and flood risk perceptions have no effect on whether respondents store two weeks of supplies (Table 6). Older respondents are more likely to store supplies in the hurricane Bonnie (1998) model. Respondents with higher incomes are less likely to store supplies in the hurricanes Dennis and Floyd (1999) model. In the panel model, older respondents are more likely to store supplies. Respondents with higher educations and incomes are less likely to store supplies. With hurricane experience respondents are less likely to store supplies.

Table 6. Probit Models of Hurricane Preparedness: Store Supplies

	Bonnie (1998)		Dennis/Floyd (1999)		Panel	
	Coeff.	t-ratio	Coeff.	t-ratio	Coeff.	t-ratio
Constant	0.825	1.847	0.740	1.734	1.119	2.48
Wind Risk	0.023	0.266	0.066	0.820	0.074	0.97
Flood Risk	-0.007	-0.079	-0.010	-0.122	-0.016	-0.21
White	-0.078	-0.465	0.070	0.436	0.002	0.01
Female	0.132	1.119	-0.155	-1.342	-0.023	-0.19
Age	0.007	1.922	0.004	1.167	0.007	1.95
Education	-0.042	-1.492	-0.036	-1.325	-0.050	-1.80
Income	-0.002	-1.136	-0.004	-2.169	-0.004	-2.18
Hurricane Experience					-0.285	-3.16
ρ					0.393	6.06
$\chi2$	12.65		12.86		60.66	
Sample Size	533		533		533	
Periods	1		1		2	

In the hurricane Bonnie (1998) prepare property model, white and higher income respondents are more likely to prepare their property (Table 7). In the hurricanes Dennis and Floyd (1999) model, those who perceive higher wind risks and white respondents are more likely to prepare their property. In the panel model respondents who perceive higher wind risks are more likely to prepare their property in advance of a storm. White and higher income respondents are also more likely to prepare property. With hurricane experience respondents are less likely to prepare their property.

Table 7. Probit Models of Hurricane Preparedness: Prepare Property

	Bonnie (1998)		Dennis/Floyd (1999)		Panel	
	Coeff.	t-ratio	Coeff.	t-ratio	Coeff.	t-ratio
Constant	0.773	1.21	0.137	0.246	0.774	1.07
Wind Risk	0.132	1.06	0.255	2.221	0.261	1.78
Flood Risk	-0.025	-0.20	-0.041	-0.342	-0.072	-0.45
White	0.522	2.65	0.790	4.365	0.992	3.98
Female	0.166	0.96	-0.201	-1.228	-0.073	-0.35
Age	0.002	0.40	-0.003	-0.746	-0.002	-0.32
Education	-0.043	-1.00	0.039	1.037	0.013	0.26
Income	0.014	2.95	0.0004	0.159	0.007	1.94
Time (=1 if 1999)					-0.257	-1.65
ρ					0.547	5.86
$\chi2$	23.57		32.18		73.80	
Sample Size	533		533		533	
Periods	1		1		2	

CONCLUSIONS

We find that respondents perceive slightly higher wind and flood risks after hurricane Bonnie (1998) than after hurricanes Dennis and Floyd (1999). The reduction in risk perceptions may be due to the misleading effects of hurricane Floyd, which approached North Carolina as a category 4 storm but landed as a category 2 storm on the ocean-bordering counties producing less wind than expected. The rain-induced flooding from hurricanes Dennis and Floyd occurred primarily in the inland coastal plain counties. This experience may have led coastal North Carolina residents to revise their perceived wind and flood risks downward.

Some of the determinants of risk are similar across both types of risk. Those who face the highest risks from hurricanes, residents of islands, storm surge zones, and flood plains, are more likely to perceive greater wind and flood risks. Those who have incurred property damages perceive greater wind and flood risks. We also find differences in risk perception across the type of risk. Mobile home owners perceive higher wind risks but not flood risks. Females perceive lower wind risks. Those who are older perceive lower flood risks. Those with higher incomes perceive greater wind risk but not flood risk. This result may be due to the higher potential economic damages from wind in high-income neighborhoods. We find some geographic differences in wind and flood risk perception.

We find that risk perceptions differ across storm season. Demographic and geographic factors influence risk perceptions after hurricane Bonnie (1998) but not after hurricanes

Dennis and Floyd (1999). One area of concern is that mobile home owners perceive the same risks from wind as those in fixed structures after experiencing hurricanes Dennis and Floyd. Again, this downward reduction in risk perceptions may be due to the misleading effects of hurricane Floyd. Homeowners and apartment dwellers perceive lower risks in 1999 but not in 1998. Another finding is that the property damage that occurred in 1998 increases flood risk perceptions in 1999, but current property damage does not. This result perhaps reflects the greater flooding in the ocean-bordering counties after hurricane Bonnie relative to flooding after hurricanes Dennis and Floyd.

In terms of evacuation planning respondents are better prepared for evacuation after hurricanes Dennis and Floyd (1999) than before. Somewhat surprisingly, respondents are less well prepared for a hurricane in terms of preparing property and storing supplies after hurricanes Dennis and Floyd than before. Perceived wind and flood risks are factors that are considered when preparing for a hurricane. However, these results are not stable over time. Also, the effect of demographic variables on hurricane preparedness changes over time.

Several of these findings should be of concern to emergency managers. The first is that risk perceptions are not stable over time. Perceived hurricane risks are lower after the experiences of two hurricanes in 1999. Perhaps, hurricane risk perceptions decrease when negative impacts from hurricanes are less than expected. The converse may also be true. Risk perceptions may increase when negative impacts are greater than expected.

Second, hurricane preparedness is not stable over time. Respondents are better prepared for evacuation but less prepared for weathering a storm in their home and protecting their home from a storm after experiencing hurricanes Dennis and Floyd. These contrasting results may be consistent. If respondents are more likely to evacuate after hurricanes Dennis and Floyd they may consider property preparation and supply storage to be less important mitigation activities.

Third, objective measures of risk, those that do not change over time, are taken into account when forming hurricane risk perceptions. Those at the most risk, those in mobile homes and those who suffer property damage, perceive lower risks than are warranted.

These results have policy implications. Hurricane preparedness is important for effective risk mitigation. Since reductions in perceived risk lead to lower levels of hurricane preparedness, better risk communication methods are needed to improve preparedness. Coastal residents may experience storms that weaken as they approach the coast or upon landing where hurricane damage and mortality is less than expected. At these times, residents should be better informed that not all major storms weaken as they approach the coast. As in many risk communication problems, however, the information is readily available to those who choose to seek it. Therefore, incentives that lead to the consumption of the risk information are needed.

REFERENCES

Avila, Lixion A. (1998) *Preliminary Report, Hurricane Bonnie 19-30 August 1998*, National Hurricane Center, *http://www.nhc.noaa.gov/1998bonnie.html*, October.

Baker, Earl J. (1991), and "Hurricane Evacuation Behavior," *International Journal of Mass Emergencies and Disasters*, Vol.9: 287-310.

Beven, Jack (2000), *Preliminary Report: Hurricane Dennis 24 August – 7 September 1999,* National Hurricane Center, http://www.nhc.noaa.gov/1999dennis_text.html, January.

Dow, Kirstin, and Susan L. Cutter (1997), "Crying Wolf: Repeat Responses to Hurricane Evacuation Orders," *Coastal Management,* Vol.26: 237-251.

Greene, William H. (1998), *LIMDEP Version 7.0 User's Manual,* Revised Edition, Econometric Software, Inc. Plainview, New York.

Greene, William H. (1999), *Econometric Analysis,* Third Edition, Prentice Hall, Upper Saddle River, New Jersey.

Ozdemir, Ozlem and Jamie Brown Kruse, (2000), *Relationship between Risk Perception and Willingness-to-Pay for Low Probability, High Consequence Risk: A Survey, Discussion Paper 2000-04,* Department of Economics and Geography, Texas Tech University.

Pasch, Richard J., Todd B. Kimberlain, and Stacy R. Stewart (2000), *Preliminary Report: Hurricane Floyd, 7– 17 September 1999.* National Hurricane Center, *http://www.nhc. noaa.gov/1999floyd_text.html,* January.

Riad, Jasmin K., Fran H. Norris, and R. Barry Ruback, (1999), "Predicting Evacuation in Two Major Disasters: Risk Perception, Social Influence, and Access to Resources," *Journal of Applied Social Psychology,* Vol.29: 918-934.

Simmons, Kevin M. and Jamie Brown Kruse (2000), "Market Value of Mitigation and Perceived Risk: Empirical Results," *Journal of Economics,* Vol.26: 41-51.

Tropical Prediction Center (1999), *The Saffir-Simpson Hurricane Scale.* National Hurricane Center, *http://www.nhc.noaa.gov/aboutsshs.html,* July 14.

Whitehead, John C., Bob Edwards, Marieke Van Willigen, John Maiolo, Ken Wilson, and Kevin Smith (2000), "Heading for Higher Ground: Factors Affecting Real and Hypothetical Hurricane Evacuation Behavior," *Environmental Hazards,* Vol.2: 133-142.

In: Psychology of Decision Making in Risk Taking …   ISBN 978-1-60021-854-5
Editor: Rachel N. Kelian   © 2008 Nova Science Publishers, Inc.

Chapter 9

RISK AVOIDANCE AND RISK TAKING IN MENTAL HEALTH SOCIAL WORK

Shulamit Ramon

Interprofessional Health and Social Studies, School of Community Health
and Social Studies, Anglia Polytechnic University, Cambridge, UK

ABSTRACT

This chapter will look at issues related to risk in mental health social work, especially the over-focus on risk avoidance and the need to create space for calculated risk taking. Examples from Britain and continental Europe will be utilised.

INTRODUCTION

The discourse on risk in British mental health social work (MHSW), and beyond it into the multidisciplinary context, is presently prolific. Nearly all of it focuses on *risk avoidance.* This focus can be observed in training for MHSW, research, policy and legislation.

This is less so in continental Europe. We therefore need to understand better the factors underlying the British preference, which largely omits serious consideration of *risk taking* in its policy and practice.

This chapter will explore the above-mentioned issues, and look at some relevant practice examples from the perspectives of social workers, mental health service users and their carers.

THE GENERIC RISK DISCOURSE

The discourse about risk does not emanate from the mental health system. Conceptually it is located in the debate about freedom and control, citizenship, crime and deviance, health and illness, with modernity and postmodernity (Giddens, 1991, Beck, 1992, Furedi, 1997, Rose, 2000). Its protagonists argued that each Western society copes with the increased uncertainty, which has been brought about by the growing gap between technological development and social fallibility, by increasing risk control, or by avoiding it. Thus control has become a synonym of avoidance. These eminent writers see risk control as an extension of social control, something to be lamented but to be taken for granted.

One does not need to disagree with the assumption of increasing, and ever more refined, social control to notice that risk is never considered in their discourse as worth taking individually and socially, as a buzz which stimulates people to give their best to a shared objective. Instead, the focus is on the increase in visible and less visible means of social control as an inevitable consequence of living with uncertainty.

This position goes against the grain of everyday life in the same societies in which ordinary people admire risk taking by a minority, and at times have a go at it themselves. Although a cliché, it is virtually impossible to live by adhering only to risk avoidance as a major strategy for living, without the utilisation of risk taking as a complimentary framework. This applies to the most banal risk such as crossing the road, extending to the more serious risks such as choosing a partner, or whether to be operated on when seriously ill. Some would go further to say that life is not worth living if it does not have some elements of risk taking, which put the spice of excitement into living. While some risk taking is what makes non-conforming or even illegal behaviour seen as worthwhile taking, most risk taking behaviour is within the narrow legal boundaries and the wider ones of conformity.

As a society we admire some types of risk taking, such as:

- Mountain climbing
- Explorers to unknown territories
- Marathon runners
- Diving
- Motor racing
- Writing a first successful novel
- Business gambling which pay off
- Inventors who risk all but succeed in becoming famous and successful
- Surgeons
- "Falling in love"

Moreover, these sociological approaches to risk negate the fact that risk taking also offers *the promise of new opportunities to become what one feels s/he has the potential to be.* This is well analysed by Harry Ferguson (2001) in his paper *"Social work, individualisation and life politics".*

Interested in emancipatory politics, Ferguson looks at how the lack of permanency in life in our time offers us also more diverse options, such as different types of intimate relationships, work, leisure and communication. All of these choices necessitate a greater degree of personal responsibility.

In his framework, a normal biography *can* become:

- the elective biography
- the reflexive biography
- the do-it-yourself biography
- the "tight-rope" biography

While aware that the possibilities we can exercise are limited by our past and present history, we have also become more aware that we usually have more than one option at most junctions in our life, and that to make a choice a reality risk would need to be taken. These risks can be financial (e.g. re-mortgaging our house to take a trip around the world); social (loss of status if we opt for a lower ranked occupation, a partner of the same sex); physical (being an explorer entails at times physical endurance); and psychological (the success of a first novel cannot be assured; moving to another country can lead to isolation). Yet more people are ready to take these risks for the sake of turning their dreams into reality. Thus life at present has become more risky for most people, in part due to the opening up of more possibilities for them to choose from.

It could be argued that the increase in possibilities also leads to increased stress levels, and inevitably to an increase in ill mental health, as it undermines the sense of coherence we need in order to live at peace with ourselves and others. Yet we know from the world of work that taking risk while *being in control* enables people to do more, do it better, and be more able to innovate (Bunce and West, 1996).

MENTAL HEALTH RISK DISCOURSE

The risk discourse is particularly developed within Anglo-Saxon societies, where it is assumed that the ideology of individual freedom and autonomy is based on *regulation from within,* in which those who do not conform are regulated through a series of inclusionary and exclusionary mechanisms and processes. Prominent writers (e.g. Rose, 2000) further assume that the inclusionary discourse of people with disabilities (e.g. inclusion within education and employment), including those with mental illness, is no more than an attempt to ensure their conformity and hence the reduction of risk to their society and to themselves. Within this perspective, empowerment is no more than a fiction and a con, because it is aimed to offer the illusion of being in control over one's life, when one is merely toeing the line in terms of being a good – i.e. conforming – citizen.

Given this line of argument, it is not surprising that people who embody mental illness are perceived only as a threat to social cohesion and hegemony. Professionals working with them are seen as mandated to ensure the reduction of the threat, the return to the fold of responsible, self-regulated citizens, and if this is not possible then the application of exclusionary sanctions follows. The fascination within post-modernity with courting the irrational in particular, as expressed in literature, films, plays, poetry and the visual arts, has escaped the notice of these sociologists, as did emphatic approaches to understanding mental illness and the (temporary) excitement/liberation it offers – side by side with suffering – to those experiencing it. Even the possibility of the co-existence of threat with excitement is not recognised, let alone that of crediting users with having valuable expertise in experiencing this ambiguity to offer to the rest of us.

There are *important* reasons for focusing on risk avoidance in mental health, which include:

- Fear of others being hurt by people suffering from ill mental health.
- Fear of harm to self due to mental ill health.
- Media coverage of mental health users and of professional activities has focused mainly on homicide, and a little on suicide, by users.
- Politicians are very sensitive to issues related to public protection.
- Professionals have responded to the media and the politicians' stand by becoming defensive and have been instructed to assess and manage risk avoidance.
- As a result of the above, fear of the unpredictable element in some mental illness has been extended to all mental ill health categories.

Politicians in the Western world are perceiving risk policies and measures as one of the two most important core issues of mental health policy, the other being *cost containment* (Shera, Healy, Aviram and Ramon, 2002). The current debate in the UK on the proposals for the introduction of community treatment orders (CTOs) and of the preventive removal from the community of people diagnosed as having antisocial personality disorder highlights the direction in which the British government wishes to go, following that of many North American states and Australia (Brophy, Campbell and Healy, 2003, Hiday and Scheid-Cook, 1989, Home Office and the Department of Health,1999). Continental Europe has not gone down the same route as the English-speaking world in terms of risk avoidance. None of the EU countries apart from Britain has legislated for CTOs, and the issue of risk avoidance does not seem to preoccupy their politicians, professionals or informal carers. The statistics of self harm and harm to others are often unreliable, but there is little to suggest that the rate of such incidents is lower in other Western European countries. Some of them – e.g. the Netherlands and the Scandinavian countries – have more developed alternatives to hospitalisation in a crisis, while others do not (e.g. Spain, France, Germany, Greece). Some countries – such as Italy – have developed more extensive methods of both solidarity and attention to underlying social issues, even though the level of financial benefits is lower than in Northern Europe. These approaches explain some of the reasons for the relative lack of interest in risk avoidance, but not all. There is some evidence that the media in Italy demonises people with severe mental illness less than in the UK (Ramon and Savio, 2000).

British MHSWs are the only group among social workers in Europe to have extended legal power and duties pertaining to risk avoidance in mental health. Since the introduction of the role of the Approved Social Worker (ASW) in 1983, ASWs have had to focus on their role in compulsory admission, which entails assessment through interviewing and documentary evidence, and reaching the decision as to whether to recommend such an admission or not in the light of availability of the least restrictive alternatives to hospitalisation, in conjunction with the decisions taken by psychiatrists and GPs (Barnes, Bowel, Newton and Fisher, 1990).

Insufficient time is left to engage even in the other tasks required by the legislation, such as following up clients, let alone in risk taking professional activities. While in the majority of cases the social worker is likely to recommend compulsory admission when a request for assessment has been made, in those minority cases in which the social worker does not recommend compulsory admission, s/he has to calculate – and take – the risk of what will happen to the client, to relatives and friends near to him/her, and to unknown others without such an admission. S/he needs also to calculate at any such application for compulsory admission the risk to the client from the admission itself – his/her self and social identity, relationships with others, the deprivation of civil rights during the admission, and the likelihood of drifting into a cycle of admissions and chronicity.

Care managers in countries such as Australia, Britain and Canada – likely to be social workers or nurses – collate evidence on risk and make decisions as to the boundaries of everyday life activities of service users.

Risk taking and risk avoidance issues are particularly acute for those, such as assertive outreach teams, or voluntary sector organisations (e.g. Turning Point, a British organisation focused on personalised work in the community with people who have mental illness and/or addiction). They are working with clients described as "hard to engage" in the community – people who have opted not to be in touch with statutory mental health services, usually after years of unsatisfactory contact from their perspective, who are nevertheless assessed as having serious mental health difficulties, and often also have substance misuse problems too.

In a recent study of four Turning Point projects, the key workers expressed their concerns about being on their own with the clients, while praising the ethos of the service and being mainly satisfied with the work they willingly engage with (Ramon, 2003b).

A recent research project (Williams, 2002) has highlighted the low morale among ASWs and the shortage in numbers in the north of England. If anything, one can predict that the situation in the rest of the country is at most no better, and is probably much worse in London, where the number of applications for compulsory admission is higher than elsewhere. The study does not go on to analyse the reasons for the low morale beyond the cumulative impact of an insufficient number of ASWs. I would argue that in addition to this burden, it is the nature of focusing on one narrow aspect of mental health work which contributes significantly to the low morale.

While ASW work has given MHSW more power (albeit largely of coercive nature), higher salary and greater prestige among mental health professionals, in its current stage it has also deprived them of the opportunity of engaging in the more caring, therapeutic, empowering and innovative work of which social workers are capable. Risk taking ranks high among the types of work ASWs have been discouraged from undertaking, as will be discussed below.

MHSW in continental Europe covers a wide range of emphases. In some countries these social workers focus on the financial eligibility of clients; in others they are part of a therapeutic team focusing on in-depth work with users and their families (e.g. Sweden), and/or they engage in building the links with relevant community groups (France, Germany), or in initiating and managing voluntary organisations (The Netherlands).

RISK AVOIDANCE PRACTICE AND POLICY ISSUES FOR USERS

It is important to identify risk avoidance practice and policy issues, as risk taking would be about reversing them in some instances. They include admission to a special environment where the user is under constant observation and supervision and deprived of his/her freedom of movement and association with others. The more confined the setting, the greater the threat to other patients and staff, as well as to the index user, as there are fewer alternatives in which to channel the tension.

Although it is recognised that the more occupied the patient is with pleasant activities the lower the level of risk, little by way of fun or stimulating activities is available in acute admission settings for high risk patients, as distinct from some more long-term secure settings.

Thus the *organisational facet* feeds on unhelpful attitudes and modes of working (Bowers, 2002). An erosion of belief in the value of the system and of professional contribution to it is likely to follow, leading to burn-out and cynicism. Indeed, the rate of staff retention on acute wards and high security services is poor. Consequently, what they offer to users is a distancing, controlling practice.

The importance of the *physical environment* to the sense of safety and consequently to feeling empowered has emerged as one of the most significant dimensions in a study of empowerment components on different wards (acute, rehabilitation, long term), in which the dimensions originated from interviews with users (Schafer, 2003).

Social workers are not usually based in acute admission wards, and hence are spared their impact. However, this turns them into outsiders from the ward staff's and users' perspectives.

The realisation that the high tariff settings are not the most effective ones for the purpose of negative risk reduction has led to the introduction of community treatment orders (CTOs) in Australia (Brophy, et al, 2003), Canada, New Zealand, the United States (Hiday, 1989) and the United Kingdom (Foster, 2002) (where they are currently titled "supervision orders" and "guardianship"). These are compulsory orders focused on where people should live, their presence in intervention settings, their daily activities, the control of their finances, and their entitlement to support additional to that provided to other people with mental health problems who are not subject to these orders. The major sanction for not obeying is a return to hospitalisation.

Mental health service users in all of the countries which have established CTOs of one type or another oppose this new invention, primarily on grounds of the deprivation of civil liberties. They see the CTOs as yet another facet of the *medicalisation* of mental illness as much as a mechanism of greater coercive control, and prefer interventions focused on personalised relationships between staff and users, mutual support, and safe crisis facilities in the community as alternatives to hospitalisation (May, Hartley and Knight, 2003).

Women users have been vocal in expressing their views about acute admission wards and high secure hospitals as *unsafe* places for women (Mental Health Media, 2003). When Labour came to power in Britain in 1997, the government promised the end of wards in which accommodation is shared by men and women, and the forced socialisation of women with men on such premises. Thus far, however, little has been achieved in phasing out mixed wards. This raises the issue, which is embarrassing and difficult to confront, of users harming other users, and of a philosophy which women see as harmful.

Black users' and carers' associations, and a number of both black and white professionals, have protested since the 1980s against the fact that black people, especially young black men, are more likely to be compulsorily admitted, over-medicated, and less likely to be given talk therapies than white users (Thomas, Stone, Osborn, Thomas and Fisher, 1993).

People to whom a diagnosis of *personality disorder* has been attributed have become the newest group to be stigmatised by the British media, but not in continental Europe. A study in which user researchers with personality disorder interviewed other users with the label has demonstrated this (Ramon, Castillo and Morant, 2001, Castillo, 2002). Most of the respondents reported being treated considerably less well after being given the diagnosis than before. More subtle differences emerge when their own perceptions of their difficulties are compared with the diagnosis. Eighty per cent of the respondents reported depression and impact of child abuse as their major problems, and the same percentage had depression or anxiety attributed as their secondary diagnosis, while having personality disorder as their first (Castillo 2002). It is likely that what has tilted the professional decision in the direction of PD rather than that of depression relates to assumed risk to others and self, coupled with moral apprehension about their socially unacceptable behaviour.

The issue of fear from potential violence lies behind the political agenda in the context of personality disorder. Fear of black young men is more rooted within professional practice, where it is not articulated as it is embarrassing for mental health professionals, many of whom are from ethnic minorities, to admit to accepting racist beliefs. Although women constitute a clear majority of mental health professionals, the overwhelming focus on risk within acute and secure facilities leads to a particular type of blindness to the impact of admission to these same facilities.

POLICY ISSUES FOR CARERS

A recent study of ASWs, users and the Nearest Relative (NR) (the nominated relative who has some legal powers within the British legislation to ask and agree to compulsory admission and discharge) (Rapaport, 2003) has illustrated the element of poor communication and poor information-giving in potential risk situations between the NRs and the ASWs who have the responsibility to provide this information. This process is taking place against a background of increased tension between users and their relatives, which in part has led to the request for an assessment for compulsory admission, at times to a sense of being betrayed by the users, and being neglected and unheard by the NR, who feels unable to achieve any positive conflict resolution. In addition, the legal information is written in a language incomprehensible by lay people, and receiving it in at a time of crisis is doomed to failure.

Carers perceive professionals' attempts to not share information with them, and to doubt their perspective on what is happening to their family member, as indications of disrespect of their contribution and of attempts to exclude them as key people in this context (Hugman and Pearson, 1995).

Carers in Anglo-Saxon countries seem to welcome CTOs as providing a much needed structure and support. In fact, organisations such as NAMI (National Alliance of the Mentally Ill) in the US have led the demand for CTOs. Yet the largest British carers' organisation, –

Rethink (formally the National Schizophrenia Fellowship) – has opposed the latest proposal to allow preventive hospital detention for people with antisocial personality disorder as a step too far in deprivation of civil liberties.

RISK TAKING

Value and Theory Framework

Attention was paid in the introduction to the integral part of risk taking to our lives, and especially to its emancipatory component. Given the justified focus on risk avoidance in the work with people experiencing mental ill health, the question as to the place of risk taking within this context becomes central. Risk taking within mental health is based on values which are an integral part of universally accepted social work values. The theoretical framework and the specific values are embedded in the following:

- The Strengths approach
- Social role valorisation
- The right to self determination
- The right to fail

The Strengths Approach

This approach was developed in the US by Saleebey (1992) and by Rapp for working with users of mental health services (Rapp, 1998), in the wake of psychiatric hospital closure in the late 1960s and early 1970s. The closure was in part premised on the belief that the resettled patients do not only have weaknesses, but also have abilities and potential that have not been utilised within the institution.

Within this approach the following is assumed:

- The focus is on individual strengths rather than pathology.
- Client-worker relationships are primary and essential.
- Interventions are based on client self-determination.
- Community is viewed as an oasis of resources, not as an obstacle.
- Aggressive outreach is the preferred mode of intervention.
- People suffering from severe mental illness can continue to learn, grow and change.

The focus on strengths rather than on pathology is not a tautology. It is a shift in emphasis which does not deny that people may have difficulties and problems, but accepts that unless we focus simultaneously on the abilities that they possess, we will not manage to reveal the latter and will not motivate users, carers and professional providers to focus on the strengths. This was revolutionary at the time, and remains so for a large number of lay and professionals who are yet to shift from the pathology-only position.

There are consequences of these assumptions in everyday practice, which entail:

– Paying more attention than before to enhancing the individualisation of clients
– Facilitating of partnership rather than adversary
– Fostering empowerment
– Blending societal, programmatic, and client goals

We will look at how these are in fact implemented in the practice examples section.

The protagonists of the strengths approach do not discuss social control or risk taking issues *per se*. The unabashed focus on assertive outreach perhaps indicates that the critique of this intervention as too intrusive in people's lives has either not been heard by them, or has been rejected without an open debate.

Social Role Valorisation

Social Role Valorisation (SRV) was developed within the field of learning difficulties by Wolfensberger in 1983 (Wolfensberger, 1983). This principle pinpoints disabled people's right to a socially valued place amidst the rest of us. It analyses the tragedy of institutionalisation as one which segregated residents from ordinary living and ordinary people, thus depriving them of opportunities to develop further their social and personal knowledge and skills, and in turn rendering them incapable and thus justifying the stigma attached to their disability by society (Ramon, 1991). The framework takes it for granted that people, including those disabled, have both weaknesses and strengths, abilities and disabilities. Those recognised as disabled may need more support to bring to the fore their abilities, and, for them to have a genuine place, our emphasis on economic success and work prestige needs to be revised to include basic human qualities such a loving and giving.

SRV has developed an audit of services which looks at whether these are enabling or disabling; do away with stigma or perpetuate it in the way they use language in connection with their users; the way the physical environment is giving the message of respect or lack of it; whether users have real choices in what is on offer to them or not. Wolfensberger used harsh words in describing the damage professionals do to disabled people, especially mental health professionals, by treating them as bundles of pathology.

This has impacted on the process and outcomes of psychiatric hospital closure and resettlement in some British settings (Wainwright, 1992), as well as on care management (Brandon D., Atherton, and Brandon A., 1996; Brandon, 1997).

SRV has been criticised as being too white and middle-class in its aspirations for disabled people. Also, it does not have a critical dimension concerning the type of social control which the adherence to a socially valued role brings with it. Issues of risk avoidance, however, have been part of its application to practice with a variety of disabled people. There, risk avoidance has been treated pragmatically, with minimum fuss and maximum respect to the disabled person.

SRV developed initially in Denmark, Sweden and Norway in the late 1950s and early 1960s, under the heading of normalisation and in the field of learning difficulties. Scandinavian social workers have therefore taken for granted this philosophy.

Although Italian social workers were not using the same terminology, the emphasis in the Italian psychiatric reform, from its inception in the late 1960s onwards, on full de-institutionalisation, de-stigmatisation, and full and respectful integration of people with mental illness into the community implied a very similar conceptual and value framework. If anything, the Italian perspective has been less psychologically focused in relation to mental ill health and more preoccupied with removing social barriers to the rehabilitation of people with mental illness, and the disruption of the connections between poverty and mental illness.

Self-determination and the Right to Fail

The right to self-determination is a core value specific to social work, guiding workers to enable service users to exercise choice as to every aspect of their lives. Rooted in an individualistic and liberal society, the potential conflict with socially desirable choices vs. individual choices has been handled early on in the literature of social work by arguing that there is always a range of choices which are compatible with both demands/requirements. This amounts to accepting social preferences as morally better than individual choices in principle. This principle has been criticised as "naïve" or hypocritical insofar as social workers are only too aware of the many constraints put on clients wanting to exercise their self-determination as against the views of professionals, not to mention constraints which arise out of their family and social background. Yet there are social workers who take this principle seriously and who do their best to enable clients to exercise it (McDermott, 1975).

This right is also a part of the legacy of social work, having been recognised as a principle subsumed under the right to self-determination in social work in Sawyer's 1975 article (Sawyer, 1975). Sawyer argued that it is both difficult and unrealistic to expect clients to grow and develop without taking calculated risks, and without failing from time to time. His argument is echoed in Brandon's writings (1991) for people with mental health problems.

I do not know of any other helping profession which accepts failure as a *right*, rather than as an inevitable price we may pay when our calculated risk-taking strategy has failed. This recognition within social work does not necessarily mean that most social workers enable the exercise of this right, but it does mean that the issue is acknowledged and at times debated. In the original discussion, Sawyer looked at the underlying reasons which prevent social workers from enabling their clients to exercise this right. These include:

- the wish to protect the client from new failure, given that many of them would come with a history of failures;
- the wish to protect one's professional reputation as someone who fosters success and prevents failure;
- the fear that the client will collapse if s/he failed yet again.

All of these reasons are highly relevant within the field of mental health, and underline the focus on risk avoidance. However, those who accept the principles of strengths and SRV would consider that people experiencing mental ill health can take calculated risks with more support than other people would need, rather than that they should not take any risks.

It is only when *calculated* risk taking is allowed to be considered that the right to fail can be exercised. Socially, our attitude to people who fail when they take a risk is less favourable than it should be logically. More often than not they are blamed for miscalculating the risk and therefore for the failure. Often, those who knew them well at the height of their success are ashamed to be seen with them at the time of failure. As a society, it would seem that we are thus afraid of failure.

TYPES OF RISK TAKING

Risk taking is necessary in each aspect of mental health where the primary purpose is that of improving the quality of life of service users; yet each aspect brings with it somewhat different issues and considerations. A secondary purpose is that of improving the quality of the working life of front-line workers.

Below, I shall look at a number of relevant examples of projects established by British MHSWs, attempting to tease out the issues related to risk taking.

a. *Training and engaging local women* as leaders of groups of isolated women by the Family Welfare Association (FWA) in the 1970s.

   This project was the first to apply the lessons of George Brown's work on the social origins of depression (Brown and Harris, 1978) by training local women in two London boroughs to lead groups of women who were single parents and isolated. The meetings took place at the leaders' homes, and were run as a social event which enabled discussion. Refreshments and child-minding were on offer. The projects were successful in enabling the participants to create their own social networks and thus to reduce the level of isolation and vulnerability by using very modest means.

   Running these groups entailed risk taking for the leaders, the participants, and the social workers at the FWAs who were responsible for them. The main risk taken was believing that a six-week training module was sufficient to enable the lay leaders to run a group of vulnerable people, yet it worked well and empowered the local community (Knight, 1978).

   This has been one of the few preventive measures taken at a level in which the lay community could actively participate.

b. *Creating the first user forum* in mental health (Iris Nutting, then team leader of Camden mental health team at Friern Hospital) in the early 1980s.

   Responding to the beginning of the process of hospital closure, Ms. Nutting – literally on her own with one volunteer who did not work for social services – decided to establish this first forum. She invited some of the more articulate ex-patients of Friern, who were also members of Camden Mind, for a consultation process around the closure policy, aiming to achieve a policy recommendation document.

   The results surpassed these expectations. Not only did the users prepare the document, but many of them became involved in the management of resettlement projects in the area, and a number moved on to become leaders of the British user movement. One became a qualified social worker; another a researcher who is running a user-led research unit.

The risk taken here was that the users might not live up to the challenge, might not come on a regular basis, might not find the policy exercise useful, or might have a mental health crisis and not come back (indeed some participants had a crisis, but most of them did come back).

c. *The Chesterfield support network,* in which users run their own groups within a large community centre and are members of the centre's management committee since 1982 (Hennelly 1990).

This service enables the users to run their own activities on their own, inclusive of budget and constitution. Paid workers are available for individual consultation if needed. It is based in a generic community centre, and its users send representatives to the management committee of that centre.

The risk taken is to put to the test the Strengths approach by letting users lead their own groups, within an environment which is ordinary and not geared specifically to the needs of users with mental health problems.

Users are proud of the achievements of the network, which are theirs not less than the workers'.

d. *Residential crisis facilities* (Greenwich, 1980s, Kettering, 1990s).

These facilities were established by social services, offering both a drop-in and a respite option.

Although psychiatrists come on a sessional basis, they are not staff members. People in crisis require considerable attention, and things can go wrong in terms of harm to self and property, and less so in harm to others. Indeed, the Greenwich facility closed down after a couple of years due to the burnout of its staff group (Brangwen, 1990), while the Kettering facility is still going strong. Perhaps the differences lie in the type of support provided to the workers.

Such facilities top the users' agenda as an alternative to hospitalisation when in crisis.

e. *The Building Bridges project* (Diggins, 2000) began in the late 1990s. It offers children and parents (who have a mental illness) tailor-made support of different kinds.

This project was initiated in a south London borough by senior social workers in consultation with users and members of other professions, in response to the high number of black children going into care when their parents had a mental health crisis. It is run by a voluntary organisation with joint funding and initial Department of Health funding. The project offers casework, counselling, group work, weekends away and liaison with schools. The main feature is ensuring that each member of the family is attended to and gets the intervention method appropriate to her/his needs.

The risk taken here include child protection going wrong, parents who may harm their children, and children whose growth may be harmed by staying with the parent who has a mental illness. The project takes care of young carers, and enables parents to remain in the parenting role.

This project provides both measures of risk avoidance and risk taking, preventive and crisis response.

f. *The Family Group Conference* in mental health project as a risk taking enterprise.

The Family Group Conference follows the New Zealand Maori custom in which the community elders made joint decisions, having listened to each individual involved. Family and friends are invited to a meeting or series of meetings if need be, chaired by an independent chairperson. They are informed of the concerns raised by the professionals and the range of available options to meet these concerns. The family group decisions are to be followed by the professionals too.

In the Essex Social Services project (2002) the focus has been on an adult with serious mental health problems in Essex, and his/her family and friends. These meetings are perceived as high, but worthwhile, risk due to a three-fold baseline reasoning. When they are taking place, the family group has reached the point of "no-return", as the adult, or a child, may have to be taken out of the family, symbolising the family group's failure to look after itself and its own. It is judged that without a real shake-up no change is going to take place; the meetings can shake up and unstuck the "status quo" in which the group has been paralysed or acting in a destructive way, even though this is a high risk-taking strategy.

Negative risks may entail the following:

- Some family members have come reluctantly.
- Painful secrets may be revealed.
- The level of pain will be so high that the family group will never be able to work together again.
- The group is unable to reach a decision.
- The decision reached is beyond the menu of possibilities outlined by the professionals.
- However, if the risk taking is successful, then:
- Group members came because they care about each other.
- Good experiences will be shared too.
- The group discovers it has more strengths than it thought before the meeting.
- The group reached a decision shared by most members.
- The decision is within the menu of possibilities outlined by professionals.

It is assumed that with the shake-up that the family group conference brings about, the abilities within the family group have a much better chance of coming to the fore, even though the emotional burden has not been worked through. With an agreement, a commitment to put it into action, and a sense of ownership of the solution, as well as of being in control, there is a much better chance that things will move in the right direction.

The specific study of sixteen family group conferences demonstrates positive views of the process, and bodes well for the future, which was bleak up to the point of having the family group conference. It also highlights the fact that carers can be meaningful and equal partners to major decision-making.

g. *User researchers and risk taking*

Encouraging mental health service users and enabling them to become researchers is a risk taking strategy insofar as the following may happen:

- Users may drop out during the training due to personal crisis or disillusionment with research.
- The research work with other users may lead them to reliving painful experiences.
- They may be less good researchers than fully qualified ones, and hence carry out their research work at a lower level of quality than qualified researchers.

As against these risks stands the wish to redress the serious imbalance in our knowledge about mental ill health and mental health services, namely the fact that most of our current knowledge has not included users' perspectives, and if anything had invalidated their perspectives.

Furthermore, the perceiving of users as researchers can be contemplated only by those believing in the Strengths approach, in the ability of users to learn to the sophisticated level most research tasks require within a short time, and in the validity of users' views.

It therefore becomes a challenge – or a risk taking strategy – to develop good enough support networks and project methods to reduce the risks outlined above, while enhancing users' abilities to be good researchers (Castillo, 2002, Ramon, 2003).

Summary

Risk is an emotive issue in mental health practice, as well as for the lay public in all European societies. The emotive layer relates to the fear that the unpredictable behaviour of people experiencing mental illness will lead to physical hurt of others primarily, but also of themselves, pushing into the direction of risk avoidance.

Nevertheless, I hope a convincing case has been made in this chapter as to:

- why risk taking is inherent in mental health social work;
- why it should be focused upon and developed further;
- the fact that it can be carried out while taking into account risk avoidance issues, but without letting the latter dictate the agenda.

Social workers are better equipped than other mental health professionals to do so, as they have the initial values, the knowledge and the skills required, and a history of doing so successfully. Yet the retrenchment into risk avoidance, canonised by the role of the ASW, has meant that very little of their time and energy is spent on this necessary element of good mental health work, despite the historical legacy.

I would like to argue that it is high time to re-claim this ground, at a time when the mental health system has become more open to preventive and promoting mental health work, and at the time when the role of social workers in mental health is re-examined. As we know well, this shift would require the commitment of social workers first and foremost, as other professions are keen to claim this ground for themselves.

REFERENCES

Barnes, M./Bowl, R./Fisher, M. (1990): *Sectioned*; London: Routledge.

Beck, U. (1992): *The Risk Society*; London: Sage.

Bowers, L. (2002): *Dangerous and Severe Personality Disorder – Response and Role of the Psychiatric Team;* London: Routledge.

Brandon, D./Atherton, K./Brandon, A. (1996): *Handbook of Care Planning; London*: Positive Publications.

Brandon, D. (1997): *The Trick of Being Ordinary;* Cambridge: Anglia Polytechnic University.

Brangwyn, G. (1990): *Constructing a Crisis-Focused Social Service*; in: Ramon, S. (ed.) Psychiatry in Transition, London: Pluto Press.

Brophy, L./Campbell, J./Healy, B. (2003): Dilemmas in the Case Manager's Role – Implementing Involuntary Treatment in the Community; in: *Special Edition on Psychiatry, Psychology and Law of the Journal of the Australian and New Zealand Association of Psychiatry,* Psychology and Law.

Brown, G.W., Harris. T. (1978): *The Social Origins* of Depression; London: Tavistock Publications.

Bunce, D./West, M.A. (1996): Stress Management and Innovation Interventions at Work; in: *Human Relations*, 49, 209-232.

Campbell, J. et al (2001): The Management and Supervision of Approved Social Workers – Aspects of Law, Policy and Practice; in: *The Journal of Social Welfare and Family Law*.

Castillo, H. (2003): *Personality Disorder: Trauma or Temperament?*; London: Jessica Kingsley.

Department of Health (1999): *The National Service Framework for Mental Health*; London: HMSO.

Diggins, M. (2000): Innovation as a Professional Way of Life – the Building Bridges Project for Parents-Users of Mental Health Services and their Children; in: Ramon, S. (ed.) *A Stakeholder Approach to Innovation in Mental Health Services*, Brighton: Pavilion.

Essex Social Services Department (2002): *Essex Family Group Conference in Mental Health*, Essex County Publications.

Ferguson, H. (2001): Social Work, Individualisation and Life Politics; in: *British Journal of Social Work*, 31, 41-55.

Foster, N. (2001): Involuntary Outpatient Commitment: Managing Mental Health Risks the New Hampshire Way; in: *Journal of Mental Health and Learning Disabilities Care*, 4, 11.

Foster, N. (2002): Control, Citizenship and "Risk" in Mental Health: Perspectives from UK, US and Australia; *Paper presented at the Socrates European Conference on Risk and Mental Health*, University College Cork, May 9th 2002.

Furedi, F. (1997): *Culture of Fear: Risk-Taking and the Morality of Low Expectation*; London: Cassell.

Giddens, A. (1991): *Modernity and Self-identity*; Cambridge: Polity Press.

Healy, B./Brophy, L. (2002): Law, Psychiatry and Social Work; in: Swain, P.A. *The Shadow of the Law: The Legal Context of Social Work Practice*, New South Wales: The Federation Press.

Hennelly, R. (1990): Mental Health Resource Centres; in: Ramon, S. (ed.) *Psychiatry in Transition*; London: Pluto Press.

Hiday, V.A./Scheid-Cook, T.L. (1989): A Follow-up of Chronic Patients Committed to Outpatient Treatment; in: *Hospital and Community Psychiatry*, 40, 4, 52-58.

Home Office and the Department of Health (1999): *Managing Dangerous People with Severe Personality Disorder: Proposal for Policy Development*; London: HMSO.

Hugman, G./Pearson, G. (1995): *The Silent Partners*; London: National Schizophrenia Fellowship.

Knight, C. (178): *Neighbourhood Support Groups*; London: Family Welfare Association.

May, R./Hartley, J./Knight, T. (2003): Making the Personal Political; in the *Psychologist*, 16, 4, 182-183.

McDermott, R. (ed.) (1975): *Self Determination in Social Work*; London: Routledge and Kegan Paul.

Mental Health Media (2003): What Women Want – Mainstreaming Women's Mental Health; Mental Health Media, *www.mhmedia.com.*

Rose, N. (2000): *Powers of Freedom – Reframing Political Thought*; Cambridge: Cambridge University Press.

Ramon, S. (ed.) (1991): *Beyond Community Care – Normalisation and Integration Work*; Basingstoke: Mind Macmillan.

Ramon, S. /Savio, M. (2000): A Scandal of the 80ws and 90s – Media Representations of Mental Illness Issues in Britain and Italy; in: Ramon, S. (ed) *A Stakeholder's Approach to Innovation in Mental Health Services: A Reader for the 21st Century*, Brighton: Pavilion Publishing.

Ramon, S./Castillo, H. Morant, N. (2001): Experiencing Personality Disorder – A Participative Research; in: *International Journal of Social Psychiatry*, 41, 4, 1-15.

Ramon, S. (2003a) (ed): *Users Researching Health and Social Care – An Empowering Agenda?;* Birmingham: Venture Press.

Ramon, S. (2003b): *Evaluating Three Turning Point Projects – A Multi-stakeholder Perspective*; Unpublished Report, July.

Rapaport, J. (2003): The Ghost of the Nearest Relative under the Mental Health Act 1983 – Past, Present, and Future; in: *Journal of Mental Health Law*, 51-65.

Rapp, C.A. (1998): *The Strengths Model – Case Management with People Suffering from Severe and Persistent Mental Illness*; Oxford University Press.

Rose, N. (2000): *Powers of Freedom – Reframing Political Thought*; Cambridge: Cambridge University Press.

Saleebey, D. (ed.) (1992): *The Strengths Approach in Social Work Practice*; Longman.

Sawyer, P. (1975): The Right to Fail; in: McDermott, R. (ed.) *Self Determination in Social Work*, London: Routledge and Kegan Paul.

Schafer, T. (2003): Researching Empowerment; in: Ramon, S. (ed.) *Users Researching Health and Social Care: An Empowering Agenda*, Birmingham: Venture Press.

Shera, W./Healy, B./Aviram, U./Ramon, S. (2002): Mental Health Policy and Practice – A Multi-country Comparison; in: *Journal of Health and Mental Health Social Work*, 35, 1-2, 547-575.

Thomas, C.S./Stone, K./Osborn, M./Thomas, P./Fisher, M. (1993): Psychiatric Morbidity and Compulsory Admission among UK-Born Europeans, Afro-Caribbeans and Asians in Central Manchester; in: *British Journal of Psychiatry*, 163, 91-99.

Wainwright, T. (1992): The Changing Perspective of a Resettlement Team; in: Ramon, S. (ed.) *Psychiatric Hospital Closure – Myths and Realities*, London: Chapman Hall.

Williams, C. (2002): A *Survey of Approved Social Work Services*; Durham: Northern Centre for Mental Health.

Wolfensberger, W. (1983): The Principle of Social Role Valorisation; in: *Mental Retardation*, 21,6, 234-9.

In: Psychology of Decision Making in Risk Taking ...   ISBN 978-1-60021-854-5
Editor: Rachel N. Kelian   © 2008 Nova Science Publishers, Inc.

Chapter 10

DO OUTSIDER-DOMINATED BOARDS AND LARGE BOARD SIZE CURTAIL FIRM RISK TAKING?

Michael Graham[a] and Alfred Yawson[b]

[a]School of Economics, Finance and Marketing, Royal Melbourne Institute of Technology (RMIT) University,
Melbourne, Victoria 3001, Australia
[b]School of Banking and Finance, The University of New South Wales,
Sydney, NSW 2052 Australia

ABSTRACT

This chapter examines the impact of board composition and board size on three firm risk taking variables; strategy risk, stock returns risk, and income instability risk. There is recognition in the literature that corporate governance processes need to encompass mechanisms for motivating board and managerial behavior towards enhancing firm risk taking. Agency theory and regulatory recommendations advocate for an increasingly greater roles for outsiders on the board of directors. The evidence documented here indicates a positive relationship between majority independent board composition and firm risk taking. The literature also suggests board size affects firm activities independent of other board attributes and that there are biases against risk taking as board size grows. We do not, however, find any evidence to support the proposition that large board size influences firm risk taking. Thus, whereas the recommendation of increasing independent members on board of directors by regulatory bodies as well as the Cadbury (1992) and Hampel (1998) facilitate wealth creation by firms, the total representation on the board of directors does not exert any measurable influence on firms' wealth creation.

Keywords: agency theory, board of directors, board size, corporate governance, risk taking, firm enterprise.

1. INTRODUCTION

Short et al (1999) provide a framework of corporate governance and stress the need for governance processes to encompass mechanisms for motivating managerial behavior towards increasing the wealth of the business. That is, to enhance economic enterprise activities or risk-taking[1]. Firm risk-taking is generally a high risk-high return strategy that is attractive to stockholders given that they expect a positive effect on performance. Furthermore, stockholders can reduce their inherent risk by diversifying their investment portfolios.

Agency theory assigns the task of checking self-serving and value-decreasing behaviors by managers to the board, and in particular outside members of the board of directors. Generally, there is the expectation that board of directors composed primarily of outside directors should be superior to boards composed of insider directors in minimizing agency cost and contributing to managerial effectiveness and organizational performance. This view is supported by a number of empirical studies (see e.g. Baysinger and Butler 1985 for outside directors and firm performance, Weisbach 1988 for CEO turnover, Byrd and Hickman 1992 for tender offer bids, and Brickley et al. 1994 for poison pill adoptions and control auctions). Along this line, Rosenstein and Wyatt (1990) document positive investor reactions to appointment of outside directors. An important development on this front relates to recent regulatory activity in many countries, for example Finland, UK, and Australia that recommends that majority of the board of listed firms should be outside directors.[2] The root of this recommendation can be traced to the Cadbury (1992) and the Hampel (1998) reports.

A critical agency issue involving the recommendation of greater representation by independent directors on the board of listed firms as a means of minimizing agency cost that has not been given much attention in the literature is their impact on firm risk taking. We believe this is an important area that needs evidencing and this chapter examines this issue. Furthermore, this chapter investigates the impact of board size on firm risk taking. The number of directors on a board has been theorized to affect corporate governance independent of other board attributes. Jensen (1993) theorizes that boards of directors that are too large may not be able to operate effectively because the co-ordination and information processing problems outweigh the advantages of having a large number of people to draw on. Lipton and Lorsch (1992) point to the dysfunctional nature of board intra-relations and deliberations and suggest curbing board size. This suggestion is based on the conviction that the problems associated with the dysfunctional nature of the board are amplified as board size gets larger. Although Lipton and Lorsch's (1992) recommendation did not specify the optimal board size, the proposal amounts to a supposition that even if the board's capacity for monitoring increases with its size, the benefits are outweighed by such costs as biases against risk-taking.

The Cadbury (1992) and Hampel (1998) reports have shaped the various changes in corporate governance principles and practices around the world. However, to the best knowledge of the authors, the academic literature has not captured the relationships studied in this chapter prior to the last of the two reports. For this reason, this chapter limits the data used in the empirical analysis to the year 1998 to capture important aspects of the

---

[1] Enterprise activities and risk-taking are used interchangeably to mean the same thing in this chapter.

[2] See, for example, corporate governance recommendation of The Nordic Exchange and the Australian Stock Exchange.

relationships that led to the recommendation of having majority outsiders on firms' board of directors.

Miller and Bromiley (1990) suggest that firm risk taking measures used in the literature can be grouped into three categories: income instability risk, strategic risk, and stock return risk. Following that, this chapter studies the effect of board composition and board size on these three measures of firm enterprise. This chapter examines the issues raised above using data from Finland.

We find a positive relationship between outside dominated board of directors and firm risk taking when the relevant measures of risk taking are the proxies for stock returns (measured by beta) and strategic (measured by capital intensity). Board composition relates differently to different risk taking measures and the relationship is strongest when the relevant risk measure is capital intensity. There is no evidence found to support the assertion that board size influences firm risk taking. This chapter contributes to the body of empirical literature that examines whether boards of directors, affect firm enterprise activities. Mayer (1997 p.152) remarked that "corporate governance has become a subject on which opinion has drowned fact". To play a part in enhancing factual representation in the subject, the findings in this chapter add to the existing stock of empirical knowledge on how some elements of the governance process may influence the economic performance of companies. The contributions of this chapter to the existing literature enhance our understanding of the governance process and business prosperity, an important aspect of corporate performance.[3]

The remainder of the chapter is structured as follows: We examine agency theory and firm control and follow that up by looking into the impact of outsider-dominated boards on firm enterprise. We then investigate board size and firm enterprise. The sample construction, methodology and results from our empirical investigations follow. We then conclude the chapter.

2. AGENCY THEORY AND FIRM CONTROL

Agency theory views the board as a potentially effective element of corporate governance and, hence internal control (Fama and Jensen 1983). The issue of control is very important in agency theory, where the traditional interest lies in contracting. Agency theory considers the optimal contract form for that ubiquitous control relationship in which the principal delegates work to the agent (the principal-agent relationship is mediated by the board of directors). Eisenhardt (1985) formalize the agency problem that determines the optimal contract for the agent's service. The theory can be stated in two cases. Firstly, when the behavior of the agent is observed, a behavior-based contract is optimal because the agent's behavior is the purchased commodity. In this case, there is complete information. The two parties, principal and the agent, know what the agent has done. The second is a situation of incomplete information. Agents are aware of their behavior but the principal is not. A quandary arises because the principal cannot determine if the agent has acted appropriately. If the agent is to be rewarded based upon agreed job behaviors, but without confirmation of those behaviors by

---

[3] For example, the literature suggests that earlier studies involving board size have centred on its effect on CEO compensation (see e.g., Holthausen and Larcker 1993), and firms performance (see for instance, Yermack 1996, Eisenberg et al. 1998, and Conyon and Peck 1998).

the principal, the agent may shirk. Given this, the agent cannot be relied on to perform as agreed. In this case of incomplete information, the principal has two alternatives to put things right. First, information about the agent's behaviors could be purchased and rewards directed at those behaviors. This requires employing surveillance mechanisms such as cost accounting measures, budgeting systems, or additional layers of management. On the other hand, the principal can reward the agent based on outcomes (e.g., profitability). Such outcomes are surrogate measures for behaviors. In this alternative, however, the agent is rewarded or punished for outcomes partially outside his or her control. That is, good results could be attained despite poor efforts and poor results can occur despite good efforts.

Agency theory, thus, suggests two underlying strategies of control. These are behavior-based and outcome-based strategies of control. Both of these strategies rely on performance evaluation. Performance-based control strategies emphasize monitoring, evaluating, and rewarding an agent's performance and thus focus on the information aspect of control. Agents' performance can be evaluated on inferences concerning the quality of their decisions or on the measurable outcomes of decision-making process. Senior level corporate managers make decisions under uncertainty that are not programmable as other non-managerial tasks. Hence, following Baysinger and Hoskisson (1990), the terms strategic controls and financial controls, respectively, are used in this paper to convey behavioral and outcome control concepts in the context of controlling corporate managers. Gupta (1987) describes what is referred to here as strategic control in terms of openness in the relationship between corporate-level managers and division managers and the willingness of management to rely on subjective information when evaluating division managers' performances. That is, under a system of strategic controls, division managers are evaluated on the basis of how strategically desirable their decisions were before implementation and on the basis of performance of the firm after the decisions were implemented. On the other hand, in a system employing financial controls, managers are evaluated solely on the basis of their success in meeting performance criteria. Given the detailed nature of strategic controls, putting them into practice requires the controller to have more information than is required for implementing financial controls.

3. OUTSIDER-DOMINATED BOARDS OF DIRECTORS AND FIRM RISK TAKING

The effect independent members of the board of directors have on firm enterprise activities flow from the control strategies they adopt in monitoring firm management, including the direction the firm takes in its risk taking activities. The composition of the board of directors determines the control strategies employed. Baysinger and Hoskisson (1990) suggest that outside directors usually have different types of information from inside directors. Hence, they are likely to differ in the control strategies they employ to advance firm events. Inside directors, in their position as participants in the decision processes, have access to information relevant to assessing strategic desirability of enterprise activities, regardless of their long or short run performance outcomes. Given that insiders and the CEO frequently interact in ways that are relevant to assessing the quality of the decision-making process, relations between the two parties are more likely to be open and subjective. Hence, in terms of information processing, it could be expected that the inside party of any board would evaluate firm enterprise proposals on the basis of strategic controls.

The outside board members usually have few of these informational advantages and this reduces the likelihood of using strategic controls. Outside directors, by definition, have limited contact with the day-to-day decision process of the firm. Their evaluation of firm processes and enterprise activities is limited to board interaction, at which point the strategic plans may be at their final stage, needing only ratification by the board. Thus, in terms of information processing, Baysinger and Hoskisson (1990) suggest that outside directors lack the type of subjective information needed for evaluating managerial decisions. Jensen (1993) also points to the severe information problems that limit the effectiveness of outside board members. For example, the top management of firms headed by the CEO almost always determines the information given to the board. This limitation on information severely hinders the ability of even highly talented outside board members to significantly contribute to the evaluation of company's risk taking strategy.

It must be noted that outside directors may be able to reach detached conclusion about quality of firm's wealth creation strategies through years of experience. However, Mintzberg et al. (1976) suggest that the very nature of strategic risk taking decisions makes them unique and unstructured. Consequently, for outside directors to fully appreciate the quality of decisions, they may need supplemental experience with that firm's process. This knowledge is what is not available to the truly independent outside director. On the other hand, outside directors who are former executives of the firm will be well informed. However, such directors are not truly independent and advocates for outside directors in the composition of the board of directors have independent outsiders in mind. Hence, former company employees do not fit into the category of outsiders on the board of directors. Consequently, whereas relations between inside directors and top management may be open and subjective, relations between outside directors and top management in discussing firm enterprise activities may be more objective and formulaic. In other words, it is expected that the predominance of outside directors on boards will be associated with financial controls in board-management relations. Along these lines, Hoskisson et al. (1995) argue that outside directors may favor expansion, a risk taking action, via external means, such as acquisitions to enter new markets as these are better suited to evaluation using financial criteria.

Given the type of information available to outside directors and their likely emphasis on financial controls, outsider-dominated boards may skew the direction of managerial effort away from optimally risky strategies that many shareholders prefer and the long-term orientation that is required for competitive advantage. From the perspective of top management, financial controls correlate managerial rewards directly with short-term variations in the market value of the firm (see e.g. Demski 1987, Gupta 1987). Functionally, this is achieved either by disciplinary practices that are highly sensitive to short-term cash flow, net profit, growth, or market share results or by compensation schemes that tie much of the pecuniary rewards to quarterly earnings (see Baysinger and Hoskisson 1990). Along the same line of reasoning, Fischel and Bradley (1986) discuss behavioral implications of alterations in corporate law, which increases management's liability for short-term performance declines. They argue that if managers are penalized whenever risk taking decisions that were optimal ex ante turn out poor ex post, they will tend to avoid risky projects.

Increasing managers' liability for financial performance in the short run may increase their diligence in maximizing short-term profits. It may, however, lessen their incentive to take risks and enhance firm enterprise activities. A greater outsider representation on the board of directors may have the same effect because the insiders' influence on the decision-control process is reduced. This chapter examines this relationship.

4. BOARD SIZE AND FIRM RISK TAKING

This chapter also examines the relationship between board size and firm risk taking. The board of directors, at the apex of the internal control system, has the responsibility for the firm's risk taking activities. There is the recognition that an active board can improve decision-making and, thus, firm enterprise activities. John and Senbet (1998) argue that the effectiveness of board is determined, among other things, by its size. Lipton and Lorsch (1992) and Jensen (1993) contend that board size affects corporate governance and firm activities independent of other board attributes. Their arguments focus on the productivity losses that arise when work groups grow large, an insight borrowed from organizational behavior research such as Hackman (1990). Jensen (1993) states that "… as groups increase in size they become less effective because the coordination and process problems overwhelm the advantage from having people to draw on…" Lipton and Lorsch (1992) also state that ". . . the norms of behavior in most boardrooms are dysfunctional", because directors rarely criticize the policies of top managers or hold candid discussions about corporate performance, including the direction of firm enterprise activities. Jensen (1993) further suggests that larger boards lead to less candid discussion of firm enterprise direction. This situation arises because, according to Jensen (1993), there is "great emphasis on politeness and courtesy at the expense of truth and frankness in boardrooms". This implies that firms with large boards can reduce the board's ability to resist CEO control of firm agenda. Yermack (1996) suggests that "… CEO performance incentives provided by the board through compensation and the threat of dismissal operate less strongly as board size increases…"

Indeed empirical results presented by Yermack (1996), Eisenberg et al. (1998), and Conyon and Peck (1998) suggest that board size affects firm profitability in both large and small firms. To reduce the problems of communication and co-ordination and the decreased ability of the board to set firm agenda, including risk taking, Lipton and Lorsch (1992) recommend limiting the membership of boards of directors. Implicitly this suggests costs, such as biases against risk taking, to large board sizes.

5. SAMPLE CONSTRUCTION AND METHODOLOGY

Data is collected over a nine-year period, from 1990 to 1998, with focus on two sample periods, 1994 and 1998, for the empirical analyses. The estimation of the variables used in this chapter includes all the years between 1990 and 1998. As noted above, the second of the two reports, namely the Cadbury Report (1992) and the Hampel Report (1998), that has significantly influenced global corporate governance principles and practices was published in 1998. Therefore, this chapter limits the data used in the empirical analysis to the year 1998 to capture an important aspect of the relationships that led to the recommendation of having majority outsiders on firms' board of directors.

Generally, firms are selected from publicly traded companies in Finland satisfying two basic data requirements. First, the firm is required to have ownership data available for each sample year. Data regarding board members, institutional investors and block owners are obtained from the respective firms' annual reports. A further requirement is that firms included in the dataset should have five consecutive fiscal years of stock market and financial statement data, including the focus year, for each sample. The final sample consists of 48 firms in the 1994 sample and 68 firms in the 1998 sample.

Following previous research (for example, Gilson 1990 and Zahra 1996), this chapter considers outside directors as those who are not former employees (officers) of a firm or its subsidiaries (divisions), or do not possess contractual relationship with it. The only formal association between the outside directors and the firm are their duties as directors. The outsider-dominated boards are those boards that have higher numbers of independent outside directors than inside board members. In other words, it is measured by dividing the number of independent outside directors by the total number of directors on a board. The samples for years 1994 and 1998 are both dominated by outsider-dominated boards. There are 43 outsider-controlled boards in the 1994 sample, representing 89.6% of the firms in consideration, and 58 outsider-controlled boards in the 1998 sample, representing 85% of the firms under consideration. Data on the board of directors are accessed from the respective firm publication (annual reports). Table 1 presents summary statistics on the board of directors. From Table 1, it could be seen that there were, in total, 215 outside directors in the 1994 sample and 358 outside directors in 1998.

The board size is the total number of persons on the board of directors. This number is also accessed from company publications (annual reports) for the respective years. Table 1 also presents a summary statistics of the variable board size (under all directors). The average number of directors on the board was about the same for the two sample periods, 6.5 and 6.6 for 1994 and 1998, respectively. There were, in total, 310 directors in 1994 and 453 directors in 1998.

Table 1. Summary statistics of the board of directors: 1994 and 1998

Variable	Mean	Median	STDEV	Mode	Min	Max	No. of directors	No. of firms
Panel A: 1994 Sample								
Outside directors	4.5	4	2.78	2	0	10	215	48
Inside directors	2	1	2.05	1	0	8	95	48
All directors	6.45	6	1.76	5	4	10	310	48
Panel B: 1998 Sample								
Outside directors	5.3	5	2.2	6	0	10	358	68
Inside directors	1.4	1	1.58	1	0	8	95	68
All directors	6.6	7	1.37	7	5	10	453	68

Outside directors are independent directors who have no affiliations with the firm. Inside directors are managers in the firm.

Following Miller and Bromiley (1990) this chapter uses 3 measures of risk-taking to examine the hypothesized relationships. These are the proxy for income stream risk (the standard deviation of return on equity (ROE)), the proxy for industry or strategic risk (capital intensity), and risk based on stock returns (beta). Analogous to the methodology employed by Bowman (1980 and 1982), and Miller and Bromiley (1990), the standard deviation of return on equity over a five-year period for each sample firm is used in calculating the proxy for income stream risk. Capital intensity is calculated as the ratio of total assets to sales. This variable is calculated as the mean value over a five-year period. Capital intensity increases risk in two ways (see for instance Brealey and Myers 2006, Shapiro and Titman 1986). If capital inputs are less variable than labor inputs in the short run, a company choosing to produce a given output with large amounts of capital and low amounts of labor increases its fixed costs and lowers its variable cost. The firm consequently will experience larger variations in profits if demand fluctuates (see Lev 1974 for a detailed derivation of this point). In addition, a firm using large amounts of capital runs a high risk of capital obsolescence-the possibility that technological change will make its capital investment worth little or nothing. Beta, the risk-taking measure for stock returns data, is estimated from the conventional market model regression equation (see Sharpe 1964) over a three-year period using weekly returns. In the capital asset pricing model (CAPM), systematic risk reflects the sensitivity of return on a firm's stock to general market movement. Table 2 presents a summary statistics for the variables used in this chapter.

Table 2. Summary statistics of risk taking measures and control variables

Variable	Mean	Median	Standard Deviation	Minimum	Maximum
Panel A: 1994 Sample					
ROE (STDV)	14.37	9.61	18.47	1.1	98.22
Capital intensity	1.99	1.16	2.84	0.52	14.96
Beta	0.81	0.84	0.3	0.17	1.5
Firm size	1070	423	1422	26	5840
CEO and board ownership	3.1	0.1	9.3	0.00	56.00
Panel B: 1998 Sample					
ROE (STDV)	8.03	4.07	17.15	0.903	43.18
Capital intensity	1.81	0.95	3.37	0.002	19.17
Beta	0.68	0.69	0.33	0.04	1.37
Firm size	1326	345	2840	21	15414
CEO and board ownership	7.4	0.37	14.3	0	61.2

The 1994 and 1998 samples included 48 firms and 68 firms, respectively. ROE (STDV) is the standard deviation of return on equity measured over a five year period; capital intensity is measured by the ratio of total assets to sales, averaged over a five year period. Beta is estimated from the conventional market model regression equation (see Sharpe 1964) over a three-year period using weekly returns Firm size is measured by total assets (millions of Euros). CEO and board ownership is the combined equity stakes held by the CEO and the board of directors (in percentage).

The methodology employed to examine the impact of outsider-dominated board of directors and board size on firm risk taking is a cross-sectional regression analysis in which firm enterprise activities is regressed against board composition and board size. The control variables introduced in the analysis pertain to equity ownership by the board and the CEO, firm size and industry effects. Board and CEO ownership is assessed from company annual reports. Total assets capture firm size effect. For the data period, firms were grouped into fourteen industrial classifications.[4] Due to the small sample size, we combined industries using industry relatedness as criteria and reduced the industry classification to three.

Following Wright et al. (1996), we investigate the relationship between board composition and board size on firm enterprise activities, by estimating equations (1) and (2), respectively:

$$Risk_{i,t}^z = \alpha_0^z + \alpha_1^z OU_{i,t} + \alpha_2^z FS_{i,t} + \alpha_3^z BCEO_{i,t} + \alpha_4^z d_{i,t}^1 + \alpha_5^z d_{i,t}^2 + \varepsilon_{i,t} \tag{1}$$

$$Risk_{i,t}^z = \alpha_0^z + \alpha_1^z BS_{i,t} + \alpha_2^z FS_{i,t} + \alpha_3^z BCEO_{i,t} + \alpha_4^z d_{i,t}^1 + \alpha_5^z d_{i,t}^2 + \varepsilon_{i,t} \tag{2}$$

where $Risk_{i,t}^z$ is the risk-taking measure (or enterprise activities) for firm i at time t where $z = 1$ for standard deviation of return on equity, $z = 2$ for capital intensity, and $z = 3$ for beta; $BS_{i,t}$ is board size variable (logarithm of board size); $OU_{i,t}$ is the fraction of independent board of members for firm i at time t; $FS_{i,t}$ is firm size (logarithm of total assets) for firm i at time t; $BCEO_{i,t}$ is the percentage of equity held by the board and the CEO for firm i at time t; $d_{i,t}^1$ is firm i classified in industry 1 at time t; $d_{i,t}^2$ is firm i classified in industry 2 at time t; $\varepsilon_{i,t}$ is the error term.

The regression models in equations (1) and (2) are estimated using ordinary least squares regressions (OLS). We estimate the models separately for 1994 and 1998. The standard errors are corrected for heteroscedasticity (White, 1980).

6. EMPIRICAL RESULTS AND DISCUSSION

Table 3 reports the results of the estimation model examining the relationship between board composition and firm risk taking. For the 1994 sample, we find a statistically positive relationship between the two variables both for the full model (model 3) and the model (model 2) where we estimate the relationship without any control variables. This findings only relate to risk taking measured by the proxy for stock returns risk. When firm enterprise is

---

[4] The classifications were chemical, construction, energy, food, forest, investment, media, metal and engineering, multi-business, trade, transport, telecom and electronics, other industries, and other services. We combined industries into three based on relatedness of the industries, taking into consideration the GICS.

Table 3. Effect of board composition on firm risk taking measures

	Standard deviation ROE		Beta		Capital intensity	
	Model 1	Model 2	Model 1	Model 2	Model 1	Model 2
Intercept						
1998	8.37***	9.36***	0.96***	0.25	0.51	8.22**
	(0.01)	(0.07)	(0.00)	(0.51)	(0.40)	(0.04)
1994	13.64***	30.88	0.60***	-0.18	1.81***	10.71**
	(0.01)	(0.21)	(0.00)	(0.45)	(0.01)	(0.03)
OU						
1998	-2.93	-1.21	-0.19	-0.23	1.69*	0.63
	(0.40)	(0.56)	(0.18)	(0.39)	(0.08)	(0.54)
1994	1.69	3.26	0.30**	0.26**	0.19	-0.37
	(0.82)	(0.68)	(0.03)	(0.04)	(0.83)	(0.73)
BCEO						
1998		0.14		-0.08		-0.07**
		(0.27)		(0.26)		(0.03)
1994		-0.26		0.01		-0.06*
		(0.28)		(0.11)		(0.07)
FS						
1998		-0.53		-0.81***		-0.06*
		(0.31)		(0.01)		(0.06)
1994		-2.39		0.10***		-0.89*
		(0.37)		(0.00)		(0.06)
d^1						
1998		2.68		0.03		-1.20**
		(0.27)		(0.76)		(0.04)
1994		1.12		0.02		-1.66**
		(0.84)		(0.80)		(0.05)
d^2						
1998		-0.12		0.44		-3.02***
		(0.94)		(0.32)		(0.01)
1994		1.66		-0.05		-2.75**
		(0.83)		(0.66)		(0.02)
Adjusted R^2						
1998	0.01	0.12	0.02	0.02	0.03	0.16
1994	0.02	0.07	0.08	0.23	0.02	0.22
Correlation						
1998		-0.12		-0.80		0.13
1994		-0.26		0.15		-0.16

Regression analyses, model:

$$Risk_{i,t}^z = \alpha_0^z + \alpha_1^z BS_{i,t} + \alpha_2^z FS_{i,t} + \alpha_4^z BCEO_{i,t} + \alpha_4^z d_{i,t}^1 + \alpha_5^z d_{i,t}^2 + \varepsilon_{i,t},$$ where $Risk_{i,t}^z$ is risk taking measure

for firm i at time t where $z=1$ for standard deviation of return on equity, $z=2$ for capital intensity, and $z=3$ for

beta, $BS_{i,t}$ is board size for firm i at time t, $FS_{i,t}$ is firm size (logarithm of total assets) for firm i at time t,

$BCEO_{i,t}$ is the percentage of equity held by the board and the CEO for firm i at time t, $d_{i,t}^1$ is firm i classified

in industry 1 at time t, $d_{i,t}^2$ is firm i classified in industry 3 at time t, $\varepsilon_{i,t}$ error term for firm i at time t.

Probability values are in parentheses: *** significance at 1%; ** significance at 5%; *significance at 10%. In model 1, we estimate equation (1) without control variables. We estimate the full model given in equation (1) in model (2). The correlation results reported related to the correlations between board composition and the 3 firm risk taking variables.

Table 4. Effect of board size on firm risk taking measures

	Standard deviation ROE		Beta		Capital intensity	
	Model 1	Model 2	Model 1	Model 2	Model 1	Model 2
Intercept						
1998	0.23	8.69	-0.86	-1.32	0.22	5.24*
	0.89	0.26	0.43	0.35	0.89	0.09
1994	47.35**	47.65*	0.48	0.27	4.3	10.34**
	0.04	0.08	0.14	0.32	0.13	0.03
BS						
1998	0.85	-0.46	0.89	1.17	0.84	0.4
	0.36	0.91	0.18	0.33	0.35	0.76
1994	-17.85	-13.63	0.17	-0.2	-1.27	0.05
	0.11	0.12	0.33	0.41	0.36	0.96
BCEO						
1998		0.15		-0.003		-0.07**
		0.25		0.73		0.02
1994		-0.28		0.007		-0.06**
		0.25		0.25		0.05
FS						
1998		-0.48		0.05		-0.67**
		0.38		0.4		0.05
1994		0.97		0.11***		-0.88**
		0.67		0.01		0.05
d^1						
1998		2.86		-0.55		0.97**
		0.16		0.35		0.04
1994		-0.04		0.03		-1.64**
		0.99		0.78		0.05
d^2						
1998		0.16		-0.61		2.9***
		0.92		0.3		0.01
1994		0.25		-0.08		-2.7
		0.97		0.5		0.02
Adjusted R-Square						
1998	0.01	0.12	0.02	0.02	0.01	0.16
1994	0.05	0.04	0.01	0.16	0.004	0.22
Correlation						
1998	-0.12		-0.04			0.05
1994	0.03		0.34			0.02

Regression analyses, model:

$$Risk_{i,t}^z = \alpha_0^z + \alpha_1^z BS_{i,t} + \alpha_2^z FS_{i,t} + \alpha_4^z BCEO_{i,t} + \alpha_4^z d_{i,t}^1 + \alpha_5^z d_{i,t}^2 + \varepsilon_{i,t},$$ where $Risk_{i,t}^z$ is risk taking measure for firm i at time t where $z=1$ for standard deviation of return on equity, $z=2$ for capital intensity, and $z=3$ for beta, $BS_{i,t}$ is board size for firm i at time t, $FS_{i,t}$ is firm size (logarithm of total assets) for firm i at time t, $BCEO_{i,t}$ is the percentage of equity held by the board and the CEO for firm i at time t, $d_{i,t}^1$ is firm i classified in industry 1 at time t, $d_{i,t}^2$ is firm i classified in industry 3 at time t, $\varepsilon_{i,t}$ error term for firm i at time t. Probability values are in parentheses: *** significance at 1%; ** significance at 5%; *significance at 10%. In model 1, we estimate equation (1) without control variables. We estimate the full model given in equation (1) in model (2). The correlation results reported related to the correlations between board size and the 3 firm risk taking variables

measured by proxies for capital intensity and income instability enterprise variables, the results suggest that board composition do not exert any significant influence on firm risk taking. The results for the 1998 sample, on the other hand only finds a statistically positive relationship when the relevant risk taking measure is capital intensity. We also conduct a non parametric test to examine the relationship between the board of directors and firm enterprise. As reported in Table 3, the levels of correlation between the firm risk taking and board composition are relatively low, with the exception of the correlation between beta and board composition for the 1998 sample, with inconsistent signs. Table 3 also reports results for the control variables. The results show firm size is negatively related to firm enterprise. The sign and statistical significance of the industry effects are shown to be inconsistent. The results also show a statistically negative relationship between board and CEO equity ownership and enterprise activities.

Jensen's (1993) proposition lends some support to the weak empirical findings reported in this section. Jensen (1993) suggests that the factors that motivate board of directors to take actions that create value are, in general, inadequate. Two focal points of Jensen's (1993) proposition could be discerned. The first is the threat of legal liabilities, like class action suits initiated by shareholders (lawsuits which are often activated by unexpected declines in stock price), often faced by board members could make them act to cover their interest. These legal liabilities are more often consistent with minimizing downside risk rather than maximizing value. Anecdotal evidence of Jensen's proposition is the lawsuit filed against the non-executive directors of Equity Life Insurers, United Kingdom. The outside directors were sued for 3.3 billion euros under the claim that the directors failed to protect policyholders. On 17 October 2003, an English High Court ruled that the case could go ahead. Furthermore, threats of adverse publicity from the media or political and regulatory authorities also serve to inhibit actions by the board to enhance value through risk taking, although desirable.

Table 4 reports the results of the model examining the relationship between board size and firm risk taking. It could be seen from Table 4 that board size exerts no measurable influence on firm enterprise. This result holds for both the parametric and non-parametric analysis. Similar to the results reported for equation (1), we find that board and CEO equity ownership and firm size relate negatively to firm risk taking.

In related studies, Yermack (1996), Conyon et al. (1998), and Eisenberg et al. (1998) all find a negative relationship between board size and firm performance.

CONCLUSION

The separation of ownership and control in publicly owned firms induces potential conflicts between the interests of professional managers and stockholders. The board of directors, at the apex of the decision control system in organizations is assigned the task of checking self-serving and value-decreasing behaviors by managers. Many have recommended a greater representation by outside directors, on the board of directors of listed firms, as a means of minimizing agency cost. A critical issue involved in this recommendation is the impact of board composition on increasing the wealth of the firm or, simply, enterprise activities. This issue is empirically examined in this chapter. Also investigated in this chapter is the impact of board size on firm risk taking. The relationship between board size and firm enterprise activities is interesting to study because board size impacts firm activities independent of other board attributes (Lipton and Lorsch 1992, Jensen 1993).

The evidence produced in this chapter provides some support to the assertion that board composition has an impact on firm risk taking. The impact, however, depends on the risk-taking measure. Outsider-dominated boards have positive and measurable effect on strategic risk or stock return risk but not income variability, albeit weak. These effects are seen across different time periods and suggest a changing nature of firm risk taking. This suggests the need for shareholders to reconsider their approach to improving firm performance with respect to risk-taking. Rather than simply increasing the representation of independent members on a board to aid and check management, shareholders need to explore ways to enhance the motivation of outside board members to foster their commitment to wealth creation or enterprise activities of firms. The empirical examination does not lend any support to the hypothesis that there is a relationship between board size and firm enterprise activities. Lipton and Lorch's (1992) proposition does not hold in our analysis.

The positive relationship documented here confirms the recommendations of the Cadbury (1992) and Hampel (1998) reports of increasing the representations of independent board members. That is, a board dominated by independent members delivers value for shareholders.

REFERENCES

Baysinger, B. D. and H. N. Butler (1985). Corporate governance and the board of directors: Performance effects of changes in board composition, *Journal of Law, Economics, and Organisation* 1, pp. 101-124.

Baysinger, B. D. and R. E. Hoskisson (1990). The composition of boards of directors and strategic control: effects on corporate strategy, *Academy of Management Review* 15, vol. 1, pp. 72-87.

Bowman, E. H. (1980). A risk/return paradox for strategic management. *Sloan Management Review* (Spring), 17-31.

Bowman, E. H. (1982). Risk seeking by troubled firms. *Sloan Management Review*, 23 (4), 33-42.

Brealey, R., S. Myers (2006). Principles of corporate finance (3d ed.). New York: McGraw-Hill.

Brickley, J. A, J. Coles, and R. Terry (1994). Outside directors and the adoption of poison pills, *Journal of Financial Economics* 35, pp. 317-332.

Byrd, J. and K. Hickman (1992) Do outside directors monitor management? Evidence from tender offer bids, *Journal of Financial Economics* 32, pp. 195-222.

Cadbury, A. (1992). *Report of the committee on the financial aspects of corporate governance*. London: Gee Publishing

Conyon, M. J. and S. I. Peck (1998). Board size and corporate performance: evidence from European countries, *The European Journal of Finance* 4, pp. 291-304.

Demski, J. S. (1987). Managerial accounting, *The executive course*, ed. G.E Germane, Addison-Wesley, pp. 101-122.

Eisenberg, T. (1995). *Konkurs eller reconstruction*. SNS Förlag, Stockholm.

Eisenberg, T., S. Sundgren, and M. T. Wells (1998) Large board size and decreasing firm value in small firms, *Journal of Financial Economics* 48, pp. 35-54.

Eisenhardt, K. (1985). Control: Organisational and economic approaches, *Management Science* 31, pp. 134-149.

Fama, E. F. and M. Jensen (1983). Separation of ownership and control, *Journal of Law and Economics* 26, pp. 301-325.

Fischel, D., and M. Bradley (1986). The role of liability rules and derivative suit in corporate law: A theoretical and empirical analysis, *Cornell Law Review* 71, pp. 261-283.

Gilson, R. and M. Roe (1993). Understanding the Japanese keiretsu: overlaps between corporate governance and industrial organisation. *Yale Law Journal* 102, 871-906.

Gilson, S. C. (1990). Bankruptcy, boards, banks, and blockholders, *Journal of Financial Economics* 27, pp. 355-387.

Gupta, A. K. (1987). SBU strategies, corporate-SBU relations, and SBU effectiveness in strategy implementation, *Academy of Management Journal* 30, pp. 477-500.

Hackman, J. R. (1990). Groups that work Jossey-Bass, San Francisco. CA.

Hampel, R. (1998). *Committee on Corporate Governance: Final Report*. London: Gee Publishing

Holthausen, R. and D. F. Larcker (1993). Boards of directors, ownership structure and CEO compensation, Unpublished manuscript, Wharton School, University of Pennsylvania, Philadelphia, PA.

Hoskisson, R. M. Hitt, R. Johnson, and W. Grossman (1995). The effects of internal governance and ownership control on corporate entrepreneurship. University of Texas AandM, mimeo.

Jensen, M. C. (1993). The modern industrial revolution, exit, and the failure of internal control system', *Journal of Finance* 3, pp. 831-877.

John, K. and L. W. Senbet (1998). Corporate governance and board effectiveness, *Journal of Banking and Finance* 22, pp. 371-403.

Lev, B. (1974). On the association between operating leverage and risk. *Journal of Financial and Quantitative Analysis* 9, 627-642.

Lipton M. and J. W. Lorsch (1992). A modest proposal for improved corporate governance, *Business Lawyer* 48, vol.1, pp. 59-77.

March, J. G. and Z. Shapira (1987). Managerial perspectives on risk and risk taking, *Management Science* 33 (11), 1404-1414.

Mayer, C. (1997). Corporate governance, competition and performance, *Journal of Law and Society* 24, pp. 152-176.

Miller, K. D. and P. Bromiley (1990). Strategic risk and corporate performance: An analysis of alternative risk measures, *Academy of Management Journal* 33, pp. 756-779.

Mintzberg, H., D. Raisinghani, and A. Theoret (1976). The structure of "unstructured" decision processes, *Administrative Science Quarterly* 21, pp. 246-275.

Roe, M. (1994). *Strong mergers, weak owners: the political roots of American corporate finance*. Princeton University Press, Princeton, NJ.

Rosenstein, S. and J. G. Wyatt (1990). Outside directors, board independence and shareholder wealth, *Journal of Financial Economics* 26, pp. 175-191.

Shapiro, A. C. and S. Titman (1986). An integrated approach to corporate risk measurement. In J. M. Stern and D.H Chew (Eds.), *The revolution in corporate finance*, Oxford: Blackwell, 215-229.

Sharpe, W. (1964). Capital asset prices: A theory of market equilibrium under conditions of risk. *Journal of Finance* 19 (3), 425-442.

Short, H., K. Keasey, M. Wright, and A. Hull (1999). Corporate governance: from accountability to enterprise, *Accounting and Business Research* 29 (4), pp. 337-352.

White, H. (1980). A heteroskedasticity-consistent covariance matrix estimator and a direct test for heteroskedasticity, *Econometrica* 48, pp. 817-838.

Wright, P., S. P. Ferris, A. Sarin and V. Awasthi (1996). Impact of corporate insider, blockholder, and institutional ownership on firm risk taking, *Academy of Management Journal* 39 (2), pp. 441-463.

Yermack, D. (1996). Higher market valuation of companies with a small board of directors, *Journal of Financial Economics* 40, pp. 185-211.

Zahra, S. (1996). Governance, ownership and corporate entrepreneurship: the moderating impact of industry technological opportunities, *Academy of Management Journal* 39 (6), pp. 1713-1735.

In: Psychology of Decision Making in Risk Taking …   ISBN 978-1-60021-854-5
Editor: Rachel N. Kelian   © 2008 Nova Science Publishers, Inc.

Chapter 11

RISK PERCEPTION AND THE VALUE OF SAFE ROOMS AS A PROTECTIVE MEASURE FROM TORNADOES: A SURVEY METHOD

Ozlem Ozdemir

Department of Economics, Yeditepe University, Istanbul, Turkey

INTRODUCTION

Over the past thirty years, researchers have developed a theoretical framework concerning risk and the protective mechanisms chosen by individuals (e.g. insurance, seat belts, storm shelters) against disasters (Kunruether, 1978, 1996; Quiggin, 1992; Shogren and Crocker, 1999; Ehrlich and Becker, 1972; Lewis and Nickerson, 1989; Shogren 1990; Viscusi, 1992; Cook and Graham, 1979; Hirshleifer, 1966, Dong and Wong, 1996; Dixit, 1990; Arrow, 1972, 1996; Slovic, 1977). In most of these models, buying insurance is studied as the protective mechanism and monetary loss is taken as the damage from the hazard.

Since the theoretical models are not fully adequate to describe people's reactions under some uncertain and risky situations, particularly low-probability events (Camerer and Kunreuther, 1989), empirical investigations become crucial. As McClelland, Shulze, and Coursey (1993) stated, "both field and lab studies provide complementary information that will lead to a fuller understanding of insurance purchase and other protective behaviors for low-probability risks."

Numerous survey studies have examined risk perception for low-probability, high-consequence (LPHC) hazards (Smith and Devousges, 1987; Fischoff, Watson, and Hope, 1984; Slovic, 1987; McDaniels, Kamlet and Fischer, 1992; Slovic, Fischoff, and Lichtenstein, 1980; Kunreuther, 1976, 1978; Camerer and Kunreuther, 1989; Kunreuther, 1996; McClelland, Schulze, and Hurd, 1990; Kunreuther, Onculer, and Slovic, 1998). Most found divergence in risk perceptions and mitigation actions taken by individuals. While some individuals focus on the probability of the risky event, others act by looking at the extreme loss. These studies call for further investigation of the relationship between the valuation of risk and perception of risk.

The purpose of the current study is to investigate the relationship between risk perception and willingness-to-pay for increased safety in LPHC risk situations. A tornado is chosen as the LPHC risk and willingness-to-pay for an in-residence storm shelter (safe room) is specified as the mitigation measure. The probability that a damaging tornado will strike a given location is miniscule, even in "high" tornado risk areas. However, the prospect of injury or loss of life due to a tornado is frightening. Brown, Kruger and Bos (2000) place tornadoes "among the most violent and lethal of all natural disasters."

An in-residence storm shelter or "safe room" has been proposed to reduce injuries and loss of life in the event of a tornado. One such safe room design by the Wind Engineering Research Center at Texas Tech University has been promoted by The Federal Emergency Management Agency (FEMA)(2000). A safe room is an integral part of the interior of a house and located in the basement or in an interior room on the first floor of a house without a basement. The room is constructed to endure strong winds, windborne missiles, and falling objects.

Brown, Kruger and Bos (2000) report the results of on-site interviews of persons in communities that were severely damaged during the May 3, 1999, Oklahoma City tornado outbreak. 78% of the 614 persons interviewed were inside their homes when the tornado struck. The safe room provides a haven that is consistent with human behavior because it is accessible from within the home.

The question remains whether perception of risk is sufficient to prompt a several thousand-dollar investment in this protective device if it were commercially available. In that respect, first, a theoretical model is developed that uses the severity of risk (magnitude), the probability of occurrence and the protective ability of safe rooms to explain the maximum amount people are willing-to-pay. Different from previous models, the effect on health status as well as monetary loss outcomes are considered in the utility function. In addition, the independent effect of probability and magnitude of risk on WTP are investigated.

Then, a mail survey was conducted to test the conceptual model that explores the relationship between individual tornado risk perception and willingness to pay (WTP) for safe rooms. Different from other empirical research, I examine the willingness-to-pay as two independent components (whether people are willing to buy or not with an undisclosed price and the maximum amount they are willing to pay) that makes a distinction between the choice and payment decision. For perceived risk measurement, perceived exposure, perceived severity, perceived control over risk, and perceived responsibility are chosen as the components of perceived risk (Kunreuther et.al, 1990; Slovic et.al., 1980; Smith, 1986).

The rest of the paper is organized as follows. In the next section I describe prior studies related to this paper. I follow with a description of the theoretical model, the survey instrument and the data collection procedures and relate them to the conceptual model. Results and regression analysis follow with conclusions and suggestions for future research in the last section.

RELATED RESEARCH

The theoretical models used to explain behavioral responses to risk are subject to much debate. Some scholars support the use of expected utility theory to describe the judgments and choices made in LPHC risk situations (Brookshire, Thayer, Tschirhart, Schulze, 1985; Gould, 1989), while others do not (Tversky, Sattath, and Slovic, 1988; Schoemaker, 1982; Robertson, 1974; Kunreuther, 1978; Slovic, 1987; Harless and Camerer, 1994). Thus, researchers have offered alternative theories to expected utility (extended expected utility theories, generalized expected utility and prospect theory) that incorporate a behavioral tendency to overweight low-probabilities (Machina, 1982; Kahneman and Tversky, 1979).

Answering the need for empirical investigation of choice under LPHC situations, many survey studies have investigated the value of mitigation i.e. WTP for reducing the loss from hazards. Each study either has taken different risks (natural disasters, hazardous waste, accidents etc.) or different methodologies to investigate valuation of risk i.e. WTP (e.g., Randall, 1993; Bishop and Heberlein, 1990; Mansfield, 1998; Hammitt, 1990; Smith, Desvousges, and Freeman III, 1985; Brookshire and Coursey, 1987; Crocker and Shogren, 1991; Viscusi and Evans, 1990).

Willingness-to-pay for mitigation measures is highly dependent on perceptions about the uncertain hazard. For many reasons (e.g., the probabilistic information may be a challenge for humans), there has been a gap between public perceptions of risks and the real risks. For instance, members of the League of Women Voters and students were asked to estimate the number of deaths per year in U.S. from automobile accidents. Women estimate 28,000 deaths while students' estimation is 10,500 deaths. In fact, the real number was 50,000 deaths (Slovic, Fischhoff, and Lichtenstein, 1979).

The reasons for biased judgments of risk have always been an interesting research question in many fields (Fischer, Morgan, Fischhoff, Nair, and Lave, 1991; Slovic, Kraus, Covello, 1990, and many others). Slovic (1987) states that risk perception is affected by the length of delay between cause and effect, the degree of control over the risk, the potential magnitude of its effect, and whether the risk is faced voluntarily. Additionally, biased evaluations of risks may be because of unfamiliarity with an event, overconfidence about judgments, and the divergence of opinions about risk (Slovic, et. al, 1980). Whatever the reasons behind the gap between the statistical risk and perceived risk, we are compelled to accept it and must search for an appropriate measurement of perceived risk.

Previous studies determine the perceived risk by stating different components. In Kunreuther, Easterling, Desvousges, and Slovic (1990), four components of perceived risk are: perceived seriousness, control, dread, and trust of the federal government. Slovic, Fischoff, and Lichtenstein (1980) not only claim" perceived risk is quantifiable", but also they list five determinants of perceived risk: frequency of death, subjective fatality estimates, disaster potential, qualitative characteristics, judged seriousness of death. According to Smith (1986), perceived attributes of hazards can be identified as: the extent of knowledge about a hazard, whether it is a source of dread, and the perceived exposure to the hazard.

Alternatively, a "risk ladder," a numerical base comparing risks in terms of their annual mortality probabilities is used in some studies to detect perceived risk (Hammitt, 1990; Mitchell and Carson, 1989; Smith, Desvousges, and Freeman III, 1985; McClelland, Schulze, and Hurd, 1990). A "risk ladder" is a numerical base comparing risks in terms of their annual mortality probabilities (Hammitt, 1990; Mitchell and Carson, 1989; Smith, Desvousges, and Freeman III, 1985; McClelland, Schulze, and Hurd, 1990). Respondents estimate the annual number of deaths per million from tornadoes [the basic premise is the same as the "determinants of perceived risk" from Slovic, Fischoff, and Lichtenstein (1980, page 190)]. Providing the information to respondents in the form of a "risk ladder" has not been examined precisely by previous studies. However, Camerer and Kunreuther (1989) argue that the degree of uncertainty associated with these risk estimates should be explained; otherwise, people may distrust the entire analysis. Slovic, Kraus, and Covello (1990, p.389) offer the following comment on the usage of a "risk ladder":

> .... simplicity and intuitive appeal of comparisons of unrelated risks may be highly deceptive. Many factors appear to play a role in determining whether such comparisons will be useful. Whether these kinds of comparisons ultimately generate more light than heat will depend on the degree to which both the context of risk communication and the content of the messages are sensitive to those factors.

In order to see whether using a "risk ladder" fits the current study, I included a risk ladder question in the survey and concluded that it is statistically inappropriate for this case. One possible reason behind this may be the high variation in the values stated for perceived number of deaths per million per year for tornadoes compared to other risks. Further, the stated number on the risk ladder may capture the combination of exposure and severity; however, the inability to separate exposure from severity seriously limits the explanatory power of this measure.

Previous studies of low-probability, high-consequence risks find divergence in risk perceptions and mitigation actions taken by individuals. While some individuals focus on the probability of the risky event, others act by looking at the extreme loss. For example, Indians near Santa Barbara, California, still live without any fear next to a liquefied natural gas terminal that is shown to be dangerous to health by experts (Kasper, 1980). Individuals tend to buy insurance only when the probability is above some threshold (Camerer and Kunreuther, 1989; Kunreuther, 1996). On the other hand, people "perceive other technological risks, such as a nuclear plant accident, to be more likely than do experts" according to Camerer and Kunreuther (1989). Slovic, Fischoff, and Lichtenstein (1980) explain the overreaction to low-probability risks by emphasizing the importance of the amount of loss rather than the frequency. Consistent with their result, Slovic, et. al (1980, p. 184) states tornadoes to be among the most overestimated risks in terms of the gap between judged frequency and actual number of deaths.

The inconsistent perception of low-probability risks becomes more remarkable in McClelland, Shulze, Hurd (1990). They find some people to perceive the risk of a hazardous waste site as if no hazard exists, while others rate a low-probability risk equal to more frequent risk exposure. These studies call for further investigation of the relationship between WTP and perceived risk.

THEORETICAL AND CONCEPTUAL MODELS

For this study, a theoretical model is developed in the spirit of Ehrlich and Becker (1972) to generate testable hypotheses regarding the value of mitigation measures (willingness to pay for increased safety) in risky situations. The theoretical model can be found in Appendix I. Adoption of a safe room is taken as self-insurance type of mitigation, since having a safe room does not affect the probability, but can influence the consequences of the risk. Monetary compensation would not necessarily restore health status in the same way other physical assets can be replaced, thus, market insurance is not a perfect substitute for self-insurance. The theoretical model yields three testable implications: (1) maximum willingness to pay for the protective measure is increasing in the probability (exposure) of the harmful event, (2) maximum willingness to pay for the protective measure is increasing in the magnitude (severity) of the loss and, (3) maximum willingness to pay is increasing in the protective ability of the measure (safe room).

For the empirical investigation, first a conceptual model is built to test in our hypotheses.

$$WTP = \alpha + \sum_{n=1}^{n} [B_{1n}Exposure + B_{2n}Severity + B_{3n}Experience + B_{4n}Control + B_{5n}Re sponsibility + B_{6n}Age +$$

$$B_{7n}Sex + B_{8n}Education + B_{9n}Children + B_{10n}Riskaversion + B_{11n}Timeinresidence + B_{12n}\Pr otectivebility$$

$$+ B_{13n}\Pr ecaution + B_{14n}Possess + \varepsilon$$

In this model the maximum amount that people are willing to pay for a safe room is described as a function of perceived risk of a tornado and some socioeconomic variables. Then a survey described in the following section is constructed.

SURVEY DESIGN AND MEASUREMENT

In this section, important variables used in the survey are classified by topic and discussed with their associated survey questions.

DEGREE OF RISK AVERSION

Do you have a smoke alarm?	YES_____	NO_____
a burglar alarm?	YES_____	NO_____
a car alarm?	YES_____	NO_____
natural disaster insurance?	YES_____	NO_____
life insurance?	YES_____	NO_____
emergency items/ food	YES_____	NO_____

This question is a modified version of the one used for a "risk index variable" in Singh and Thayer (1992). The index is calculated by summing "yes" responses to yes/no questions for six different "revealed preferences about risk behavior." These are listed precautions *already taken* against potential risks that a person/family may be exposed to in daily lives. According to their "relative risk aversion" measurement, the individuals that possess 5 or 6 items are considered "relatively risk averse" and those who have 0,1, or 2 index values are risk lovers.

In the present risk index version, I first modify the items that an individual possesses for protection. For that reason, I chose natural disaster insurance vs. earthquake home insurance, then add life insurance for health concern, and finally include the possession of emergency items/food as the last category. This measurement of risk aversion differs from the previous study in the sense that it uses an ordinal scale. In addition, each individual is placed on a risk attitude scale in terms of the relative degree of risk aversion. For example, a person who has 5 items is considered to be more risk averse than people who scored 0, 1, 2, 3 or 4.

PERCEIVED EXPOSURE TO TORNADO RISK

In your view, how likely is it that *your house* will be hit by a tornado?

	Not Very Likely			Very Likely	
This Year	1	2	3	4	5
Within the next 5 years	1	2	3	4	5
Within the next 10 years	1	2	3	4	5

Personal exposure is considered rather than public exposure for two reasons; first, it is a common sense that "the individual is primarily concerned with its own exposure to danger" (Bohnenblust and Pretre, 1990). This is different from McDaniels, Kamlet, and Fischer's study (1992). The authors use seven-point psychometric scale reflecting exposure to measure subjective probability. It is also important to note that a similar exposure question was used in "South Florida Mitigation baseline Survey" (1998) by DCA. International Hurricane Center, Institute for Public Opinion Research. Second, it is more appropriate to detect the effect of perceived probability of occurrence on the willingness-to-pay for in-residence shelter, because purchasing a shelter is considered to be an individual decision. Factor analysis (factor scores for each period) is used to determine the linear combination of three periods. Factor scores are not found to be significantly different from each other (and are not shown here). Accordingly, the direct average of three periods is deemed appropriate for the regression analysis.

PERCEIVED SEVERITY OF RISK

Please rank the following activities in terms of the threat (risk) they pose on human life in general.

(1=highest risk, 5=lowest risk)

Motor vehicle accident	_____
Airline crash	_____
Floods	_____
Tornadoes	_____
Home accident	_____

In Slovic, Fischoff, and Lichtenstein (1980), 110 people were asked to rank 30 different risks ("activities, substances, and technologies") from each activity/technology from least to most risky. The ranking is by the death rate in the U.S. population. Risks included in their list were unrelated in terms of the exposed setting/ cause of the risk. The ordinal scale question in the present study focuses on the individual's perceived severity of tornado generally compared to the other selected risks from the "safety" category. The risk category "safety" is one of the risk classifications in Fischer, Morgan, Fischoff, Nair, and Lave (1991). In their study, subjects were asked to rank five risks "of greatest concern" ranging from "1=greatest concern to 5=least concern" and their categories were: health, safety, environment, society, and other. I use two natural hazards, including tornadoes, and three other selected risks from "safety category." The reason for selecting the risks from the same category is to eliminate the fact that "the simplicity and intuitive appeal of comparisons of unrelated risks may be highly deceptive" (Slovic, Kraus, and Covello, 1990). Note that rank is coded as (6 – the number stated for tornado) for the analysis.

CONTROLLABILITY OF TORNADO RISK

To what extent do you feel that you can *do something (anything)* to protect yourself and your family from a possible tornado?

I can't do much			I can do a lot	
1	2	3	4	5

This question is a reworded version of the question used to measure perceived "personal efficacy" in Fischer, Morgan, Fischoff, Nair, and Lave (1991).

PERCEIVED RESPONSIBILITY

In your opinion, what degree of responsibility each individual/institution below has to undertake to protect you and your family from the damage of a possible tornado?

	Not Responsible At All			Very Responsible Myself	
Local/state government	1	2	3	4	5
Federal government	1	2	3	4	5
Media (newspaper, TV)	1	2	3	4	5
Homebuilders/owners	1	2	3	4	5
Others (Please specify)	1	2	3	4	5

I not only modified the alternatives of responsible entities, but also measured the degree of responsibility each individual/institution has to undertake from Fischer, Morgan, Fischoff, Nair, and Lave (1991) study.

PERCEIVED PROTECTIVE ABILITY OF SAFE ROOM

Do you think this shelter can protect you and your family from a possible tornado? (Please circle one).

Not at all   Very much
     1   2   3   4   5

Individuals that have a response below 3 are assumed to be *weak believers* of a shelter's protective ability, above 3 to be *strong believers*, and the ones who circled 3 are considered to be *neutral believers*.

WILLINGNESS-TO-PAY (WTP) MEASURES

Would you be willing to purchase the safe room (in-residence shelter) described above?

Certainly Not   Certainly
     1   2   3   4   5

How much, *at most,* would you be willing to pay for *a safe room inside your house?*
❑   Less than $1000
❑ $1000-$2000
❑ $2000-$3000
❑ $3000-$4000
❑ $4000-$5000
❑ $5000-$6000
❑ $6000-$7000
❑ $7000-$8000
❑ $8000-$9000
❑ $9000-$10,000
❑   More than $10,000

Consistent with the previous survey studies, contingent valuation method is used for the value of WTP. Different from the studies that used an open-ended question (e.g., McDaniels, Kamlet, and Fischer, 1992; Brookshire and Coursey, 1987) or a percent stated as a portion of current income or a dichotomous type of question (e.g., Bishop and Heberlein, 1990) to measure WTP, for this study, the payment-scale is found to be more appropriate. One reason is that respondents do not have any idea about ranges of safe room price (safe rooms were not available in the market when this study was done). In addition, an open-ended question can be appropriate for a well-known good, but the range of the values that individuals state may become so diverse for a new good that the researcher may not be able to interpret the result (Donaldson, Thomas, and Torgerson, 1997).

In addition to the maximum willingness to pay question, before giving monetary information about the safe room, subjects are asked to indicate whether they were likely to purchase this kind of good regardless of its price (with an undisclosed price). While the former is considered to be a choice decision, the latter is a payment decision.

SAMPLING PROCEDURE

A sample of one thousand homeowners from Lubbock was selected to be the potential respondents to the mail survey. The addresses were randomly selected from the population of homeowners by a research company called "InfoUSA". A tornado hit Lubbock on May 11, 1970, killing 27 people. The city is considered by FEMA to be in a high-risk wind zone where shelter is suggested as an effective protective mechanism for tornadoes.

The response rate is 20% with no compensation provided to respondents and with no follow-up method used. According to Dillman (1978), this rate is acceptable as an initial response In order to assess sample representative ability, I conducted two different tests. First, I compared the demographics of the homeowners in the general sampling frame (homeowners in the city of Lubbock) with those of my respondents. This test resulted in no significant differences. Second, in order to evaluate the degree of non-response bias in my data, I compared the early ($n1=125$) and late ($n2=75$) respondents in the sample in terms of the mean values of the variables in the research. This test is also suggested that non-response bias may not be a critical problem in the data since I found no statistically significant differences.

DESCRIPTIVE STATISTICS

There are 138 male and 62 female respondents in the data pool. The median age of a respondent is 38. Almost half of the respondents have a college education (42.33%). The median family income is $45,000. Thus, the demographic description of the respondents is very similar to the general makeup of Lubbock's population. It is interesting to note that less than 15% of the respondents have any kind of shelter. However, 85% report that they would choose to go to safe place *inside* their houses after notice of an approaching tornado. This is consistent with the evidence reported by Brown, Kruger and Bos (2000). Individuals responding to the survey perceive themselves as the most responsible entity to protect themselves and their family from the damage of a possible tornado (68.5% of respondents). The average maximum willingness to pay in the sample is $2449. This amount is lower than the estimated average cost of building a safe room ($4000).

The correlation matrix (not shown) gives the strength of the association between variables. We find a highly positive correlation between willingness to purchase and maximum willingness to pay (p-value of 0.000). Relative severity and perceived exposure are uncorrelated and thus useable for the two-component measure of risk perception. Numerous survey and experimental studies suggest that women are more risk-averse than men in financial decisions (for a review see Schubert, Brown, Gysler, and Brachinger, 1999). The correlation of the degree of risk aversion and gender variables is -0.066 with p-value of 0.360 indicating no strong gender component of risk attitude here. However, the presence of children has a significant positive relationship to willingness to purchase and maximum willingness to pay (Max WTP).

REGRESSION ANALYSIS

The focal variable of the present study is risk perception; however, in order to conduct a stronger test of the effects of risk perception on willingness to pay, several control variables are included. The analysis is based on estimated linear regressions after checking the OLS assumptions. Two regression equations are estimated with dependent variables, willingness to purchase and maximum willingness to pay. The effect of perceived severity and perceived exposure that are the two main components of perceived risk out of four, are examined both as a multiplicative effect and independent effect of each separately.

Table 1. Regression Results

	WTP (Choice Decision)	MaxWTP (Payment Decision)
Intercept	1.560	-3535.0
Expected time to live in residence	-0.019	-7.6
	(0.058)	(0.668)
Risk Aversion	-0.093	51.0
	(0.231)	(0.711)
Severity	0.1510	373.0
	(0.136)	(0.038)
Experience	-0.026	-328.0
	(0.879)	(0.277)
Controllability	-0.206	98.0
	(0.013)	(0.503)
Precautions	0.188	42.0
	(0.011)	(0.744)
Protectivity	0.411	315.0
	(0.000)	(0.093)
Have any shelter	-1.006	-68.0
	(0.000)	(0.878)
Income	-0.000	0.009
	(0.232)	(0.110)
Have Children	0.272	995.6
	(0.249)	(0.018)
Age	0.003	22.9
	(0.688)	(0.088)
Sex	-0.178	-506.6
	(0.311)	(0.104)
Education	0.020	475.0
	(0.844)	(0.010)
Exposure	0.217	140.0
	(0.012)	(0.354)
R-square	27.5%	18.0%
F-statistic	4.62	2.67
p-value	0.000	0.001

The multiplicative effect of perceived exposure and severity is found to have a positive effect on willingness to purchase a safe room however no statistical significance is detected for maximum willingness to pay. McDaniels, Kamlet, and Fischer (1992) note that empirical studies have shown that it is applicable to use additive and multiplicative functions for eliciting multi-attribute utility and value. Slovic (1987) describes the similarity between the multiplicative model and analytical representation of risk perceptions.

The results of the regression analysis are summarized in Table 1. Perceived exposure has a significant positive effect on willingness to purchase the safe room, but not on the maximum willingness to pay (p-values are 0.012 and 0.354 respectively). Perceived severity has a significant positive influence on the maximum amount respondents are willing to pay, but not their willingness to purchase the shelter (p-values are 0.136 and 0.038 respectively).

For the analysis on the control variables, the degree of risk aversion has no significant effect on either of the WTP measurements. The belief that individuals can exert some control over the losses from a tornado has a significant positive effect on their maximum willingness to pay. If people believe that safe room protects them from a tornado, then they respond with higher values for both WTP measurements. Income does not have a significant effect on the WTP measurements. The presence of dependent children is a significant factor with a positive influence on the maximum WTP (p-value 0.018). Contrary to many previous studies but consistent with Fischer, Morgan, Fischoff, Nair, and Lave (1991), male respondents stated higher values for WTP measurements. The maximum amount male respondents are willing to pay for the shelter is $500 higher on average than the amount stated by females. Finally, Max WTP is positively related to the level of education (p-value 0.010).

CONCLUSIONS

The present study examines the relationship between individual risk perceptions and willingness to pay for a safe room for tornado protection. The theoretical model based on expected utility predicts that the probability of loss, the severity of loss, the protective ability of the safe room have a positive effect on the willingness to pay for a safe room. The empirical results are consistent with the theoretical predictions in some dimensions but not in others. The results of the survey study are based on a small segment of the population and so may not generalize. However, they are remarkable in many aspects.

First, theory predicts a positive relationship between perceived protective ability of the safe room and willingness to pay. Empirically, individuals who have a stronger belief about the protective ability of the shelter i.e. strong believers stated significantly higher values for both WTP measures. Second, the theory predicts a positive relationship between the probability of the harmful event and willingness to pay. Accordingly, willingness to purchase the shelter (choice decision) is positively related to perception of the hazard's probability (perceived exposure). Third, theory predicts that willingness to pay is increasing in the size of the loss (severity of the hazard). Empirically, there exists a significant positive relationship between perceived severity and maximum willingness to pay (payment decision). Lastly, the presence of dependent children has important explanatory power on both WTP measures. On average people with dependent children in the home state a maximum willingness to pay nearly $1,000 higher than other respondents.

One of the most interesting facets of this study is the distinction evidently made between the action (or choice) decision and the valuation (or payment) decision embodied in the different descriptions of WTP. Economic theory does not distinguish the WTP measures along these lines. However, respondents do distinguish and react to the two components of risk differently depending on whether they are making a choice or a payment decision. Further research is necessary in many aspects. First, the determinants of perceived risk needs deeper investigation for a precise and more exploratory identification of risk. Second, the questionnaire can be conducted on different samples with a better follow-up procedure. In addition an analysis of different types of disasters (e.g. hurricanes) would be useful.

APPENDIX 1
THEORETICAL MODEL

Let $U(H_i, W_i)$ represent preferences in state i, where $U(.,.)$ is an increasing concave function of health status, H_i, and wealth level, W_i. For the following analysis, there are two states of the world, 0 and 1. In state 0, a damaging tornado occurs. The probability of state 0 is p. The maximum loss of health status due to tornado as loss of life is denoted as $H_0=0$. Further, assume $H_1 \geq H_0$, $W_1 \geq W_0$ and $U(0,W)=0$.

Expected utility of the tornado risk is:

$$pU(H_0, W_0) + (1-p)U(H_1, W_1) \tag{1}$$

H_{0s} is defined as health status in the event that a tornado occurs with access to a safe room. The safe room protects health status, thus, $H_{0s} > H_0$. The maximum willingness-to-pay (WTP), c solves

$$pU(H_0, W_0) + (1-p)U(H_1, W_1) = pU(H_{0S}, W_0 - c) + (1-p)U(H_1, W_1 - c) \tag{2}$$

For the simplest case, assume that wealth is unaffected by the tornado. Further, suppose that health status is zero in the event of the tornado (i.e. the health outcome is death). The safe room, however, provides complete protection leaving health status the same as in the no-tornado state. Mathematically, $W_1=W_0$, $H_0=0$, and $H_{0s}= H_1$. With these simplifications, equation (2) becomes:

$$(1-p)U(H_1, W_1) = U(H_1, W_1 - c) \tag{3}$$

$$F(p,c) = (1-p)U(H_1, W_1) - U(H_1, W_1 - c) = 0 \tag{4}$$

Using the implicit function theorem, we can derive the relationship between maximum willingness-to-pay and the probability of a tornado. So,

$$\frac{\partial c}{\partial p} = -\frac{F_p}{F_c} = \frac{U(H_1, W_1)}{U_W(H_1, W_1 - c)} > 0. \tag{5}$$

Thus, maximum willingness-to-pay for a safe room is increasing in probability, p. Now, suppose the perceived reduction in health status due to tornado is some level of harm, but not necessarily death, thus, $H_1 \geq H_{0s} > H_0 \geq 0$. The maximum willingness to pay for this case, c^*, solves

$$pU(H_0, W_0) + (1-p)U(H_1, W_1) = pU(H_{0S}, W_0 - c^*) + (1-p)U(H_1, W_1 - c^*)$$
$$p[U(H_0, W_0) - U(H_{0S}, W_0 - c^*)] + (1-p)[U(H_1, W_1) - U(H_1, W_1 - c^*)] = 0 \tag{6}$$

Again, by the implicit function theorem,

$$\frac{\partial c^*}{\partial p} = \frac{-[U(H_0, W_0) - U(H_{0S}, W_0 - c^*)] + [U(H_1, W_1) - U(H_1, W_1 - c^*)]}{pU_W(H_{0S}, W_0 - c^*) + (1-p)U_W(H_1, W_1 - c^*)} \tag{7}$$

$$= \frac{[U(H_1, W_1) - U(H_1, W_1 - c^*)] + [U(H_{0S}, W_0 - c^*) - U(H_0, W_{01})]}{pU_W(H_{0S}, W_0 - c^*) + (1-p)U_W(H_1, W_1 - c^*)} > 0 \tag{8}$$

By concavity of U and where U $(0,w) = 0$, thus, a positive relationship is illustrated between the probability of tornado risk and the maximum willingness to pay. H_1-H_0 is defined as unprotected health loss. In the event of a tornado, the safe room will improve health status up to, but not exceeding the health status in state 1. Further, let θ be the level of protection afforded by the safe room against tornado, where $0 < \theta \leq 1$.

$$H_{0s} = (1-\theta) H_0 + \theta H_1. \tag{9}$$

Trivially, $\partial H_{0s} / \partial H_0 = (1-\theta) \geq 0$ and $1 > (1-\theta) \geq 0$. $\tag{10}$

A larger θ implies greater protection. Recall the simplified framework described by equation (3). This is the case where $\theta = 1$. We can examine changes in H_0 for a sense of the level of harm or severity of the tornado. Thus,

$$\frac{\partial c^*}{\partial H_0} = \frac{-p[U_H(H_0, W_0) - U_H(H_{0S}, W_0 - c^*)\partial H_{0S}/\partial H_0]}{pU_W(H_{0S}, W_0 - c^*) + (1-p)U_W(H_1, W_1 - c^*)}$$
$$= \frac{-p[U_H(H_0, W_0) - (1-\theta)U_H(H_{0S1}, W_0 - c^*)]}{pU_W(H_{0S}, W_0 - c^*) + (1-p)U_W(H_1, W_1 - c^*)} < 0 \tag{11}$$

This means that as unprotected health status increases (decreases) within the bounds, $0 \leq H_0 \leq H_1$, willingness-to-pay decreases (increases). Decreasing H_0 relative to H_1 implies greater severity of the loss. Greater severity implies a higher maximum willingness-to-pay. Lastly, substituting $(1-\theta) H_0 + \theta H_1$ for H_{0s} into equation (6), we have

$$p[U(H_0,W_0) - U[(1-\theta)H_0 + \theta H_1, W_0 - c^*]] + (1-p)[U(H_1,W_1) - U(H_1,W_1 - c^*)] = 0.$$

$$\frac{\partial c^*}{\partial \theta} = \frac{p[U_H(H_{0S},W_0 - c^*)](H_1 - H_0)}{pU_W(H_{0S},W_0 - c^*) + (1-p)U_W(H_1,W_1 - c^*)} > 0 \tag{12}$$

Therefore as the ability of the safe room to protect individuals from a possible tornado increases, the higher the maximum willingness to pay for a safe room. To summarize, the simple theoretical model yields three testable implications. They are maximum willingness to pay is:

1. increasing in the probability of the harmful event,
2. increasing in the perceived severity of the loss and
3. increasing in the protective ability of the safe room.

REFERENCES

Bishop, R.C., T.A. Heberlein (1990), *Economic valuation of natural resources: Issues, theory, and applications*, edited by R.L. Johnson and G. V. Johnson, Boulder CO, Westview Press.

Brookshire, D. S., D. L. Coursey (1987), "Measuring the value of a public good: an empirical comparison of elicitation procedures", *American Economic Review,* Vol.77: 554-6.

Brown, S., E. Kruger, and J. Bos (2000), *Injury Update: A Report to Oklahoma Injury Surveillance Participants*, Injury Prevention Service, Oklahoma Department of Health, Oklahoma City, OK.

Camerer C. F., H. Kunreuther (1989), "Decision Processes for Low Probability Events: Policy Implications", *Journal of Policy Analysis and Management*, Vol.8 (4): 565-92.

Churchill, G.A. Jr. (1991), *Marketing Research Methodological Foundations*, Fifth edition, The Dryden Press.

Crocker, T.D., J. F. Shogren (1991), "Preference Learning and Contingent Valuation and Revealed Preference Methodologies: Comparing the Estimates for Quasi-public Goods", *Land Economics,* Vol.72: 80-90.

Crouch, E.A.C., R. Wilson (1982), *Risk/Benefit Analysis,* Cambridge, Balinger.

Dillman, D.A. (1978), *Mail and Telephone Surveys – The Total Design Method.* New York, Wiley.

Donaldson, C., R. Thomas, and D. Togerson (1997), "Validity of Open-ended and Payment Scale Approaches to Eliciting Willingness to Pay", *Applied Economics,* Vol.29: 79-84.

East Bay Seismic Retrofit Survey (1998), University of California, Berkley and University of Pennsylvania.

Ehrlich, I, G. S. Becker (1972), "Market Insurance, Self-insurance and Self-protection." *Journal of Political Economy,* Vol. 80: 623-48.

FEMA Mitigation Directorate (1999), Taking Shelter from the Storm, Building a Safe Room Inside Your House.

Fischer, G.W., M.G. Morgan, B. Fischoff, I. Nair, and L.B. Lave (1991), "What Risks Are People Concerned About?", *Risk Analysis,* Vol.11 (2): 303-14.

Fischoff, B., S. Watson, and C. Hope (1984), "Defining Risk", *Policy Sciences,* Vol.17: 123-139.

Hammitt, J. K (1990), "Risk Perceptions and Food Choice: An Exploratory Analysis of Organic-versus Conventional-produce Buyers", *Risk Analysis,* Vol.10 (3): 367-74.

Harless, D., C. Camerer (1994), "The Predictive Utility of Generalized Expected Utility Theories", *Econometrica* Vol.62: 1251-89.

Hasher, L., R.T. Zacks (1984), *Automatic Processing of Fundamental Information*, American Psychologist.

Kunreuther, H. (1976), "Limited Knowledge and Insurance Protection", *Public Policy* Vol.29 (2): 227-61.

Kunreuther, H. (1978), *Disaster Insurance Protection*, Public Policy Lessons, John Wiley, New York.

Kunreuther, H. (1996), "Mitigating Disaster Losses Through Insurance", *Journal of Risk and Uncertainty,* Vol.12 (2/3): 171-87.

Mansfield, C. (1998), "A Consistent Method for Calibrating Contingent Value Survey Data", *Southern Economic Journal,* Vol.64 (3): 665-81.

McClelland, G.H., W.D. Schulze, and B. Hurd (1990), "The Effect of Risk Beliefs on Property Values: A Case Study of a Hazardous Waste Site", *Risk Analysis,* Vol.10 (4): 485-97.

McDaniels, T.L., M.S. Kamlet, and G.W. Fischer (1992), "Risk Perception and the Value of Safety", *Risk Analysis,* Vol.12 (4): 495-503.

Mitchell, R. and R.T. Carson (1989), *Using Surveys to Value Public Goods: The Contingent Valuation Method,* Resources for the Future, Washington, DC.

Randall, A. (1993), "Passive-use values and Contingent Valuation – Valid for Damage Assessment", *Choices,* Vol.2: 12-15.

Schubert, R., M. Brown, M. Gysler, and H.W. Brachinger (1999), "Financial Decision-making: Are Women Really More Risk-averse?", *American Economic Review,* Vol.89 (2): 381-86.

Singh, H., M. Thayer (1992), "Impact of Seat Belt Use on Driving Behavior", *Economic Inquiry,* Vol.30: 649-658.

Slovic, P., N. Kraus, and V.T. Covello (1990), "What Should We Know About Making Risk Comparisons?", *Risk Analysis,* Vol.10 (3): 389-92.

Slovic, P. (1987), "Perception of Risk", *Science,* Vol.236: 280-85.

Slovic, P., B. Fischoff, and S. Lichtenstein (1980), *Facts and Fears: Understanding Perceived Risk. Societal Risk Assessments: How Safe is Safe Enough?* Edited by Richard C. Schwing and Walter Albers, Jr. Plenum Press, New York.

Smith, V.K. (1986), "Benefit Analysis for Natural Hazards", *Risk Analysis,* Vol.6: 325-34.

Smith, V.K., and W. Devousges (1987), "An Empirical Analysis of the Economic Value of Risk Changes, *Journal of Political Economy,* Vol.95: 1.

Smith, V.K., W.H. Desvousges, and A.M. Freeman III (1985), *Valuing Changes in Hazardous Waste Risks: A Contingent Valuation Analysis*, Research Triangle Institute, Research Triangle Park, North Carolina.

South Florida Mitigation Baseline Survey (1998), DCA, International Hurricane Center,
    Institute for Public Opinion Research.
Underwood, B.J. (1971), "Recognition Memory" In H.H. Kendler and J.T. Spence, 313-335,
    Appleton-Century-Crofts, New York.
Viscusi, W.K., W. N. Evans (1990), "Utility Functions that Depend on Health Status:
    Estimates and Economic Implications", *American Economic Review,* Vol.80 (3): 353-74.

ACKNOWLEDGEMENTS

This work was performed under the Department of Commerce NIST/TTU Cooperative
Agreement Award 70NANB8H0059.

INDEX

A

abdominal, 6, 67
abortion, vii, viii, 29, 30, 47, 49, 59
abstinence, vii, 29, 30, 31, 32, 33, 34, 35, 36, 38, 39, 40, 41, 42, 43, 44, 45, 46
abuse, 137
abusive, 2, 4, 5, 8, 9, 11, 12, 15, 20, 23, 63
academic, 10, 150
access, 6, 152, 176
accessibility, 9
accidents, 167
accommodation, 6, 23, 136
accountability, 163
accounting, 8, 152, 161
accuracy, 36
achievement, 10, 30
acquisitions, 153
activities, 134, 135, 136, 142
actual risk, ix, 75, 80
acute, 12, 18, 19, 135, 136, 137
addiction, 135
adjustment, 104, 106
administration, 40
adolescence, viii, 2, 4, 8, 47, 48, 49, 59, 70, 76, 83
adolescent problem behavior, 58
adolescents, vii, viii, 1, 5, 12, 14, 26, 29, 30, 31, 33, 34, 36, 37, 39, 44, 45, 47, 49, 50, 51, 52, 53, 54, 55, 56, 57, 58, 59, 81
adult, 6, 7, 11, 12, 18, 44, 49, 50, 62, 70, 76, 81, 143
adulthood, 12, 14, 49
adults, viii, 3, 11, 12, 24, 25, 26, 29, 32, 33, 34, 37, 38, 50, 62, 68, 69, 71, 72, 87
advocacy, vii, 1, 42
affect, 3, 10, 11, 21, 50
affective disorder, 10
African American, 77, 78, 80, 81

age, viii, 2, 5, 8, 17, 22, 31, 32, 38, 44, 45, 48, 49, 50, 51, 55, 56, 57, 58, 65, 69, 70, 79, 80, 82, 121, 122, 126, 173
agent, 103, 151, 152
aggregates, 85, 88
aggregation, 103
aggression, viii, 5, 9, 11, 12, 57, 61, 64, 65, 70
aggressive behavior, 5, 10, 12, 68
aid, 85, 161
AIDS, 32, 38, 39, 44, 46, 49, 56, 79, 82
alcohol, viii, ix, 5, 31, 48, 51, 54, 55, 56, 57, 58, 75, 77, 79, 80
alcohol consumption, 55, 56
alcohol use, viii, 48, 55, 56, 57
alpha, ix, 75, 78, 79
alternative, vii, 5, 15, 105, 142, 152, 162, 167
alternatives, 8, 79, 134, 136, 152, 171
alters, 85
ambiguity, 32, 34, 43, 134
American Academy of Pediatrics, 26
American Civil Liberties Union, 30
American Psychological Association, 26
analog, 102, 105, 106
anatomy, 23
anger, 5, 9, 11, 12
Anglo-Saxon, 133, 137
anorexia nervosa, 8
antecedents, 24
antisocial behavior, 7
antisocial personality disorder, 134, 138
antithesis, 3
anus, 36
anxiety, 11, 17, 63, 68, 70, 71, 137
anxiety disorder, 11
apathy, 9
application, 26, 108, 133, 135, 139
applied research, 62
Argentina, 106, 107, 108, 109, 110, 113, 114

argument, 133, 140
arousal, 6
artificial, 14
Asian, ix, 75, 77, 78, 80, 82
aspiration, ix, 75, 76, 77, 80, 81
assault(s), 4, 18, 20, 25, 26, 64
assessment, 13, 18, 62, 64, 65, 134, 135, 137
assets, 102, 104, 156, 157, 158, 159, 169
association(s), 4, 9, 12, 25, 49, 76, 136, 137
assumptions, 139, 174
asthma, 4
Atlantic, 40, 118
attachment, 7, 9, 50
attacks, 69
attention, 10, 13, 14, 42, 81, 85, 134, 139, 142, 150
attitudes, ix, 39, 42, 44, 45, 50, 51, 57, 75, 76, 77,
    78, 79, 80, 81, 82, 136
attractiveness, 86
atypical, 71
audio, 65
Australia, 2, 15, 134, 135, 136, 145, 149, 150
authority, 19
autolysis, 71
autonomic, 11
autonomy, viii, 47, 133
availability, 31, 134
averaging, 109
aversion, x, 86, 101, 102, 103, 104, 105, 108, 109,
    113, 114, 170
avoidance, x, 18, 131, 132, 134, 135, 136, 138, 139,
    140, 142, 144
avoidant, 5
awareness, 3, 5

B

babies, 9
backlash, 5
Bali, 178
banks, 162
barrier(s), 39, 140
basic needs, 3, 14
Bayesian, 88
beating, 4
beer, 79
behavior, vii, viii, ix, x, 1, 4, 5, 7, 8, 10, 12, 14, 15,
    25, 29, 30, 32, 33, 34, 35, 36, 37, 38, 39, 42, 43,
    44, 45, 47, 48, 49, 50, 51, 52, 55, 56, 57, 58, 59,
    67, 69, 75, 76, 77, 79, 80, 81, 85, 88, 90, 94, 95,
    96, 97, 98, 102, 105, 117, 132, 137, 144, 149,
    150, 151, 152, 154, 169
behavioral manifestations, 21
behavioral problems, vii, 1, 6

beliefs, 34, 43, 137
benefits, 14, 88, 117, 134, 150
beta, 151, 156, 157, 158, 159, 160
betrayal, 6
bias, 9, 16, 21, 62, 64, 88, 173
biological, 4, 11, 50, 52, 56, 58
biological markers, 11
biological parents, 52, 56, 58
biological systems, 11
biology, 42
birth(s), vii, 9, 29, 30, 42, 49, 76, 79
birth control, 42, 79
birth rates, vii, 29, 30
birth weight, 9
black, 137, 142
blame, 6, 15
bleeding, 6
blindness, 137
blood, 11, 18
blood pressure, 11
board members, 153, 155, 160, 161
body, 6, 17, 18
body image, 67, 68, 71
Boston, 46
bounds, 177
bowel, 25
boys, ix, 44, 52, 53, 54, 55, 56, 57, 62, 64, 65
brain, 10, 25
brain damage, 10
Britain, x, 45, 131, 134, 135, 136, 146
British, 131, 134, 135, 137, 139, 141, 145, 146
brutality, 63, 64
buffer, 58
bullies, 12
bullying, 54
burn, 136
burning, 4
burnout, 142
business, 78, 103, 109, 115, 118, 150, 151, 157
business cycle, 103, 115

C

California, 32, 168, 178
campaigns, 13
Canada, 82, 135, 136
cancer, 11
capacity, 5, 15, 150
capital, 151, 156, 157, 158, 159, 160
Capital Asset Pricing Model, 102
capital input, 156
caregiver(s), 3, 9
caretaker, 4, 5, 15, 24

cash flow, 153
causal model, 82
causal relationship, 58
causality, viii, 48, 63
cell, 30
Centers for Disease Control (CDC), 30, 43, 59
CEO, 150, 151, 152, 153, 154, 156, 157, 158, 159, 160, 162
chaotic, 9
chemical, 157
Chicago, 22, 23, 26
child abuse, 2, 3, 8, 9, 10, 12, 13, 18, 19, 21, 22, 23, 24, 25, 26, 27, 137
child development, viii, 8, 9, 24, 61
child maltreatment, 2, 4, 8, 9, 10, 13, 22, 24
child protection, 8, 13, 15, 16, 21, 142
child protective services, 2, 4
child rearing, 13
child welfare, 4, 15
childbearing, 30, 50, 59
childbirth, viii, 47, 49
childcare, 3
childhood, vii, viii, 1, 2, 4, 5, 7, 8, 11, 12, 14, 24, 25, 26, 47, 49, 62, 63, 76
childhood sexual abuse, 7, 24
children, vii, ix, 1, 2, 3, 4, 5, 6, 7, 8, 9, 10, 11, 12, 13, 14, 15, 16, 17, 19, 21, 22, 23, 24, 25, 26, 31, 32, 43, 48, 50, 51, 59, 61, 63, 68, 69, 70, 71, 72, 76, 142, 173, 175
Chile, 106, 107, 109, 111, 113, 114
Chi-square, viii, 48, 52
chronic, 5, 8, 11, 12, 22, 24, 62, 71
chronic disorders, 12
chronic fatigue syndrome, 8
chronically ill, 22, 24
cigarette smoking, 54, 55
cigarettes, 56, 58
citizens, 12, 133
citizenship, 132
civil liberties, 136, 138
civil rights, 135
classes, 2, 32, 51, 52, 53
classical, 70
classification, 157
classified, 3, 157, 158, 159, 169
classroom, 51
cleaning, 67
clients, 87, 135, 139, 140
clinical, viii, ix, 2, 11, 16, 18, 20, 21, 34, 37, 61, 62, 63, 65, 68, 69, 70, 71
clinical approach, 62
clinical assessment, 65
clinical examination, 68

clinician(s), vii, 1, 16, 21, 58
clinics, 8
closure, 138, 139, 141
clothing, 18
coastal zone, 117
cocaine, 51, 55, 79
codes, 78
coding, 40
coercion, 6
co-existence, 134
cognition, 68
cognitive, 10, 15, 16, 42, 49, 63, 65, 66, 67, 68, 69
cognitive process, 10, 68
cognitive processing, 10
coherence, 113, 133
cohesion, 4
coitus, 56, 69
collaboration, 61
college students, 33, 36, 42, 44, 87
colleges, 48
Colombia, 106, 107, 108, 109, 111, 113, 114
colors, 2
combined effect, 25
commercial, 5
commitment, 143, 144
commodity, 151
common law, 18, 21
communication, 14, 19, 51, 52, 53, 54, 56, 58, 66, 81, 129, 133, 137, 154, 168
communities, 2, 10, 14, 50, 166
community(ies), 4, 9, 10, 13, 14, 15, 21, 24, 35, 43, 48, 49, 62, 98, 131, 134, 135, 136, 138, 140, 141, 142, 143, 145, 146
community service, 15
community-based, 15, 43
compensation, 151, 153, 154, 162, 168, 173
competence, 9, 11, 12, 15
competition, 162
competitive advantage, 153
complement, x, 101
complementary, 67, 165
complexity, viii, ix, 21, 33, 61, 62, 64
compliance, 9
components, 12, 17, 68, 69, 105, 136, 166, 167, 174, 176
composition, x, 149, 151, 152, 153, 157, 158, 160, 161
concave, 176
concentration, 67, 112
conceptual model, 119, 120, 166, 169
conceptualization, 72
condom(s), viii, 38, 41, 42, 44, 46, 48, 50, 55, 56, 57, 79

conduct, 12
conduct disorder, 12, 63, 65, 66, 67, 68, 69
confabulation, 17
confession, 16, 26
confidence, 51, 52, 56, 63
confidence interval(s), 51, 52, 56
confidentiality, 14, 19
conflict, 7, 11, 15, 19, 137, 140
conflict resolution, 137
conformity, 132, 133
confusion, 16, 38
congruence, 6
consciousness, 68
consensus, viii, 13, 16, 29, 30, 33, 34, 36, 37, 62, 68
consent, 5, 18, 77, 89
consequence(s), 132, 139
constipation, 6
constitution, 142
constraints, 140
construction, 46, 68, 69, 71, 151, 157
consumers, 86, 88
consumption, viii, 48, 51, 55, 56, 58, 102, 103, 104,
    105, 106, 107, 108, 109, 110, 112, 113, 114, 129
context, 3, 6, 10, 16, 24, 131, 137, 138
contraceptives, 32, 41, 50, 58
control, viii, 11, 12, 13, 20, 23, 41, 42, 47, 57, 62,
    64, 67, 68, 79, 81, 82, 90, 126, 132, 133, 136,
    139, 143, 150, 151, 152, 154, 156, 157, 158, 159,
    160, 161, 162, 167, 174, 175
control group, 62, 64, 82
controlled, 9, 155
convergence, 88
conviction, 9, 150
coordination, 13, 154
coping, 7, 14, 24, 49
coping strategies, 24
core, 134, 140
coronary heart disease, 12
corporal punishment, 8
corporate finance, 161, 162
corporate governance, x, 149, 150, 151, 154, 161,
    162
corporate performance, 151, 154, 161, 162
correlation(s), 63, 70, 79, 90, 102, 106, 108, 109,
    110, 112, 113, 114, 123, 125, 126, 158, 159, 160,
    173
correlation coefficient, 79, 102, 106, 113, 114
cortisol, 11
cost accounting, 152
cost effectiveness, 98
costs, 30, 117, 150, 154, 156
courts, 18
coverage, 134

covering, viii, 32, 47, 51
crack, 79
credibility, 26
crime(s), 72, 132
criminal behavior, 10, 63
criminology, 61
criticism, 7
cross-country, x, 101
cross-sectional, 50, 58, 157
cross-sectional study, 50, 58
crying, 5, 20
cues, 5, 8
cultural, vii, viii, 4, 39, 42, 47, 57
cultural factors, vii
cultural values, 4
cumulative, 135
curiosity, 55
currency, 106
curriculum, 32, 82
cynicism, 136
cystitis, 69

D

daily living, 10
damage, 139
danger, 170
data collection, 51, 64, 65, 166
database, 90
dating, 33
death(s), 4, 7, 19, 25, 59, 167, 168, 170, 176, 177
death rate, 170
debt, 102
decision control, 160
decision making, vii, viii, 29, 143
decision-making process, 42, 152
decision(s), vii, 19, 34, 37, 57, 58, 88, 90, 134, 135,
    137, 143, 152, 153, 173
decomposition, 109
deductible, 86, 87
deductibles, 87
deficit(s), 10, 11, 24
definition, ix, 3, 5, 31, 32, 33, 34, 35, 36, 41, 62, 153
deflator, 106
degradation, 7
degrading, 7
degree, 4, 34, 70, 133, 167, 168, 170, 171, 173, 175
delinquency, 24, 57, 82
delivery, 58
demand, 85, 137, 156
demographic, viii, 48, 51, 126, 129, 173
demographic characteristics, viii, 48, 51
demographics, x, 39, 118, 173

denial, 3, 7
Denmark, 139
density, 105
Department of Commerce, 98, 180
Department of Health and Human Services, 22, 31, 32, 59, 81, 83
dependent, 88, 90, 94, 96, 119, 120, 122, 123, 167, 174, 175
dependent variable, 90, 94, 96, 119, 120, 122, 123, 174
depersonalization, 71
depressed, 9, 10
depression, 7, 8, 9, 10, 12, 15, 23, 63, 66, 67, 68, 71, 137, 141
depressive symptoms, 10
deprivation, 2, 23, 135, 136, 138
dermatosis, 69
desires, 5
destruction, 68
detection, 8, 63
detention, 138
developed countries, 107, 108
developing countries, 108
development, 132, 146
developmental delay, 10
developmental disabilities, 4
developmental milestones, 9
developmental psychopathology, 22
deviation, 3, 88, 107, 156, 157, 158, 159
diagnosis, 137
diagnostic, 2, 7, 20, 64
differences, 137, 142
differential diagnosis, viii, 61, 70
dimensions, 136
direct observation, 8
disabilities, 4, 133, 139
disability, 139
disabled, 9, 22, 139
disaster, 88, 98, 167, 169
discipline, 5, 8, 13, 14, 21, 30
disclosure, 6, 16, 17, 19, 20
discordance, vii, 29
discourse, ix, 75, 77, 79, 80, 81, 82, 131, 132, 133
diseases, 8, 82
disorder, vii, 1, 134, 137, 138
dispersion, 108
distress, 15
distribution, 49, 87, 88, 90, 93, 94, 98, 104
diurnal, 68
divergence, 62, 165, 167, 168
diversity, 77
dividends, 106
division, 72, 152

divorce, 50
DNA, 18, 26
doctor(s), 48, 69, 71
do-it-yourself, 133
domain, 78, 79
domestic violence, 3, 4, 7, 8
dominant strategy, x, 86
draft, 65
dream, 68
drinking, 51, 55
drowning, 4
drug abuse, 7
drug consumption, 51, 56, 58
drug use, ix, 5, 10, 31, 55, 75, 82
drugs, viii, ix, 48, 51, 55, 57, 75, 77, 79
DSM, 12, 63
duration, 11, 68, 103
duties, 134, 155
dysfunctional, 150, 154
dysregulation(s), 11, 12
dysthymia, 68

E

earnings, 89, 153
earthquake, 169
ecology, 24
economic, 30, 85, 102, 108, 115, 128, 139, 150, 151, 162
economic behaviour, 108
economic damages, 128
economic performance, 151
economic theory, 108
economically disadvantaged, 77
economics, 76, 85
economy, 70, 103, 108
education, vii, 3, 9, 13, 14, 18, 29, 30, 31, 32, 33, 37, 38, 39, 42, 43, 44, 45, 46, 49, 50, 76, 78, 80, 82, 121, 122, 124, 125, 126, 127, 128, 133, 173, 174, 175
educational attainment, 76, 81
educational policy, 32
educators, 33, 45
effective, 136
efficacy, vii, 1, 31, 39
elaboration, 68
elasticity, 103, 108, 113
elders, 143
electronics, 157
elementary school, 48
eligibility criteria, 37
email, 75
emergence, 38

emerging markets, x, 101, 102, 106, 107
emotion regulation, 11, 12
emotional, vii, 1, 2, 3, 6, 7, 8, 9, 10, 11, 12, 14, 19, 22, 24, 25, 143
emotional abuse, 2, 8, 25
emotional conflict, 7
emotional health, 9
emotional reactions, 24
emotional well-being, 8
emotions, 11, 12
empirical, 122, 124, 130, 179
employees, 153, 155
employment, 30, 133
empowered, 136, 141
empowerment, 133, 136, 139, 146
encouragement, 4, 15, 76
endangered, 7
endocrine, 11
endurance, 133
energy, 144, 157
engagement, 9, 34
engineering, 85, 157
England, 23, 135
English, 77, 134, 160
enrollment, 77
enterprise, 142, 149, 150, 151, 152, 153, 154, 157, 160, 161, 163
entrepreneurship, 162, 163
envelope, 89
environment, viii, 3, 6, 7, 8, 10, 11, 12, 13, 48, 50, 51, 52, 53, 56, 57, 58, 136, 139, 142, 171
environmental, 8, 42
epidemiological, viii, 61, 62, 70
epidemiology, 76, 82
episodic, 88
epistemological, 62
equilibrium, 163
equity, x, 101, 102, 103, 105, 106, 108, 113, 114, 115, 156, 157, 158, 159, 160
erosion, 136
estimating, 157
estimator, 163
ethical, 18, 19, 32, 39
ethical concerns, 39
ethical principles, 18
ethics, vii, 26, 30
ethnic groups, 2, 4, 8
ethnic minorities, 137
ethnicity, 44, 78
etiology, viii, 3, 48
Euler, 103
Europe, x, 131, 134, 135, 137
European(s), 134, 144, 145, 146, 161

European Union (EU), 134
evacuation, 98, 117, 118, 120, 123, 126, 127, 129
everyday life, 132, 135
evidence, x, 2, 6, 7, 11, 16, 18, 19, 26, 30, 31, 32, 33, 39, 42, 63, 76, 101, 102, 109, 114, 134, 135, 149, 151, 160, 161, 173
evolution, 71
examinations, 26
excitement, 132, 134
exclusion, 80
exercise, 108, 133, 140, 142
expectations, 82, 141
experimental design, x, 86
expertise, ix, 62, 134
experts, 3, 168
exploitation, 2, 5, 15, 67
exposure, viii, x, 3, 5, 11, 12, 25, 47, 58, 59, 86, 166, 167, 168, 169, 170, 173, 174, 175
expression, 9
extra help, 52, 53

F

facial expression, 67
factors, 131
failure, 2, 3, 8, 24, 66, 102, 137, 140, 141, 143, 162
false, 6, 16
familial, 6, 9, 63, 70
families, 135
family, viii, 4, 6, 7, 8, 9, 10, 11, 12, 13, 14, 15, 17, 26, 47, 48, 49, 51, 52, 56, 58, 59, 70, 82, 120, 126, 137, 140, 141, 142, 143, 145, 146, 169, 171, 173
family conflict, 15
family environment, 7, 11
family functioning, 10
family history, 11
family income, 173
family members, 6, 9, 12, 15, 143
family structure, 51
family support, 51
family system, 10
family therapy, 15
family violence, 8
family(ies), 135, 137, 140, 142, 143
fatigue, 8
fear, 5, 6, 87, 134, 137, 140, 144, 168
Federal Emergency Management Agency (FEMA), 166, 173, 179
federal government, 30, 33, 167
feedback, 10, 32, 33, 40
feeding, 5, 15, 67
feelings, viii, 6, 9, 14, 47, 49

females, 34, 35, 36, 40, 41, 42, 54, 57, 77, 175
fibromyalgia, 25
Filipino, 82
films, 133
finance, 161, 162
financial markets, 108
financial performance, 154
Finland, 150, 151, 155
firm management, 152
firm size, 157, 158, 159, 160
firms, x, 149, 150, 151, 153, 154, 155, 156, 157, 160,
    161, 162
fixed costs, 156
flexibility, 16
flood, x, 88, 117, 119, 121, 122, 124, 125, 126, 127,
    128, 129
flooding, 119, 128, 129
flow, 152, 153
fluctuations, 102
fluid, 18
focusing, 134, 135
food, 3, 63, 157, 169
forensic, ix, 3, 16, 17, 18, 21, 62, 64
fractures, 4, 11, 22
framework, 132, 133, 138, 139, 140
France, ix, 48, 61, 62, 64, 134, 135
free recall, 16
freedom(s), 7, 132, 133, 136
frequency distribution, 40
Freud, 5
friends, 9, 50, 51, 54, 56, 57, 58, 135, 143
friendship, 54, 56
funding, 37, 38, 39, 142
funds, 32, 44

G

gambling, 132
gauge, vii, 29, 38
gay marriage, 30
gay men, 39
GDP, 106, 107
GDP deflator, 106
gender, 35, 36, 39, 40, 41, 42, 50, 52, 53, 54, 55, 80,
    96, 173
gender differences, 35, 39, 42, 53, 54, 55
generation, 16, 37
genetic, 11, 18
genetic marker, 18
genital herpes, 45
Germany, 48, 134, 135
ghost, 146
gift, 34

gifted, 77
girls, ix, 33, 52, 53, 54, 55, 56, 57, 62, 64, 65, 81
global education, 82
goals, 3, 76, 139
going to school, 52
governance, x, 149, 150, 151, 154, 161, 162, 163
government, 14, 30, 33, 85, 118, 134, 136, 171
GPs, 134
grades, 30
gradings, 132, 133, 134, 135, 139, 143
grain, 132
grants, 43, 44
graph, 90, 94, 95
Greece, 101, 134
group work, 142
groups, 2, 3, 4, 8, 10, 14, 64, 82, 87, 125, 135, 141,
    142, 154
growth, 48, 49, 102, 104, 105, 107, 108, 109, 110,
    112, 113, 114, 142, 153
guardian, 19, 79
guidelines, 18, 32, 44, 117
guilt, 6

H

handicapped, 24, 38
handling, 18
happiness, 49
harassment, 64
harm, 4, 8, 134, 142, 177
harmful, 4, 31, 136, 169, 175, 178
hazards, 49, 165, 167
health, vii, viii, ix, x, 1, 2, 3, 4, 7, 8, 9, 11, 12, 13, 14,
    15, 16, 18, 21, 25, 29, 30, 31, 32, 33, 34, 35, 37,
    38, 39, 41, 44, 45, 48, 49, 50, 51, 57, 58, 59, 75,
    76, 77, 78, 79, 80, 81, 82, 131, 132, 133, 134,
    135, 136, 137, 138, 139, 140, 141, 142, 143, 144,
    166, 168, 169, 171, 176, 177
Health and Human Services (HHS), 22, 31, 32, 43,
    44, 59, 81, 83
health care, 9, 14, 16, 18, 58
health care professionals, 16
health care workers, 14
health clinics, 8
health education, 32
health effects, 11
health insurance, 3
health problems, vii, 1, 8, 11, 15, 31, 136, 140, 142,
    143
health services, vii, 1, 48, 57, 135, 138, 144
health status, 25, 166, 168, 176, 177
heart disease, 11, 12
heart rate, 11

heat, 168
hegemony, 133
height, 141
hematoma, 22
heroin, 79
herpes, 45, 69
heterogeneity, 3
heteroscedasticity, 157
heteroskedasticity, 163
high risk, vii, 9, 10, 13, 24, 29, 57, 113, 114, 119,
    121, 123, 136, 143, 150, 156, 173
high school, 32, 46, 57, 78, 80
higher education, 76, 82, 127
hip(s), 9, 81, 160
Hispanic, ix, 75, 77, 78, 80
history, 133, 140, 144
HIV, viii, 25, 32, 38, 44, 47, 49, 59, 78
Holland, 114
homeowners, 122, 173
homes, 14, 88, 122, 124, 126, 129, 141, 166
homicide, 134
horizon, 109, 112, 113
hospital(s), 4, 70, 136, 138, 139, 141
hospitalisation, 134, 136, 142
hospitalized, 9
host, 34, 37
hostility, 4, 12
household(s), 11, 25, 106, 118, 120, 121, 122, 126,
    127
household income, 121, 122
housing, 117
human(s), 2, 3, 4, 5, 14, 24, 25, 30, 31, 38, 39, 49,
    85, 139, 166, 167, 170
human actions, 2
human behavior, 166
human brain, 25
human development, 3
Human Papilloma Virus (HPV), 30
human rights, 39
humiliation, 7, 63, 70
hurricane, x, 85, 98, 117, 118, 119, 120, 121, 122,
    123, 124, 125, 126, 127, 128, 129
Hurricane Andrew, 85
hurricanes, x, 98, 117, 119, 120, 121, 122, 124, 125,
    126, 127, 128, 129, 176
hygiene, 8
hypersensitivity, 68
hypertension, 12
hypothalamic, 11
hypothesis, ix, 62, 81, 161

I

identification, 18, 21, 40, 176
identity, ix, 20, 35, 63, 68, 69, 70, 72, 86, 89, 135,
    145
ideology, 133
illusion, 133
implementation, 152, 162
impulsive, 9
impulsiveness, 67
impulsivity, 66
in situ, 8
inadmissible, 19
inattention, 3, 8
incentive(s), 20, 89, 129, 154
incest, viii, 5, 6, 61, 62, 63, 64, 68
incidence, 2, 8, 13, 67, 70
inclusion, 34, 133
income(s), x, 23, 121, 122, 124, 125, 126, 127, 128,
    149, 151, 156, 160, 161, 172, 174, 175
independence, 88, 162
independent variable, 90, 94, 96, 122, 125
India, 1, 25, 59
Indian(s), 23, 168
indication, 89, 112
indicators, 7, 67
indices, 15, 106
individual development, 49
industrial, 157, 162
industrial revolution, 162
industry, 156, 157, 158, 159, 160, 163
infancy, 2, 4, 5, 14
infants, 22, 24
infection(s), viii, 6, 7, 23, 30, 38, 39, 44, 47, 49
inferences, 34, 152
infinite, 109, 113
inflammatory, 25, 69
inflammatory bowel disease, 25
influence, 10
information, 179
information processing, 150, 153
informed consent, 5
infrastructure, 37
inhibition, 68, 69
inhibitors, 6
initiation, 39, 49, 50, 58
injury(ies), xi, 4, 5, 6, 8, 17, 64, 166
innocence, 21
innovation, 145, 146
insecurity, 68
insight, 50, 98, 154
insomnia, 63
inspection, 48, 124

instability, x, 66, 94, 149, 151, 160
institutionalisation, 139, 140
instruments, 62, 102
insurance, ix, 3, 85, 86, 87, 88, 89, 98, 99, 165, 168, 169, 178, 179
integration, 140, 146
integrity, 32
intellectual development, 68
intensity, 11, 69, 70, 71, 117, 118, 151, 156, 157, 158, 159, 160
intentions, 34, 82
interaction(s), ix, 4, 8, 9, 14, 15, 24, 64, 70, 75, 76, 80, 81, 153
interdisciplinary, 21
interest, 134
interference, vii, 1, 68
internal consistency, 78
international, x, 76, 101, 102, 106
International Monetary Fund, 106
internet, 33
interpersonal relationships, 9, 10, 15
interpersonal skills, 14
interpretation, 33, 37, 40, 59
interval, 51, 56, 107
intervention(s), 4, 10, 13, 15, 26, 77, 136, 138, 139, 142
interview, 16, 17, 19, 37, 65, 71, 118
interview methodology, 37
interviews, 8, 16, 17, 26, 34, 118, 136, 166
intimidating, 16
investment, 49, 76, 98, 103, 150, 156, 157, 166
investors, 102, 103, 155
irritable bowel syndrome, 25
ischemic heart disease, 11
island, 120, 122, 124, 126
isolation, 9, 10, 12, 13, 15, 24, 67, 68, 133, 141
issues, x, 131, 134, 135, 136, 139, 141, 144
Italy, 134, 146

J

JAMA, 25
Japanese, 162
Jordan, 29, 34, 35, 36, 37, 46
judgment, 9
judiciary, 14
jury, 18, 21
justice, 21

K

Kaiser Family Foundation, 32, 37, 44

keiretsu, 162
killing, 173
knowledge, 8, 9, 21, 139, 144

L

labeling, 18
labor, 156
language, viii, 16, 29, 37, 38, 67, 68, 137, 139
Latin America, x, 101, 102, 106, 107, 108, 113, 114, 142
Latino, 78, 80
law(s), 3, 4, 8, 13, 16, 18, 19, 21, 26, 30, 65, 153, 162
law enforcement, 3, 4, 13, 18
lawsuits, 160
lawyers, 21
lead, ix, 3, 6, 8, 9, 14, 16, 17, 30, 50, 62, 64, 68, 69, 76, 102, 121, 129, 133, 141, 142, 144, 154, 165
leadership, 21, 142
learning, 10, 67, 68, 69, 139
learning difficulties, 139
learning process, 68, 69
legal, 132, 134, 137
legal issues, 21
legislation, 131, 135, 137
leisure, viii, 48, 51, 133
lesions, 4
liberal, 140
liberalization, 142
liberation, 134
lice, 65
licenses, 89, 93
lien, 72
life expectancy, 142
lifestyles, 50
lifetime, 51
light, 134
likelihood, 12, 16, 50, 126, 127, 135, 153
limitation(s), ix, 21, 25, 58, 62, 80, 142, 153
linear, 94, 104, 106, 170, 174
linear function, 94
linear regression, 174
links, 67, 135
lipid, 68
liquefied natural gas, 168
liquor, 79
literacy, 142
literature, x, 21, 37, 69, 80, 81, 86, 101, 102, 103, 133, 140, 149, 150, 151
Lithuania, 142
litigation, vii, 1, 19
liver disease, 11

lobbying, 142
local community, 89, 141
location, xi, 98, 166
lognormal, 104
London, 22, 23, 46, 48, 82, 114, 135, 141, 142, 145, 146, 147, 161, 162
loneliness, 9
longitudinal studies, 68
long-term, 4, 10, 11, 12, 102, 136, 153
Los Angeles, 25
losses, 7, 85, 86, 87, 88, 117, 154, 175
lotteries, 86
love, 8, 43, 55, 79, 132
low risk, 123
lung disease, 11

M

macroeconomic, 106
Maine, 32
males, 34, 35, 36, 41, 42, 54, 57, 77
maltreatment, 2, 3, 5, 7, 8, 9, 10, 13, 14, 15, 19, 22, 23, 24, 26
management, 3, 15, 21, 120, 130, 139, 141, 142, 145, 146, 152, 153, 161, 166, 178
management committee, 142
manipulation, 86
Maori, 143
marijuana, ix, 51, 55, 75, 79, 80
market, ix, 85, 88, 94, 97, 102, 105, 106, 107, 108, 153, 155, 156, 163, 169, 172
market prices, 88
market share, 153
market value, 153
markets, x, 101, 102, 106, 107, 108, 113, 114, 115, 153
marriage, viii, 30, 31, 39, 47, 49, 57
Maryland, 29
mask, 121
mass media, viii, 13, 47
maternal, 23, 81, 82
Mathematica, 31, 45
matrix, 105, 106, 163, 173
mean, 122, 140
measurement, 22, 162, 166, 167, 169
measures, ix, 38, 41, 45, 75, 77, 80, 85, 98, 108, 120, 123, 125, 129, 134, 141, 142, 151, 152, 156, 158, 159, 162, 167, 168, 175, 176
media, viii, 13, 47, 85, 134, 137, 157, 160
median, 173
mediators, 25
medical care, 3
medications, vii, 1, 4, 8

medicine, 18, 21, 48, 69
Medline, 38, 45
membership, 154
memory, 16, 17, 68
men, 34, 39, 45, 57, 89, 96, 98, 136, 137, 173
menarche, 49
menopause, 72
menstruation, 79
mental disorder, 26
mental health, vii, x, 1, 3, 4, 7, 8, 11, 13, 14, 15, 131, 132, 133, 134, 135, 136, 137, 138, 139, 140, 141, 142, 143, 144
mental health professionals, vii, 1, 135, 137, 139, 144
mental illness, 12, 133, 134, 135, 136, 138, 140, 142, 144
mental retardation, 9
mergers, 162
messages, 38, 39, 168
methodology, 59
Mexican, 78, 80
Mexico, 98, 106, 107, 108, 109, 111, 113, 114
middle schools, ix, 46, 75, 76, 77
mimicking, 6
Minnesota, 59
minority(ies), 98, 132, 135, 137
mirror, 69
miscarriages, 21
misconceptions, 50
misleading, vii, 128, 129
missiles, 166
mode, 10, 138
modeling, 12, 15, 82
model(s), x, 56, 63, 80, 93, 94, 95, 102, 114, 118, 122, 124, 125, 126, 127, 146, 157, 165, 166, 176
modernity, 132, 133
money, 86, 89, 106
monitoring, 11
monograph, 23
moral standards, 6
morale, 135
morality, 30
morbidity, 70
morning, 30, 52, 53
mortality, 12, 82, 129, 167
mortality risk, 82
Moscow, 48
mothers, 9, 12, 15, 23, 24, 25, 43, 45, 82
motion, 12
motivation, 6, 161
motives, 32
mouth, 35
movement, 30, 136, 142, 156

multidisciplinary, 13, 14, 131
multivariate, x, 52, 105, 118
mutations, 71
mutual, 136

N

national, viii, 2, 29, 30, 32, 34, 37, 50
National Hurricane Center, 129, 130
National Institutes of Health, 82
National Youth Survey, 78
natural, xi, 33, 108, 166, 167, 169, 171, 178
natural disasters, xi, 166, 167
natural hazards, 171
natural resources, 178
NBC, 33, 37, 45
needs, 2, 3, 4, 6, 8, 9, 10, 13, 14, 15, 20, 135, 139,
    142
negative attitudes, 39
negative consequences, 38
negative relation, 9, 81, 160
neglect, vii, 1, 2, 3, 4, 5, 7, 8, 9, 10, 11, 12, 13, 15,
    18, 19, 21, 22, 23, 24, 25, 26, 27
negotiating, 44
negotiation, 3
nervous system, 11
Netherlands, 44, 134, 135
network(s), 70, 142, 144
neuroendocrine, 25
New Jersey, 32, 130
New Mexico, 98
New South Wales, 145, 149
New York, 26, 43, 44, 45, 59, 82, 130, 161, 178,
    179, 180
New York Times, 45
New Zealand, 136, 143, 145
Newton, 134
nightmares, 63
NIST, 98, 180
normal, 3, 6, 11, 49, 87, 90, 98, 123, 133
normal distribution, 87, 98, 123
norms, 154
North America, 134
North Carolina, x, 32, 45, 117, 118, 120, 128, 179
Norway, 139
nuclear, 168
nudity, 69
nurses, 135
nursing, 18

O

observations, 8, 90, 94, 106, 123
odds ratio, 52, 56
Oedipus, 70
Oklahoma, 166, 178
omission, 2, 3, 4, 7
online, 82
openness, 152
opposition, 67
oral, ix, 6, 32, 33, 34, 35, 36, 37, 39, 46, 62, 65, 67,
    68
organization(s), 13, 50, 70, 118, 135, 137, 142, 160
organizational behavior, 154
orgasm, 39
orientation, 153
oscillations, 103
overweight, 98, 167
ownership, 143, 155, 156, 157, 160, 162, 163
ownership structure, 162

P

packaging, 18
pain, 6, 24, 67, 68, 143
paper, x, 32, 43, 45, 71, 85, 101, 103, 117, 118, 130,
    132, 145, 152, 166
paradox, 161
parameter, 93, 95, 108, 109, 114, 122
parental control, 81
parental involvement, 7, 76, 82
parent-child, 8, 9, 10, 24, 76
parenthood, 9, 59
parenting, 8, 10, 13, 14, 15, 24, 76, 142
parents, ix, 3, 8, 9, 11, 13, 14, 15, 19, 23, 24, 31, 32,
    50, 51, 52, 53, 56, 58, 75, 76, 77, 78, 79, 80, 81,
    141, 142
Paris, 72, 73
parole, 73
partnership, 77, 139
passive, 9
pathogenic, 68, 70, 71
pathologists, 3
pathology, 64, 67, 138, 139
pathways, 11, 12, 76
patients, 19, 25, 69, 70, 71, 136, 138, 141
pay off, 132
pediatric, 4, 5, 9, 22
peer, viii, 6, 34, 48, 51, 52, 55, 56, 58
peer group, 6
peers, vii, 5, 6, 10, 29, 30, 48, 49, 50, 59, 81
pelvic, 24, 69

pelvic pain, 24
penalty, 86
penis, 33, 34, 35, 36
Pennsylvania, 32, 86, 162, 178
per capita, 106, 107
perceived control, 166
perception, 68, 80, 87, 119, 121, 126, 127, 128, 165, 166, 168, 174, 175
perceptions, viii, ix, x, 10, 33, 44, 46, 48, 51, 75, 76, 77, 79, 81, 82, 117, 119, 121, 125, 128, 129, 137, 165, 167
performance, 52, 53, 77, 150, 151, 152, 153, 154, 160, 161, 162
perinatal, 24
periodic, 88
periodicity, 102
permit, 6, 67
personal, 3, 5, 15, 23, 39, 41, 42, 106, 107, 133, 139, 144, 171
personal efficacy, 171
personal problems, 5
personal responsibility, 133
personality, viii, 7, 61, 134, 137, 138
personality disorder, 134, 137, 138
perspective, 3, 22, 23, 76, 81, 133, 135, 137, 140
Peru, 106, 107, 108, 109, 112, 113, 114
pets, 121, 124
Philadelphia, 43, 86, 162
philosophy, 136, 139
phobia, 63, 71
physical abuse, 2, 4, 5, 11, 12, 15, 22, 25
physical aggression, 57
physical environment, 136, 139
physical health, 11, 12, 25
physicians, 3, 5, 48
physiological, 23, 63
Piagetian, 68
pilot study, 25
pituitary, 11
planning, viii, 9, 47, 129
plasticity, 72
play, 14, 15, 151, 168
plurality, 38
poison, 150, 161
poisonous, 3
polarity, 38
polarized, 30
police, 14, 16
policy makers, 32
policy(ies), 131, 134, 136, 137, 141, 142, 145, 146, 178, 179
politeness, 154
political, 30, 32, 39, 57, 137, 160, 162

politicians, 42, 134
politics, 46, 57, 132
poor, 6, 9, 11, 12, 31, 57, 76, 136, 137, 152, 153
poor health, 12, 76
population, 2, 13, 25, 34, 36, 49, 52, 67, 98, 106, 170, 173, 175
population growth, 49
portfolios, 150
positive correlation, 173
positive interactions, 15
positive relationship, x, 149, 151, 157, 160, 161, 173, 175, 177
post-traumatic stress disorder, vii, 1, 63
poverty, 3, 4, 10, 13, 30, 140
power(s), 49, 103, 104, 134, 135, 136, 137, 168, 175
pragmatic, 31
prediction, ix, 75
predictive model, 79
predictors, ix, 75, 80, 117, 126
pre-existing, 63, 70
preference, 38, 44, 87, 131
pregnancy, vii, viii, 5, 10, 29, 30, 31, 34, 37, 38, 39, 42, 44, 47, 49, 50, 55, 58, 59, 78, 79, 82
pregnant, 50, 58, 79
prematurity, 9
premium, x, 86, 87, 101, 102, 103, 104, 105, 106, 108, 109, 113, 114, 115
premiums, 87
preparation, 8, 117, 120, 123, 129
preparedness, x, 117, 118, 120, 123, 126, 129
prepubertal, 26
President Clinton, 33
pressure, 6, 11, 16, 32
prestige, 135, 139
presumption of innocence, 21
prevention, 12, 13, 14, 21, 23, 26, 32, 34, 39, 42, 45, 57, 58, 59, 76, 77, 78, 82
preventive, viii, 13, 26, 47, 134, 138, 141, 142, 144
price changes, 106
prices, 88, 94, 163
primary care, 3
principle, 139, 140
private, ix, 61
proactive, 14
probability, xi, 18, 20, 86, 87, 88, 89, 90, 93, 94, 95, 96, 97, 98, 99, 118, 123, 130, 165, 166, 168, 170, 175, 176, 177, 178
probation, 4
probit models, 123, 126
problem behavior, 58
problem solving, 9, 24
problem-solving skills, 9
procedures, 8, 18, 166, 178

procreation, 32
production, 5, 63
productivity, 154
profession(s), 14, 18, 140, 142, 144
profitability, 152, 154
profit(s), 153, 154, 156
prognosis, 5, 7
program, 15, 31, 32, 36, 76, 77
programming, 30, 31
progressive, 68
promote, 76
property, 4, 88, 98, 113, 114, 117, 120, 121, 124, 125, 128, 129, 142
proposition, x, 149, 160, 161
prosocial behavior, 4
prosperity, 151
prostitution, 5, 8
protection, 3, 8, 13, 14, 15, 16, 21, 32, 40, 41, 42, 68, 76, 81, 88, 97, 98, 134, 142, 169, 175, 176, 177
protective factors, 50
protective mechanisms, 165
protocol(s), 16, 18, 50, 51, 62, 77, 89
proxy, 156, 157
psychiatric diagnosis, 24
psychiatric disorders, vii, 1, 8, 12, 25
psychiatrists, 18, 134, 142
psychiatry, vii, 1, 70
psychological, vii, viii, 2, 4, 7, 8, 15, 18, 24, 31, 49, 61, 63, 64, 67, 72, 133
psychologist(s), 18, 71
psychology, vii, 26, 41, 42, 43
psychopathology, viii, 22, 61, 63, 70
psychosocial, viii, 11, 26, 30, 39, 48, 51, 57, 61
psychosomatic, 63, 68, 69
psychotherapeutic, 69
puberty, viii, 47, 70
public, vii, ix, 1, 4, 5, 12, 13, 32, 33, 35, 37, 38, 42, 44, 51, 57, 61, 89, 134, 144, 167, 170, 178
public awareness, 5
public health, vii, 1, 4, 12, 37, 57
public schools, 32, 38, 44, 51
public service, 13
punishment, 6, 8

Q

quality of life, 10, 141
questionnaire(s), viii, 35, 36, 37, 45, 46, 47, 51, 52, 77, 78, 176

R

race, ix, 44, 49, 75
radiologists, 3
rain, 128
random, 80, 118, 123, 125, 126
range, 3, 5, 7, 11, 15, 33, 89, 105, 107, 108, 113, 114, 135, 140, 143, 172
rape, ix, 5, 20, 25, 49, 62, 63, 64
rate of return, 103
rationality, 88
reactivity, 11
reading, 67, 70
reality, 69, 133
reasoning, 143, 153
recall, 16
recognition, x, 3, 16, 30, 140, 149, 154
reconcile, 102
reconstruction, 161
recovery, 12
recreational, 10
recurrence, 13, 63
recurrent respiratory papillomatosis, 44
reduction, 38, 128, 129, 133, 136, 177
regression(s), viii, x, 48, 52, 56, 90, 94, 95, 96, 114, 118, 156, 157, 166, 170, 174, 175
regression analysis, 56, 118, 157, 166, 170, 175
regression equation, 156, 174
regular, 55, 142
regulation(s), 8, 11, 12, 46, 133
regulatory bodies, x, 149
rehabilitation, vii, 1, 136, 140
rejection, 7, 12
relationship, ix, x, 6, 11, 19, 31, 33, 34, 39, 55, 69, 81, 82, 85, 94, 102, 117, 124, 149, 151, 152, 154, 155, 157, 160, 161, 165, 166, 168, 175, 176
relationships, viii, 6, 7, 8, 9, 10, 11, 12, 14, 15, 47, 48, 50, 58, 71, 76, 133, 135, 136, 138, 150, 155, 156
relatives, 135, 137
relativity, 2, 70
relevance, 50
reliability, 20, 26, 36, 38, 40
religion(s), 2, 30
religious, 8, 30, 32, 39, 57
reputation, 39, 140
research, vii, viii, ix, 1, 2, 9, 22, 23, 26, 29, 30, 31, 33, 34, 36, 37, 40, 42, 48, 50, 51, 57, 58, 61, 62, 63, 64, 65, 68, 69, 70, 71, 72, 76, 77, 80, 81, 82, 85, 88, 131, 135, 142, 144, 154, 155, 166, 167, 173, 176
Research and Development, 82
research design, 31

researchers, vii, 29, 31, 33, 34, 36, 37, 62, 137, 143, 144, 165, 167
resettlement, 139, 141
resilience, 24, 61, 81
resistance, 6
resolution, 15, 58, 137
resources, vii, 1, 2, 4, 10, 13, 14, 130, 138, 179
respiratory, 44
response, 142
responsibility, 8, 13, 133, 137
responsiveness, 7
retardation, 9
retention, 136
retrenchment, 144
return on equity (ROE), 156, 158, 159
returns, x, 102, 104, 105, 106, 107, 108, 109, 110, 112, 113, 114, 115, 149, 151, 156, 157
revolutionary, 138
rewards, 6, 152, 153
rice, 94, 97, 172
rights, 2, 14, 21
risk aversion, x, 86, 96, 101, 102, 103, 104, 105, 108, 109, 113, 114, 169, 173, 175
risk behaviors, viii, ix, 25, 34, 37, 48, 49, 56, 57, 58, 75, 76, 77, 78, 79, 80, 81
risk factors, x, 8, 9, 12, 13, 44, 50, 117
risk perception, x, 117, 118, 119, 120, 121, 122, 123, 124, 125, 126, 127, 128, 129, 165, 166, 167, 168, 173, 174, 175
risk-taking, 6, 38, 140, 143, 150, 156, 157, 161
rods, 30
romantic relationship, 12

S

safe room, xi, 166, 168, 169, 172, 173, 175, 176, 177, 178
safeguard, 19
safety, x, 10, 15, 85, 136, 166, 168, 171
salary, 135
sales, 156
saliva, 18
sample, viii, 29, 33, 34, 35, 36, 43, 47, 51, 62, 63, 79, 90, 105, 106, 118, 120, 121, 122, 124, 125, 126, 127, 128, 151, 154, 155, 156, 157, 160, 173
sample design, 51
sampling, 51, 173
sanctions, 39, 133
Sarin, 163
satellite, viii, 48
scarcity, 94
schizophrenia, 138, 146

school, vii, viii, ix, 4, 7, 8, 14, 22, 29, 30, 31, 32, 38, 44, 46, 48, 50, 51, 52, 53, 54, 56, 57, 58, 59, 66, 68, 69, 75, 76, 77, 78, 79, 80, 81, 82, 142
school failure, 66
school learning, 69
school performance, 52, 53
schooling, 121
science, 18, 82
scientific, 5, 18, 21, 32, 39
scientists, 32
scores, 170
scripts, 16
search, 16, 42, 43, 167
secondary, 137, 141
secrets, 143
security, 136
selecting, 171
self, ix, 5, 7, 12, 14, 22, 25, 66, 75, 77, 79, 80, 133, 134, 135, 137, 138, 140, 142, 145, 146, 178
self worth, 14
self-confidence, 63
self-destructive behavior, 5, 25
self-discipline, 30
self-esteem, 22, 63
self-mutilation, 71
self-protection, 178
self-report, ix, 37, 75, 77, 79, 80
self-worth, 7
semantic, 71
sense of coherence, 133
sensitivity, 15, 49, 90, 108, 156
separation, 7, 160
sequelae, 4
Serbia, 47
series, x, 16, 33, 38, 101, 102, 105, 106, 107, 109, 112, 114, 115, 133, 143
serotonergic, 11
serotonergic dysfunction, 11
serum, 11
service provider, 21
services, vii, 1, 2, 4, 10, 13, 14, 15, 16, 20, 23, 24, 48, 57, 76, 135, 136, 138, 139, 141, 142, 144, 157
severity, 3, 4, 11, 63, 166, 168, 169, 171, 173, 174, 175, 177, 178
sex, viii, ix, 11, 29, 30, 31, 32, 33, 34, 35, 36, 37, 38, 39, 40, 41, 42, 43, 44, 45, 46, 48, 49, 50, 52, 54, 55, 56, 57, 58, 61, 64, 72, 79, 80, 82, 133
sex role, 11
sexual abuse, vii, 1, 2, 5, 6, 7, 14, 15, 16, 18, 20, 21, 22, 23, 24, 25, 26, 49, 63, 64, 70, 72
sexual activity(ies), viii, ix, 5, 6, 15, 30, 31, 33, 35, 38, 39, 41, 42, 46, 47, 48, 51, 56, 57, 58, 61, 81
sexual assault, 18, 20, 26, 32

sexual behavior, vii, viii, ix, 29, 30, 32, 33, 34, 36, 37, 38, 39, 42, 43, 47, 49, 50, 52, 55, 56, 57, 58, 59, 75
sexual contact, 18, 38
sexual health, ix, 25, 37, 39, 41, 75, 76, 77, 78, 79, 80, 81
sexual intercourse, viii, 30, 31, 33, 35, 36, 37, 39, 42, 48, 51, 55, 56, 57, 58, 66, 67
sexual risk behavior, viii, 47, 48
sexual transmitted diseases, viii, 47, 58
sexual violence, 63
sexuality, vii, viii, 29, 30, 31, 32, 33, 34, 37, 38, 39, 42, 44, 46, 47, 49, 50, 57, 61, 81
sexually abused, 7, 16, 23, 24, 65, 68, 69, 72
sexually transmitted disease(s) (STD), 20, 39, 43, 49, 50, 56, 79
sexually transmitted infections (STIs,) vii, 29, 30, 32, 34, 37, 38, 39, 42, 58, 78
shame, 63
shape, 4, 42, 68, 87, 90, 98
shareholders, 153, 160, 161
shelter, xi, 3, 166, 170, 171, 172, 173, 174, 175
short run, 102, 113, 152, 154, 156
shortage, 135
short-term, 102, 106, 107, 112, 113, 153, 154
short-term interest rate, 106
siblings, 57
sign(s), viii, 2, 61, 65, 89, 96, 160
similarity, 175
singular, 35
situation, 135
skills, 9, 11, 12, 13, 14, 15, 42, 139, 144
skin, 68
sleep, 67, 71
small firms, 154, 162
smoke, 51, 169
smokers, 51, 54
smoking, 51, 54, 55, 56, 58
smoothing, 106
smoothness, 108
sociability, 63
social, x, 2, 3, 4, 5, 7, 9, 10, 11, 12, 13, 14, 15, 18, 23, 24, 26, 31, 39, 42, 46, 49, 63, 67, 69, 70, 72, 131, 132, 133, 134, 135, 138, 139, 140, 141, 142, 144
social activities, 7
social care, 2
social class, 2
social cohesion, 133
social competence, 11, 12
social construct, 46
social control, 132, 139
social development, 49

social environment, 12
social factors, viii, 61, 63
social identity, 135
social isolation, 9, 10, 13, 15
social networks, 141
social policy, 26
social psychology, 42
social regulation, 12
social relationships, 7, 11, 12
Social Security, 31, 46
social services, 4, 23, 24, 141, 142, 143, 145
social skills, 42
social stress, 15
social support, 12
social welfare, 49
social work, x, 18, 131, 134, 135, 138, 139, 140, 141, 142, 144
social workers, 18, 131, 134, 135, 139, 140, 141, 142, 144
socialisation, 136
socially, 5, 12, 14, 49, 58, 132, 137, 139, 140
society, 2, 10, 30, 31, 43, 46, 49, 132, 133, 139, 140, 141, 171
sociocultural, 49
socioeconomic, 4, 8, 169
socioeconomic status, 4, 8
sociological, 62, 132
sociologists, 133
sociology, 76
Socrates, 145
sodomy, 5
software, 123
solidarity, 134
solution, 143
somatic symptoms, 68
Spain, 134
special education, 3
specificity, viii, 37, 61, 70
spectra, 102, 105, 106, 109, 112
spectral analysis, 102, 105, 114
spectrum, 105, 109, 112, 113, 114
sperm, 18, 42
sphincter, 67
spontaneity, 20
sporadic, 56
spouse, 9
stability, 30, 83, 94, 114
staff, 136, 142
stages, 8
stakeholder, 146
standard deviation, 107, 156, 157, 158, 159
standard error, 157
standards, 4, 6, 16, 21

statistical analysis, 31, 46
statistics, viii, 3, 13, 23, 48, 52, 107, 126, 134, 155, 156, 173
statutory, 135
stem cell research, 30
stigma, 34, 139
stochastic, 114, 115
stock, x, 102, 104, 105, 107, 109, 113, 114, 149, 151, 155, 156, 157, 160, 161
stock markets, 102, 107, 113
stock price, 160
stomach, 66, 68
storage, 129
storm resistant construction, 85
storm shutters, 121, 122, 125
storm surge, 121, 122, 124, 125
storms, 85, 117, 121, 129
strategic, 151, 152, 153, 156, 161
strategic management, 161
strategies, vii, 1, 11, 13, 24, 71, 152, 153, 162
strength, 96, 173
stress, 8, 9, 11, 13, 19, 25, 133, 150
stress level, 133
stress reactions, 25
stressors, 8
student group, 87
students, viii, ix, 29, 31, 32, 33, 34, 35, 36, 40, 41, 42, 44, 45, 46, 48, 51, 54, 55, 57, 75, 77, 80, 86, 87, 167
study, 135, 136, 137, 143
subdural hematoma, 22
subjective, 39, 43, 117, 152, 153, 167, 170
subjective experience, 43
subjective judgments, 39
subjectivity, 34
subsidy, 86
substance abuse, vii, 1, 8, 9, 11, 12, 13, 15, 50, 59, 76
substance use, 55, 82
substances, 18, 51, 170
substitution, 104
suffering, 22, 69, 134, 138
suicidal, vii, 1, 12, 25, 63, 68
suicidal behavior, vii, 1, 12, 25
suicidal ideation, 68
suicide, 5, 12, 25, 134
suicide attempters, 12
suicide attempts, 12, 25
summer, 118
superposition, 106
supervision, 3, 6, 136
supplemental, 153
supply, 129

support services, 15
surgeons, 132
surgery, 8
surveillance, 34, 37, 45, 152
survey, 130, 147, 165, 169, 170, 178, 179, 180
survival, 2
susceptibility, 11
Sweden, 48, 135, 139
symbolic, 68
sympathetic nervous system, 11
symptom(s), 2, 6, 7, 10, 11, 15, 16, 17, 23, 63, 68, 70
syndrome, ix, 6, 8, 9, 16, 23, 25, 62, 70, 98
syntactic, 71
synthesis, 26, 82
systematic, 16, 156
systems, 10, 11, 34, 152

T

talent, 83
tariff, 136
teachers, 3, 8, 32, 51, 52, 53, 58
teaching, 16, 31, 38, 42, 45
team members, 21, 40
technological, 132, 156, 163, 168
technological change, 156
technology, 170
teenagers, 30, 68, 69, 71, 72
teens, 46, 50
telecommunications, 49
telephone, 118
tension, 136, 137
territory, 62
testimony, 18, 26
Texas, 75, 77, 85, 89, 130, 162, 166
theoretical, 63, 102, 103, 138, 162, 165, 166, 168, 175, 178
theory(ies), x, 13, 88, 102, 108, 149, 150, 151, 152, 163, 166, 175, 176, 178, 179
therapeutic, ix, 8, 62, 70, 135
therapy, 15, 19
thinking, 45
third party, 85
threat(s), 3, 6, 49, 71, 133, 136, 154, 160, 170
threatened, 71, 85
threatening, 3, 7
threshold(s), 3, 11, 168
time periods, 123, 125, 126, 161
time series, x, 101, 102, 114, 115
timing, 57
tobacco, viii, 48, 51, 57
toddlers, 5
top management, 153

tornadoes, xi, 98, 166, 167, 168, 171, 173
torture, 63, 70
trade, 78, 157
traditional model, 102
training, 48, 49, 131, 141, 144
trajectory, 3
transformation, 71
transition, 18, 34, 43, 49
transmission, 30, 32, 34
transport, 157
transportation, 10
transpose, 105
trauma, viii, 4, 12, 61, 62, 63, 67, 68, 69, 70, 71, 72
travel, viii, 47, 49
treatable, 8
treatment, 134, 136
trend, 109
trust, 14, 16, 167
Turkey, 165
turnover, 150

variables, x, 23, 52, 57, 58, 63, 80, 87, 102, 119, 120, 121, 122, 123, 124, 125, 126, 129, 149, 154, 156, 157, 158, 159, 160, 169, 173, 174, 175
variance, 90, 96, 102, 104, 108, 109, 112, 113, 122, 123
variation, 18, 108, 168
vector, 106, 122
victimization, 2, 6, 22, 23, 25, 65
victims, vii, 1, 2, 5, 6, 12, 13, 14, 18, 21, 26
videotape, 17
vigilante, 68
violence, 3, 4, 7, 8, 9, 12, 15, 50, 63, 73, 137
violent, xi, 15, 68, 85, 166
virus, 45
visible, 10, 68, 132
visual, 65, 133
vocational, 78
volatility, 104, 107, 108
vulnerability, viii, 6, 24, 31, 61, 71, 141
vulnerable people, 141

U

ubiquitous, 151
uncertainty, 21, 36, 132, 152, 168
undergraduate, 33, 34, 40, 86, 89
United Kingdom (UK), 8, 15, 34, 45, 46, 131, 134, 136, 145, 146, 150
United States (US), vii, 15, 29, 30, 43, 44, 45, 46, 59, 82, 136, 137, 138, 145
university students, viii, 29, 35, 36, 45
unpredictability, 63
upload, 44
urban, 77
urinary tract, 6, 23
urinary tract infection, 7, 23
US dollar, 106
users, 131, 134, 135, 136, 137, 138, 139, 140, 141, 142, 143, 144

V

vaccination, 30
vagina, 33, 34, 35, 36
vaginal, ix, 33, 34, 35, 37, 39, 44, 46, 62, 69
validity, 16, 18, 38, 103, 144
values, x, 4, 50, 86, 88, 94, 101, 102, 103, 108, 109, 113, 114, 138, 144, 158, 159, 168, 169, 172, 173, 175, 179
variability, 3, 36, 112, 113, 114, 161
variable, 53, 54, 55, 56, 90, 95, 96, 105, 121, 123, 124, 125, 126, 155, 156, 157, 169, 174

W

war, 136
Washington, 22, 23, 26, 44, 46, 59, 82, 83, 179
Washington Post, 46
waste, 167, 168
watches, 120
water, 124
wealth, x, 87, 103, 149, 150, 153, 160, 161, 162, 176
weathering, 129
welfare, 4, 15, 30, 49
welfare reform, 30
well-being, 8, 15, 49, 58
Western Europe, 134
Wikipedia, 38, 39, 46
willingness to pay (WTP), 166, 167, 168, 172, 173, 174, 175, 176
wind, x, 98, 117, 119, 121, 122, 124, 125, 126, 127, 128, 129, 173
windstorms, 85
wine, 79
winning, ix, 86
withdrawal, 67
witness, 21, 26
witnesses, 16
women, 25, 34, 39, 45, 57, 89, 96, 98, 136, 137, 141, 146, 173
words, 19, 21, 139
work, x, 12, 18, 21, 131, 132, 133, 135, 138, 139, 140, 141, 142, 143, 144, 145, 146, 147
workers, 14, 131, 134, 135, 136, 139, 140, 141, 142, 144

World Health Organization (WHO), 2, 14, 50
writing, 66

yes/no, 169

yield, 18, 88
young adults, viii, 26, 29, 33, 34, 37, 38
young men, 137
young women, 57
younger children, 68